MAFIOSO

PART 5: Getting Lucky

NISA SANTIAGO

This is a work of fiction. All of the characters, organizations, and events portrayed in this novel are either products of the author's imagination or are used fictitiously.

ISBN-13: 978-1620780848
ISBN-10: 1620780844

First Edition: March 2020

www.melodramapublishing.com

"Die the way you lived" - is a quote in Manhattan Melodrama, the last movie that was seen by the gangster, John Dillinger.

Mafioso 5 – Getting Lucky is dedicated to his memory.

—Nisa.

Chapter 1

The verdict shocked every living person within the sound of the jury's voice. The place erupted with some jeers—loud guttural noises emanating from anger, angst, or anxiety. And cheers—sounds of pure jubilation. The underworld and spectators stood up abruptly and applauded enthusiastically, agreeing with the verdict. The jury did the right thing—made a wise choice, the criminal organization believed. A few people sat there dumbfounded, a cloud of disbelief strangling their vocal cords, weighing down any sudden movement. Scott and Layla West were exonerated. They had beat the unbeatable odds and were now free to resume business as per usual. It was rare that a known criminal organization could outsmart the federal government, but Arnold Meade and Fitzgerald Spencer had skillfully accomplished that impossible feat. After a quick embrace with his codefendant, Scott stood there expressionless; his body stiff, his eyes cold as his lawyer smiled his way. Scott West had scores to settle, truthfully, he had only vengeance surging through his veins, and this acquittal brought him that much closer to retribution.

Scott steeled himself for the next chapter in his life. He knew what no one in his family knew. Maxine Henderson, a woman he had known intimately, a female that not too long ago was his fiancée, used trojan-horse deception to infiltrate his heart. Maxine now wore many hats. She was committed to his son, she was a mother who had borne Scott his first grandson—and, astonishingly, she had put the events in motion that ultimately took the lives of his youngest children. Gotti, Bonnie, and Clyde were used as collateral to pay a debt owed by their parents—disposable pawns cut down before they got to experience life. No parent should ever have to bury a child; Scott and Layla had buried three. Maxine had harbored a long-standing grudge that only murder could mitigate. The blood of three innocent children needed to be spilled to right the wrong done to her. Scott couldn't bring himself to reconcile her actions; it didn't evenly measure on the scales of justice. Maxine's scale had dipped low, and then crashed, and spilled over into depravity. *She had to be insane*, Scott thought. *Lost her fucking mind to believe she could take what was his without reproach.*

Scott remembered how he felt as each casket lowered into the ground, red roses tossed as uncontrollable tears flowed. A part of his soul was left at each gravesite; disproportionate pockets of his humanity was ripped away and buried six feet deep. His anger and rage compartmentalized, inherently stored within because he was afraid to tap into it because of what he might become. Scott couldn't think of enough ways to murder this bitch; each torturous thought wasn't gruesome or painful enough. Murder was almost too good for Maxine unless he could kill her, bring her back to life to kill her again. He wanted her murdered thrice; for each child, she viciously took away.

Scott observed his surroundings; federal agents huddled around the United States Attorney Gloria Sheindlin—whispering, plotting, revamping their strategy. They wanted another bite at the apple, to put him away for life. His attorney, Arnold Meade, grinned like the Joker, high off the win and admiration from his peers. And then there were his children, Bugsy and Lucky—the traitors who had kicked him when he was down. Scott observed the overly dramatic Layla—a ticking timebomb, who unknowingly had paid for the execution of their children, always seconds away from imploding. And finally, Maxine. The murderous minx, who only moments before the verdict, sat smugly before him, clutching her trophy son.

Scott was a foreboding figure who stood handsomely dressed in his dark blue tailored suit and 18-karat gold cufflinks and silk tie. Unaffected as the mood around him was celebratory. He'd proven he was an O.G., never cracking under pressure. He was Mr. Untouchable West, and everyone needed to know this. The not-guilty verdict didn't change a thing for Scott. The level of disrespect he experienced while incarcerated was almost unbearable. Still, he seethed within. His entire organization was predicated upon all the serious work that he'd put in *before* his kids were even born. The murders, hostile takeovers, drug distribution, it was all him—his doing with his bare hands. For Arnold to disregard it all and readily accept that Bugsy was the de facto boss, was mutiny. Arnold would have to atone for his sin against the Founding Father of the West organization.

Arnold was eager to talk to the press. He felt he had done his job with the skillful calculation that few defense attorneys could have pulled off. He had gotten a kingpin acquitted; his clientele list would grow exponentially with every narco wanting his representation. Arnold patted Scott on his back; three quick, succinct taps meant to nudge his client to open his mouth and kiss his ass. Arnold wanted praise for the exceptional job he had done. He expected Scott to nearly collapse in his arms and burst into tears just as Orenthal Simpson had done to Cochran. But Scott West was a different dude, cut from a different cloth. Scott wasn't an accident murderer or someone who killed for passion. He was skilled, methodical, and undeniably, Machiavellian. A man whose emotions, thoughts, and strategies were always kept bottled airtight, vaulted under the acumen of a man with a lot to lose.

Arnold's eyes had danced around the room and drank in what he had expected. The criminal spectators were happy, and the prosecution and judge were not. And then his eyes re-acquainted with those of a hardened criminal, and a chill ran down his spine. Arnold's body involuntarily shuttered. Scott's dark energy and icy glare nearly stopped Arnold's heart, and his broad smile dissolved into a flatline as if his vitals were being monitored.

"We did it, Scott. We did it, brother!" He said, trying to get his client to loosen up. Scott's lackadaisical demeanor didn't go over Arnold's head. "We'll talk later after you've settled back into your life. Congratulations, my friend."

Scott nodded.

"You can call me on my private line, day or night, and I'll be there. Whatever you need, Scott, I'm there for you. You're one of my most esteemed clients."

The renewed respect was too little, too late. Arnold collected his things from the defense table, loaded everything into his leather briefcase, and exited from the courtroom into a sea of reporters.

Lucky and Bugsy sat there, and they both pretended not to panic. They both sat still, unable to move as they watched both lawyers congratulate their clients with handshakes and smiles. An acquittal of their parents, it wasn't expected. Maxine couldn't believe it either. She held baby Dillinger tighter, shock on full display. What did this mean for her?

Maxine discharged early from the hospital to come to the courthouse with her baby to taunt Scott, Layla, too. She'd manipulated Bugsy into kicking Scott while he was down, and she couldn't help but wonder if her life was now in imminent danger. Could Scott ever forgive his firstborn son for hooking up with his fiancée? More important, could he ever forgive her? Leaving a man while incarcerated was a cardinal sin in the hood, but leaving that same powerful man for his *son* was on a whole other level. She would be a fool to think otherwise. As Maxine clutched Dillinger tightly in her arms, she wondered, had she finally gone too far?

Bugsy could see Maxine's fear. Her mouth gaped open as she white-knuckled Dillinger's baby blanket. Layers of terror were unraveling like a loose thread in a delicate garment; she was falling apart right before his eyes. He reached for her, taking her hand into his and squeezed, hoping to comfort her. He said, "Listen, go home. Let me handle things with my pops."

She nodded. Maxine took a deep breath—her lungs quickly filling with oxygen before slowly exhaling. From a distance, it looked like she was about to go into labor before she stood up. Maxine's legs felt wobbly; unsteady means of transportation as she tried to scurry away. Her heartbeat was fast, her nerves on edge—she had fucked up, and she knew it.

As Maxine safely departed, Bugsy knew he had to step up. He would not be intimidated by his father. He was a man, and he would show it and remind his father who he was—mentally and physically. Bugsy felt superiority over his pops—a younger, smarter version of the patriarch. He finally walked toward Scott. Scott smiled. A wide, disarming grin that looked and felt genuine.

"Bugsy," he said, and warmly embraced him. "We did it, son. Beat those pigs at their own game."

"Congratulations," Bugsy coolly admonished. "I knew this wasn't over until you said it was."

Bugsy repeated Scott's lifelong mantra and then extended his hand for a handshake. Strong grips were exchanged as each man eyed each other suspiciously. Bugsy behaved as if he didn't plunge a dagger deep into his father's back. He continued with, "When you get the chance, we need to talk, especially about Maxine and your grandson. I've missed you, Pop. I hope we can get past this. It was something that just happened, neither one of us meant to hurt you."

Scott stuffed his hands into his suit pants pockets, posturing, and stared his son directly in his eyes. His voice was leveled as he measured each word against what he *wanted* to say and what *needed* to be said.

"Hurt is the wrong categorization of how I felt; it's not in my wheelhouse. Just note there are no hard feelings about you and Maxine, and that I understand her actions now more than ever. Let's move on from this."

"She'll be glad to hear it," Bugsy said. "You should come over soon and spend quality time with Dillinger, Pop. He's the spitting image of when Clyde was a baby."

Hearing Clyde's name nearly uncorked the emotional rage Scott was holding at bay. "Family is most important to me, so I can't wait to meet my first grandchild. I'm a free man again with a lot on my agenda, but I'll make time."

Bugsy nodded, hoping that Scott's agenda didn't include heading up his former organization. If so, then there would be a problem.

Chapter 2

Layla couldn't hide her emotions. She hollered, "Thank you, Jesus!" which offended the Irish-Catholic judge's religious beliefs. Layla felt unbeatable, a queen bitch, a real Mafioso. She could live again—better yet, she could take back her businesses from her daughter, and then continue her feud with her soon-to-be ex-husband. It didn't escape her that Meyer didn't attend the trial, a retaliatory act on his part that compounded her ill feelings toward her children. They were a disrespectful trio of spoiled, ungrateful brats, but Meyer would always get another chance with Layla. He was her favorite twin, her favorite child, who could do little wrong in her eyes. But that dead-eyed, trifling bitch Lucky wouldn't get the privilege of her mother's forgiveness. Layla had dreamed of ways she would have Lucky tortured for what she had considered an unforgivable betrayal. As for her, she had always had her daughter's back no matter what, and at the first sign of tribulation, Lucky went for her crown. Layla knew that when you were in the game, you didn't get many second chances. This verdict would allow her to tighten up all loose ends and become a better criminal—a risk management assessment at the governments' expense.

Fitzgerald stood before Layla with his chiseled jawline and sharp nose punctuated with a massive grin. His legal-ease, swagger, and model-handsome face contributed to his colossal ego. Fitz had slayed more than half of the Upper East Side women, SoHo housewives, and most of his law firm. He was fortunate that no sexual harassment lawsuits had been filed up to date. Fitz, too, was waiting for his client to tell him how remarkable of a job he did. He wanted his fifteen minutes of fame to last. However, Layla was ready to get down to business. She said, "How much of that million-dollar retainer is remaining?"

Fitz was smacked back by the question. *Was she serious?* Layla wanted to talk money right now. He'd just given her her freedom, and she wanted to split hairs over a few remaining crumbs on the table. Honestly, he now felt this was a two-million-dollar defense he'd executed. Fitz thought about playing hardball. Tell this ill-bred woman she had a large balance due but quickly lost his nerve. Who was he fooling? He was no tough guy, and the West's were soaked so deep in mob-style proclivities, it transcended to their children. He stumbled with his words, "Um…well…I'm not sure, Layla. I'm going to have to check with Accounts Payable and have them look into it."

"You need to do that, asap."

"Noted," he said assertively.

Layla's voice embodied that of a boss; you had to address her with respect. In a controlled tone, her stern words spewed out and checked him. "Do we have a problem, Fitzgerald? I would hate to have you handled."

His reply was swift. "No problem at all."

Fitzgerald eyed the female thug with an equal mix of revulsion and attraction. Layla was, undoubtedly, a beautiful woman. He wasn't into black females, but under different circumstances, she could get it. Fitz assumed she was wild in the bedroom—a real stallion that few men could tame. In another lifetime, he would have loved a taste to see if her berry was unquestionably sweeter.

Layla's attention went from him to glaring at her daughter. Fitzgerald observed Layla glower at Lucky, who hadn't moved from her seat yet. Her anger almost overshadowed her acquittal. And then Layla saw the male, a looming figure sat inconspicuously by Lucky's side looking like a spectator. Who was he? And where was Maxine? Layla was positive she'd seen her in the courtroom, smugly perched in the front pew clutching her bastard child, but now the bitch was nowhere to be found. The letter Maxine sent her while she was in jail, Layla couldn't get it out of her mind. It was provocative. No one felt the way she felt about Maxine; no one saw her for who she had always been—a manipulative parasite still laying in the cut for an opportunity to advance. Layla would put all that shit to an end.

Fitz packed up his things as Layla vicariously sent threats through her hard stares. Before his exit, he turned toward his client with an afterthought. He said, "You sure you don't want to keep the money in escrow for another rainy day?"

Without hesitation, she said, "You have seventy-two hours to have my muthafuckin' money, Fitz. Don't make me ask again."

Lucky watched Fitzgerald leave and knew she needed to deal with Layla right away, and it would behoove her to do it mono-y-mono.

It didn't go unnoticed that she grimaced at her only living daughter inside the courtroom. A schism hard to ignore. Layla had a vengeful spirit, which meant her need for revenge usually superseded logic. She was cold and stone-faced with her lips twisted into a heavy scowl. Her trial was over. *Not guilty*, yes— but betrayed, embarrassed, robbed, and ridiculed, Lucky was *guilty* of it all.

Lucky cautiously approached Layla with extended arms

expecting a hug. She was snappily met with antagonism.

"You can't be serious," Layla said. "You got some balls thinking you could smile up in my face after all the shit you've pulled."

"I don't know what you're talking about."

Admittedly, Lucky hadn't thought many moves ahead when she began her uprising. Her insubordination was the byproduct of a spoiled child. The FBI had done all the heavy lifting while she reaped the benefits. Because of their takedown, Lucky fostered her own alliance with the Juarez cartel and procured her mother's fortune. She kept *getting lucky*, and those small victories had emboldened the young protégé. But mutiny came with a steep price tag. It would take more than luck and opportunity for her to stay on top. Now, with her mother acquitted, she would need to move like a boss.

"You don't want it, baby-girl," Layla said as a final warning. "Going against me while I was locked up was like fighting Ali with both hands tied behind his back. Try me now, bitch. You won't win!"

Lucky grimaced.

"You're behaving immaturely," she deduced. "Why are you taking this so personally, Layla? You taught me that business always comes first."

Lucky calling her mother by her first name didn't escape Layla. She knew Lucky was trying to hit her where it hurt. Layla was a mother of six, so to disregard her earned title was a knock to her mothering skills. Her daughter was reminding her that on her watch, she'd buried three slain children. What kind of mother was that?

"I'm putting you on notice. You started something that you won't be able to finish. I'm comin' for you, Lucky, and I'm takin' it all back."

"Taking what back, Layla? Your *drug* organization!" Lucky's voice elevated to just under a scream as it echoed off the walls of the courtroom, halting all movement and conversations. If Layla thought that Lucky would cower and fold once she was acquitted, she just got checked.

Layla snorted, and then slowly nodded. Her fury was burning holes in her stomach like acid as it had nowhere to escape.

She continued, "I'm not who I was before you went in, Layla. You and Scott have used my brothers and me long enough. We're runnin' shit now so you can either be seen and not heard or never be seen or heard of again—however you wanna do this, I'm down for whatever. But you will respect me and mine. And check this, I'm forcing you into early retirement."

Lucky had no other words for her mother. She had said her piece, and it was unequivocal; they would have problems. Lucky pivoted and sauntered toward an exit knowing her mother was clocking her every move. The unidentified male was close on her heels.

There would be no reconciliation.

Scott finally made his way toward Layla. There was urgent news she needed to hear, news that would change the trajectory of everyone's life as they had known it. As he approached, Layla frowned heavily and outstretched her arm with her palm emulating a stop sign. The action placed a barrier between the estranged couple. She snapped, "Not now, Scott! I got shit to do."

"Correction. *We* got shit to do."

"Regarding what?"

"Payback."

Layla nodded.

"You saw that lil' nigga," asked Scott.

"I want him dead."

Without hesitation, Scott replied, "Done."

Chapter 3

L ayla couldn't bolt fast enough out of the courtroom. Between the cunningness of Lucky and the vagueness of Scott, she was ready for Calgon to take her away. Her heartbeat so quick, so loud, and forcefully she heard the rhythm; *boom-boom, boom-boom*—the staccato was drowning out the jarring sounds emanating from revving motors, blaring horns, and living in general. Lucky had just threatened her life, basically told her in street terms to get down or lay down. She wanted to destroy Lucky, however, and whatever that meant, she was still undecided.

Her driver navigated his way through the city, going from Downtown Manhattan and arriving in Midtown, where rush hour traffic had thickened to a snail's pace. Layla sat silent. She thought about everything she had lost in the past few years, her children, her husband, her freedom, her empire, and her money. It was now time for her to take a few things, snatch a couple lives, settle several scores.

The black Escalade came to a rolling stop in front of The Plaza Hotel on the corner of 5th Avenue and 59th Street, right across the street from Central Park. At her request, Fitz booked Layla the hotel room for a couple weeks. Although she couldn't foresee the future, she knew Fitz was a tremendous lawyer, and she relied on him to create reasonable doubt.

Her leased driver stepped out of the truck and opened the back door for her, allowing Layla to climb out. It felt good to be treated almost like royalty again. Layla knew she was at the beginning of a comeback. Her five-inch heels were planted firmly on the ground as she took a moment to just inhale. A cool breeze tousled her hair, playfully kissed her face, and swirled under her mink, through her conservative business suit. She stared at the lavish landmark—a twenty-story luxury hotel and felt something stir inside of her. *How easily the mighty can fall*, she thought.

"You okay?" the driver asked.

"I'm golden," Layla replied, and placed her Jackie Onassis inspired shades on, and power walked through the grand lobby.

From the Metropolitan Correctional Center to The Plaza Hotel on the same day, it was an unquestionable upgrade for most. Still, for the cofounding member of the West empire, she felt ashamed. She did not make basic moves and rent basic hotel rooms by the week. At the front desk, she greeted the female receptionist.

"Layla West."

The woman typed on her computer, searching for Layla's reservation. Layla stood there coolly, her dark shades covering her tired eyes. Thanks to Lucky, she only had the clothing on her back but knew she would remedy all her issues. For now, her main concern was a manicurist, a masseuse, and a beautician.

"There you are," the receptionist uttered.

Layla went through the formalities of booking the room and was escorted upstairs. She was on the 10th floor. She knowingly strolled through the carpeted and neatly designed hallway toward her room. Inside, the space was above-average, comfortable with the latest amenities, but it wasn't what she was used too—this wasn't the penthouse suite. She noticed a burner cellphone and a closet full of clothing—Gucci, Yves St. Laurent, Escada, Chanel, Versace, and Balmain. Momentarily, she thought the gesture was thoughtful. It took forethought and anticipatory critical thinking to move five steps ahead—that's what she liked about Fitz. She disliked that he was a greedy, cheap bastard, so those clothes, the room, the driver were unequivocally out of her retainer, so she thanked herself for the shopping spree.

Layla drew the curtains closed and dialed room service. She wanted a liquid lunch for now—a bottle of champagne was ordered to celebrate her homecoming. While she waited, she peeled away her clothing and stepped into the marble shower. Layla submerged her head under the cascading waterfall and allowed the warm, steamy water to massage her scalp, the nape of her neck, and the small of her back. The complimentary shower gel was burst open, as was the shampoo and conditioner. Layla washed away the past and was more than optimistic about her future. She stepped out of the shower and slipped into the hotel's plush robe and slippers. Her wavy hair was dripping wet as she walked toward the door.

"Who is it?" she shouted.

"Room service, ma'am," he announced.

Layla quickly looked through the peephole and saw a uniformed employee in the hallway with a hotel room service cart. She opened the door, and the man pushed the cart, which held a bucket of chilled Dom Perignon into the sitting area.

"Your champagne," he stated the obvious and handed Layla a bill to sign. As she signed, the waiter immediately recognized her. Against his better judgment, he asked, "Do you mind if I get a picture for Instagram? I can't believe it's really you." The presumptuous waiter was already pulling out his cellphone. "My name's Reggie, by the way. You've been on the news all day. Is it true what they're saying about you?"

Layla scoffed. "What are they sayin'?"

Reggie didn't want to repeat it, he thought that would be rude. He said, "Some bad things."

"Yeah, well, I'ma bad bitch."

A hard knock at the door had interrupted their exchange. Layla looked to Reggie to explain the intrusion, but his eyes were equally bewildered.

She snapped, "Who?"

"It's me."

The solid wood door was forcefully swung open. The overly dramatic gesture wasn't necessary. "How'd you find me, Scott?"

Whatever her soon-to-be-ex had conjured up in his head, she wasn't here for it. In court, he claimed there was something that they needed to handle as one unit but wouldn't tell her what. Now she was staring at her husband and his two henchmen, Kane and Zaire.

"This me you talkin' to," he said. "I run New York." Scott and his entourage stepped farther into Layla's personal space without invitation.

Reggie broke all the strict rules of the hotel in terms of privacy when he fanned out. His voice elevated, "Oh my god, this is unreal," he gasped. "You're *the* Scott West!" He fiddled with his smartphone to record this event; this happenstance needed to go *Instagram live* when he noticed that all eyes were on him. Everyone was silent, but hard stares menaced the young man, and he understood what wasn't spoken.

"I should—"

"Get the fuck out." Layla finished his sentence.

As Reggie exited, she casually walked and poured herself a glass of champagne. Layla was always on her ignorant shit, so she didn't offer. She didn't have to ask questions as Scott's men went around checking the room for bugs; then, the television, telephone, and alarm clock were all unplugged before they could talk business.

"Give me your cellphone," Scott asked.

Layla nodded toward the bed, and it was confiscated. Zaire and Kane then left the room, allowing the boss to have his privacy. The room rake had taken a lot of time, so Layla was now on her third drink.

"Slow down," Scott said. "We got a lot of matters that are up for discussion."

Layla grabbed the champagne bottle out of the bucket and walked across the room, drops of ice-cold water dripped down onto the carpet, leaving a trail of defiance behind her. Scott no longer got to tell her what to do. He forfeited that right a long time ago. Layla crawled onto the bed, adjusted her robe so he couldn't see her goodies, and placed the champagne between her toned thighs. The cold sensation near her clitoris reminded her how long it had been since she had gotten fucked.

Scott grabbed the armless chair from under the desk and placed it a few feet away from his wife and sat down. His leg crossed over the other as he opened his suit jacket and made himself comfortable.

"What happened between you and Lucky? I saw and heard the exchange. I need the backstory."

Layla was livid. The mention of their daughter's name made her stomach churn wildly. She clenched her flute glass as her eyes narrowed. "You don't know? Bugsy didn't tell you?"

Scott shrugged. "Bugsy ain't tell me shit."

Layla told Scott how Lucky found her fifty million, sold her apartment, sold everything she had, and betrayed her with their connect. She filled her shoes with the Juarez cartel and left her to rot in jail.

"Juarez cartel?" The name of Scott's rival gave him pause. It was as if he had drunk a few shots of espresso and his senses; touch, sight, smell, taste, and his hearing—were now all heightened.

"You don't know shit, do you? Which worries me." Layla looked around for a Newport she knew she didn't have. "She's better than I thought."

Scott brought his hands together in a prayer position. His eyes grew dark like onyx-black stones before he spoke. Layla knew him, and she knew he was angry. "Lucky doesn't make that move against the Garcia cartel unless you make it for her."

Layla was dismissive. "I did, Scott. You know I don't give a fuck about rules. I had to eat too. And if done correctly, with Lucky under my tutelage and Meyer at my side, we would have controlled your territories."

"Do you know what you've done!" Scott had too much on his plate, and it was now compounded by her stupidity. "Now you have our daughter—"

"Your daughter," Layla corrected.

"Lucky out there thinking she can be us, outsmart a major cartel, and live?" Scott took out his pocket square and wiped his forehead. "She fucks up, and she won't see the hit coming."

"Why are you so bothered?"

Scott smirked and stared quizzically.

Layla continued. "I want her dead, Scott. On everything I love, that bitch has got to go."

"You can't be serious."

"But I am, though. Lucky can't be trusted."

"Layla…," his voice trailed off.

"Scott?" she snapped. "You taught me that if a dog snaps at you once, you gotta put it down."

"We created her, Layla. You and I, together. She's our blood. I can't sanction this hit and sleep peacefully ever again."

"You don't sleep peacefully now, nigga." Layla sucked her teeth. "You can and will cosign when I make you see things my way. Somewhere along the journey, we fucked up, Scott. As parents, we raised little monsters who turned into big threats. Our children are devoid that one virtue, and that's loyalty. I wish there was another way, but there isn't. I've thought about it nonstop right up until I walked into this shitty room. And honestly, I won't feel that bad knowing she can watch over her sister and brothers. They need her until we meet on the other side."

That last bit was bullshit. This wasn't about her three fallen children. This beef was only about Layla's ego and pride; both shredded into tiny shards of embarrassing reminders and tossed back in her face by Lucky.

"You sure about this?"

Layla was spent. Pleading and begging for permission wasn't who she was. Lucky had signed her own death certificate, and Layla would make sure the violin played, and the white doves flew at her funeral. However, she continued the negotiation.

"She wanted me to do *life*, Scott. Life in prison. I can't let that shit go. You heard her yourself in the courtroom, calling me out as a *drug* dealer. As if I was a mere block hugger, standing on the corner selling hand-to-hand. She's forgotten that our family business is what paid for her expensive education, au pairs, drivers, her privileged black lifestyle. And now I'm public enemy number one? What type of shit is that?" Layla poured the last of the champagne into her glass. Scott took her flute glass and took a mouthful before passing it back. "We forgive that who knows what she pulls next. Her next stop could be taking the witness stand against us for the federal government just as Whistler did. That little snitching, dead-eyed bitch is ruthless. I saw it in her eyes. She wants it all."

"Let me talk to her," Scott said. "I'll tell her that I'll get her out of her dealings with the Juarez cartel if she gives you back your money."

"She won't listen," Layla explained. "Besides, I know something she thinks is a secret. I found out while in lockup that apparently Lucky had a lovechild, and I would bet my life the child's father is Angel."

Scott hung his head. He knew all about the Juarez's cartel longstanding rule. "Does he know?"

"Nope," she said. "And our fuckin' kids are keeping it from

us. That shows you what type of shit they on."

"Maybe we could use this to our advantage," Scott deduced.

"Smart minds think alike."

Scott stood up and stretched his body out. This conversation was heavy, and he hadn't even gotten to the main crux of the reason he was there. This would take all night. He took the initiative and ordered room service. "And Macallan 25," he added. He needed something to take the edge off.

Layla would need to coat her stomach and absorb the champagne. He needed her mind clear so she could understand what was at stake and that if he gave the green light, there would be no going back to normal. The new norm would always be that they were parents who had their children murdered.

Chapter 4

B ugsy climbed out of his Bentley and walked briskly into the buildings' lobby. He moved toward the elevators of the swanky, thirty-story building in Midtown Manhattan, feeling astonishingly optimistic about his exchange with his father. He stepped into the elevator and pushed the top floor on the wall panel, and it ascended into the air. Bugsy had rushed home because he knew that Maxine was worried. She was such a fragile woman who had endured too much, more than him, and he was a gangsta. Since the first day they connected, he's wanted only to protect her. And when his son was born, his heart had expanded in ways he never thought possible. He'd readily give his life for either.

Inside, he found Maxine seated in the custom rocking chair, breastfeeding their son. She gently rocked back and forth, and for a moment, there was this calm about her as she held Dillinger in her arms. Bugsy stared at her until she felt his presence.

"How did it go?" The calmness he had just witnessed quickly diminished when she saw him. Anxiety passed through her body as she got up and placed her son in his crib. As Bugsy stepped farther into the room, her body noticeably dripped with fear. He couldn't help but feel emasculated that she didn't trust he would keep his family safe. He was a man, so her distress was fucking with him. Especially since his adversary was his father *and* her ex.

Bugsy looked down at his son. Dillinger was sound asleep in his crib. He was lying on his back in a muslin swaddle blanket, appearing to have sweet dreams. His little man was so cute. Bugsy thought he looked like a cherub, a baby angel that was painted in Renaissance art. Bugsy stared for a few more moments before responding. "Everything's fine, Maxine. It's handled."

"Handled?" she quizzed. "What does that mean?"

Bugsy nodded toward the door. No need for Dillinger's nap time to be interrupted. Maxine walked out of the room, her hips swaying from side to side as her backside wiggled and jiggled. Bugsy wanted to pick her up and take her into their room and make love to his woman, but it was too soon. She still had stitches from the C-section birth, and considering her state of mind, it was probably not the best moment to seek any sexual gratification.

Maxine plopped down on the leather sofa and folded her arms. The gesture was equally a barrier of exclusion as exasperation. *His lady was the antithesis of Layla*, he thought, giving him an understanding of why she was taking this situation so hard.

"Listen," he started off slowly, choosing his words. "Me and my Pops kicked it, and he said he's cool with how things turned out. He wants to come and visit his first grandchild."

"But he's not. Lucchese is," she corrected. "He meant his first grandson, right?" Maxine was sharp. She knew that every word spoken was important.

Bugsy shrugged off the drama; the labyrinth his sister had created with her poor choices were hers to sort through. "They don't know about Lulu. No one does. She's Lucky's secret."

Maxine closed her eyes and had to use all her energy to pull them back open. "Are you lying for her? Scott won't forgive you if he finds out that you kept this from him."

"Maxine, I'm going to need you to understand that Scott doesn't have any children; we're all grown and make our own decisions. Lucky will handle hers, and I will handle mine."

She looked deep into his eyes and saw a naïve little boy, not the young man she had seduced. Dismissively she got up and walked away, turning her back on the man who would give his life to protect her. Maxine's quick steps led her into the kitchen, where she reached for the bottle of whiskey and poured a three-finger glass of cognac.

"What are you doing?" Bugsy asked. "You know you can't have that while you're breastfeeding."

Maxine ignored him as she swallowed a hefty gulp of the brown juice. Truthfully, she wanted to punch Bugsy in his muthafuckin' face. What part of war did he not understand? They both played significant roles undermining Scott, and her baby daddy wanted to believe his father would just take the disrespect and not retaliate. She poured a second glass and then said, "We need to be very afraid, Bugsy. I know you don't want to believe it, and I'm not challenging your manhood. But your father won't let this just slide. Even if he can forgive you, he won't afford me that same luxury. Scott loved me, and I fucked his son while he was facing life in prison. Just take a moment and let that marinate." As she said the words, her mind quickly relived her actions. When the affair began, she felt victorious, unbeatable. Getting away with those murders had emboldened her to keep poking the bear. Maxine had spent twenty plus years in a cage. Her time with her parents was reduced to letters and fifteen-minute collect calls. The first half of her life could be summed up with one word: usurped. Maxine had to play God to get justice. Now she wanted Bugsy to choose a side. Either he would defend her beyond measure, or he would step aside and allow his father to do what he does best.

The weight of the acquittal was heavy, a measured pressure that pressed against her chest, making her breathing labored. It strangled her airwave, so her words were forced and hard to spit out. Her eyes turned cold as they observed Bugsy's cavalier demeanor. They scanned him from head to toe and deduced he was no longer worried. Why? Maxine continued her diatribe.

"If you don't do something and quick, I'm dead. Is that what you want? How will you explain to our motherless son what his grandfather did? I'm scared, Bugsy, and I need you to do something!" Tears flowed freely down the side of her flushed face. Plump, round, expressions of an emotional being. A woman on the verge of hysteria stood before him. Her tears were like diamonds to him, precious stones. He wanted to catch them all, lock them away only to be brought out for joyous occasions.

"That won't happen," he assured. He went to walk toward Maxine, he wanted to comfort her with a warm, loving embrace, but she rapidly shook her head.

"You're too smart to be this dumb," she finally admonished through sobs.

Bugsy was holding his temper at bay. He was about to become unhinged. Maxine just had a human ripped out of her body, so he wanted to be empathetic. But the way she kept whining about this situation was irritating. He stood firm. His gangsta on full display, his Balenciaga's hard bottoms planted firmly on the ground. Bugsy was unshakable, his stance was that of a boss. With his hands stuffed deep in the pockets of his Tom Ford suit, he tried again to put her worries to bed. He spoke, his deep smooth voice cut through the air like butter. "Baby, I need you to believe in me, in us. I got this. And whether you believe it or not, my father ain't that broken up about you."

Where did that come from? Maxine thought. Bugsy wasn't this petty. Sarcasm in a time like this was beneath him. That was something Meyer would have said or Lucky. He saw her cringe. That biting remark had broken her down, her exterior crumbled like discarded paper. Maxine curved over and sobbed uncontrollably, heaving her pain out through stomach contractions and loud wails. He had never seen her in such a state. Bugsy had to put her back together. He continued with, "I mean, we kicked it, and he said that he understood your actions now more than ever. He knows how much you really *love* me, and vice versa. He gets us. My Pops wants us to win, and only a real O.G. like Scott can accept the loss and move on. I would die for you baby, please believe that."

Maxine slammed her crystal glass on the granite countertop with such force the expensive goblet chipped. That seemingly cryptic statement meant something. But what? She knew Scott before Bugsy—the way he thought, his cunningness. Eventually, her cries slowed to a whimper and ultimately sniffles. Finally, she repeated, "He said he understood my actions now more than ever?"

Bugsy nodded. "Something like that."

"And you believe this? You really believe that he's moved on."

"I just said I did."

Maxine tried one more time. "Baby, I don't trust him. He's gonna do something to us…to me, I can feel it. I hate to say this, and I wouldn't if there was another way, but you must do it. You have to kill Scott."

Bugsy snorted. And then he chuckled. It was low pitched and condescending. "You can't be serious."

Maxine writhed her hands together to stop herself from balling up her fists and going full-blown MMA fighter. She still had a part to play, and that was meek. Bugsy could never meet her alter ego, Max. She was stuck playing the consummate victim, a damsel in distress he had to keep saving. Maxine continued with, "I'm serious. Your father scares me, as does your mother. They both play to win."

"It's over, baby. I beat Scott West. Me." Bugsy fisted his

chest twice and then made a slicing motion under his chin. He said, "It's a wrap. I took his woman, his bread, his empire, and his seat at the table. It's time to move on."

"Those are battles. I'm talking about the war."

Bugsy moved closer to her. His eyes powerfully met with hers, and he said with conviction, "He won't touch you. That's on my life. You're my son's mother, and Scott knows this. End of discussion."

She sighed as she watched him retreat into their bedroom, formerly her and Scott's bedroom, and shuttered. She thought Bugsy was a triggerman, a killer. Was she wrong? Maxine had given Bugsy a chance to take this situation seriously. Since he wouldn't, she would. Maxine had a child to think about. She wondered what that cryptic line about Scott understanding her actions meant. There wasn't a man alive that would *understand* why his fiancée had betrayed him with his son unless he knew her motivation. What did Scott know? She tried not to be paranoid, but the whole situation didn't sit well with her.

Maxine poured herself another drink and then curled up on the couch. As she sipped slowly, she concluded there wasn't any way Scott could have discovered the murders. Everyone involved was dead. And then that small voice inside her head, the one that tells you what you've done in the dark is about to come to light spoke. Her third eye reminded her that the ongoing threat from Wacka was that he would tell Scott West her secret. Maxine's singular thought was, *had he succeeded?*

And if that's the case, to save her life, Max had to return.

Chapter 5

I f I agree to Lucky, you will have to sanction Bugsy."

"Now, let's not get carried away," Layla began. "We can't kill our son because he fucked your bitch. She's a whore and whores do what they do. Maxine threw her aged vagina at him, and he responded like most men do when free pussy comes around. They fuck it. She's the snake."

Scott knew this to be true, but he didn't want to convolute the discussion. Bringing in her deplorable actions would sidetrack equally important issues. On the one hand, the discussion of three dead children needed to be broached. On the other, the discussion of two children—both who deserved to die was up for a vote. It was too much to cram into one evening.

"I didn't come here to discuss my son's betrayal. And I don't have to explain why I want him dead."

"Yes, you do." Layla dipped her lobster tail in the seasoned melted butter and stuffed a forkful into her mouth. The butter slid down her cheek, and instinctively Scott wiped it away with his thumb before sucking it off his finger. Her pussy jumped a few times, but she controlled her urge. There wasn't any way she would make the first move, although she desperately wanted to get fucked tonight. "Bugsy is a twin. My firstborn. Twins are special, so I need more than just your bruised manhood. Now with Lucky, she's a ticking timebomb, capable of the unthinkable."

Scott couldn't admit that his pride was driving this decision. And saying it out loud would make his tales of betrayal awfully close to those of his wife's. Bugsy had also taken over his organization and left him to rot in jail. His son now controlled his illegal empire and all his ill-gotten gains. And to punctuate those transgressions, he had made sweet love to his fiancée. Scott was a man. He couldn't help but sit in jail and wonder if Maxine's body responded to Bugsy as it did with him. Was Bugsy able to make her have multiple orgasms while she screamed his name? His son had seen her face in the throes of passion, the way she bit her lip when he entered her or moaned his name right before she climaxed. Her skills and expertise when she sucked his manhood, rode him—these intimate details his son should have never been privy too. This fucked with Scott; daily. Bugsy had clipped his balls, made his father his underling, treated him like a muthafuckin' flunky. Scott couldn't live with that. And since he wanted to live then, Bugsy couldn't. Scott gritted his teeth, and there was a slow exhale. He needed to tell Layla something, so she'd be on board.

"It's not just about Maxine," he began. "Bugsy took everything from me, too, not just my woman. He took over my soldiers, my pipeline, my bread, and my counsel. He beat me at my own game, thought ten steps ahead. I swear Layla, I didn't see it coming. I was ambushed."

Layla saw defeat in her husband's eyes, which was rare. Or was it the calm before the storm?

"Ain't this a bitch. You think they planned the takeovers together?" She didn't wait for an answer. "Yeah, they planned it. I hate this, but it's us against them. But you can't have my

33

blessing. Not right now…not without my having time to let this revelation marinate."

"I feel the same way about Lucky, but here's what we can do to make this easier on us both. You take care of Lucky, however, you see fit. I don't want to know. And I'll handle Bugsy."

Layla's head shook wildly. "If we vote to do this, we either do this together as a family, one unit, you and me like we handled everything when we were young, or we don't do it at all. If we both agree, I need you all in."

"Fair enough."

"They think they know us. What we're capable of—"

"They have no fuckin' idea how low we can go," Scott finished her sentence.

The remainder of the meal was finished with small talk. Just chitchat to help restore their bond, rebuild their trust, and help mend their splintered relationship. The enemy of my enemy is my friend manifested in that small hotel room. Scott and Layla West were now friends again.

"If you didn't know about Lucky and you didn't come here to discuss Bugsy, why did you come?" The evening felt nostalgic for her. And the few sips of Scott's cognac had stripped away her inhibitions. Layla's nether region was hypersensitive. She was horny and wanted him. Why should she have to masturbate when she had the real thing just inches away from her sweet button. Layla opened her bathrobe, and the body of a woman in her early forties was on display. Her once full, perky breasts now hung lower, large almond-colored areolas and dime size nipples had risen to attention. Layla gave birth to six children and kept a flat stomach with minimal tan-colored stretchmarks splintering across her hips and lower abdomen. Her backside had spread but was still firm enough to give any woman half her age competition. You don't get bikini waxes in prison, so her full bush was on display. Scott couldn't deny that she was still sexy, still uniquely beautiful. And an experienced, grown woman was like a fine wine not to be overlooked, tasted slow, and celebrated.

Scott walked over to his wife and parted her lips with his tongue and gave her a deep, passionate kiss. His hands slid under her robe, and he grabbed both handfuls of her juicy ass and squeezed. His dick jumped as he explored the familiarity of what was once his, would always be his, no matter who they ended up with.

He whispered, "Maybe another time," and left.

Scott walked out of Layla's room and took the elevator several floors up. He was staying in the Grand Penthouse Two Bedroom Terrace Suite. Scott had gone to Layla's room to show her the letter he had gotten and to discuss how Maxine had masterminded the assassination of their children. Yet, they negotiated the murder of his firstborn son and daughter. With Layla under the influence and blind with rage about Lucky's duplicity, he made a judgment call to withhold the information for a day or two. He needed Layla to understand that he was calling the shots; that Maxine would be dealt with *his* way on *his* terms. He would be making all unilateral decisions regarding her demise.

He opened the door, and Cha-Cha and Nina were walking around his suite in only heels. Tight, toned bodies were pacing the room waiting for Scott West—The King of New York to arrive.

Scott was silent. His eyes were gifted with the sight of two women: both half his age. Their bodies were remarkable, perfection in every way. The women were professional escorts. The upper echelon in the service industry, the epitome of no strings attached. Nina was Haitian and spoke fluent Creole.

"Alo bèl gason," she murmured her greeting.

She was model tall and slender with the darkest chocolate skin he had ever seen. Her soft hair was cropped in a short natural afro which complimented her high cheekbones. Nina was stunning. An exotic looking beauty, unlike any woman he had ever had. And then there was Cha-Cha. An equally stunning beauty with video vixen curves. Her long hair was bone straight and parted down the middle showcasing her round face and pouty lips. Her bronze-colored skin indicated a pricey spray tan, but it worked. It complimented her blond highlights and blended with her brown hair.

Scott wasted no time inside his suite, getting the party started. He had been starved female companionship for longer than he would ever again be. Both women eagerly approached him like bookends, and piece by piece, he was undressed until his manhood stood at full attention. Scott followed the pair through the massive suite, walking through the solid wood double doors where a firm, king-size bed awaited their arrival.

"What do you want?" Cha-Cha asked.

"Everything," Scott said. Tonight he felt freaky and wanted to do kinky things.

Nina asked, "Any safe word?"

Scott nodded. "Stop."

An expensive butter-soft leather duffel sat inconspicuously on the floor. So much perversion was crammed into the seemingly inconsequential luggage. A naughty bag filled with adult toys for adult things. Leather whips, nipple clamps, anal plugs, vibrators, flavored lube, edible panties, pussy pops, ball gags, deep throat numbing spray, Kama Sutra body dust with feathers, and scented massage oils. The treasure trove also had bindings: zip ties, handcuffs, and leather straps.

"Sit down, Mr. West." Nina and Scott were staring eye to eye. He didn't move, so her manicured hand had to assertively push him off his feet. "You're a powerful man, Mr. West. Used to being in control."

Cha-Cha kneeled to open the goodie bag, her legs gaped open, exposing her weekly Brazilian sugar wax. Her pussy was phat and pink, and Scott was eager to inch his way inside her. She finished where Nina had left off. "Tonight, Mr. West, you're going to get fucked."

As Cha-Cha fumbled through the bag, she coyly teased him. In her most flirty voice, she said, "What does a powerful man like yourself *really* want in the bedroom?" Her hand landed on the handcuffs but felt that would be too crude considering his recent situation. Cha-Cha slid the leather straps out of the bag and wrapped each end around the palms of her hands and pulled. It made a snapping sound before she ran her tongue across the restraint, a move meant to tantalize the drug kingpin.

"Get on with it," Scott said. He wasn't into this whole seduction scene. That wasn't what he had paid for.

The women moved the party along. Not at all offended by his outburst. They were professionals, and the client was always right. When the leather binds were tightly wrapped around Scott's wrists, he wanted to protest. But, a part of him wanted to be dominated; to see how it felt to be in a submissive, more relaxed role.

Nina liberally applied the body dust to the indomitable figure, and Scott was about to cancel these ho's until the feathers came out. Cha-Cha started at the soles of his feet while Nina began at his nipples. The ticklers had quickly sent sensations coursing throughout his whole body, and the tiny gestures, the subtle movements of the feathers gliding across his skin was phenomenal. Scott moaned his pleasure just as the women knew he would. His penis was rock solid hard and jumped in anticipatory satisfaction.

"Sit on my dick, ride me," he asked, particularly to no one. Any warm body would do. However, the women continued to ignore his request. He wasn't in charge. He wasn't calling the shots. Tightly bound, they felt more in control.

Four hands applied a liberal amount of massage oil, which heated upon contact. Every inch of Scott's muscular frame was kneaded, caressed, doted upon until two of those hands wrapped around his sizable penis. Cha-Cha placed a dental dam over Scott's penis and lathered up his magic stick with her saliva as she began to deep throat. Cha-Cha didn't gag as her head moved skillfully handling Scott's manhood, as Nina whipped him with a leather strap across his upper body. The combination of the sting from the whip, coupled with the pleasuring blowjob, had this gangsta in the palm of their hands. Cha-Cha continued to use her skills until Scott called out, "I'm about to come," — his juices erupting before sliding down his shaft.

The young women hoped that Scott was down for round two, if he could match their stamina and handle them both. Nina loved a big dick, so she motioned for Cha-Cha to switch positions. Nina's petite hands massaged his balls while her free hand jerked his penis until it responded. Cha-Cha placed clamps on his erect nipples, and Scott didn't realize how sensitive they were. He had submitted to these pros and allowed them to give him only pleasure. However, they needed to achieve that. So he had no issue when Nina lubed an anus plug and slid it deep inside Scott's mancave.

"Oh...shit...," he murmured his pleasure. The condom slid down his penis, and Nina climbed on reverse cowboy style and rode him with the expertise of someone who knew how to control a man with her pussy. His dick expanded her vagina walls and tickled her G-spot. Scott wanted his hands loose. He wanted to control the fucking, but they wouldn't let him go.

A pussy pop was placed over his mouth, and Cha-Cha lowered herself onto his face. "Eat me, daddy," she purred. And he did. While Cha-Cha slowly wound her hips, they both were gradually seeking satisfaction.

"Suck this pussy," Cha-Cha murmured. "Fuck me, daddy," Nina moaned. The erotism was unbelievable. Scott came and hardly had time to catch his breath before Cha-Cha climbed on board. As she rode him, Cha-Cha finger fucked Nina. The women gave him a show, both nasty with it. Soon Nina stood up on the bed, and as Cha-Cha handled him, she also ate Nina's pussy while slapping her hard on her ass. The optics had his mind blown, Scott couldn't believe the multiple orgasms he had. It drained him, left him spent. His breathing was hard, fast, irregular. He was ready to drift off into a peaceful sleep when the women finally loosened his binding. Cha-Cha walked over to the minibar and poured herself a glass of cognac. A light bead of sweat had formed on all bodies, indicative that a workout was just completed. She lazily walked backed over to the forty-plus-year-old Scott.

"Now, you fuck us."

They were just getting started.

The next morning Scott woke up alone. All signs of his late-night rendezvous were gone. Scott was glad that his heart was still beating. Those young women were insatiable. They had done things to him; he was surprised had never been done before.

Last night had invigorated him. He knew what needed to be done. On this day, Layla would learn the truth.

Chapter 6

The telephone number wasn't known to her, but Lucky knew the exchange, and it was New York-Presbyterian Hospital. She picked up thinking it was about her daughter or one of her brothers, maybe hurt again.

"Hello," she said frantically.

There was a pregnant pause, and then, "Ms. West?"

"Yes? Who's this? What's going on?"

"I work for New York-Presbyterian Hospital, and there's an Angel Morales here. He's saying he's the father of your child. He's downstairs in the lobby and wants to visit. We're not allowed to give out any details, but he's refusing to leave."

Lucky's heart rose to her throat. What had she done? Why had Angel ambushed her? What did he know? She swallowed hard and said, "Tell him I'll be there in an hour. Don't let him upstairs under any circumstance. My child could be in imminent danger. Do you understand that?"

The registered nurse understood. The premature baby girl was a West. She was the granddaughter of the infamous couple splattered across the news for nearly a year and was just acquitted of unspeakable things. She wanted no problems.

"Yes, Ms. West. As per hospital rules, he won't be allowed up."

Lucky didn't want to speak to her like she was the help because she needed an ally. "What's your name?"

"Mine," the nurse stalled. She didn't want to get involved, but her curiosity superseded her commonsense. She was born nosy. A person who liked to sip her tea, daily. At the nurses' station, she was the first to spread a rumor and gossip about infidelity and affairs between coworkers. "It's Pattie Jones."

"Pattie, are you located in the Neonatal Intensive Care Unit?"

"Yes, ma'am." Pattie couldn't believe she was giving this young woman so much respect, but something in Lucky's voice demanded it. Her tone was assertive, not aggressive. She spoke with confidence and a hint of impatience. "I'm one of the night nurses overseeing Lucchese. She's doing fine, she's in good hands."

Lucky got to the point. "I have a favor, and it's paid."

Despite her six-inch heels, Lucky's mink coat swept the floor while she walked. It was the symbolism of a diva, someone with large sums of money to blow. Her cavalier approach to the dire situation right in front of her would astound many. Lucky was playing a dangerous game. Her level of consciousness seemed on pause as she strolled into the hospital with Packer flanking her side.

Angel Morales, the head of the Juarez cartel, had flooded the large waiting room area with his men. He was less than pleased to be kept waiting and even less amused at Lucky's antics. Angel had called her nearly thirty times since arriving at the hospital only to get her voicemail. A slew of angry voice messages was left, threats of violence, imminent death had Lucky not come before his private jet took off at midnight.

Angel's long hair was slicked back into a tight ponytail. His tailored suit was under a full-length cashmere coat. His distaste for cold weather was written on his face, behind his eyes, through the snarl of his lips. He was pissed. Lucky could feel his heat permeating off his body; she felt smothered, unable to breathe freely. But she would persevere.

His heart pumps blood like mine, she thought. Lucky wanted to be stern but not disrespectful. "Why are you here?"

Angel lunged forward and grabbed a chunk of Lucky's hair. Her long locks were wrapped around his fist, nearly popping out all her luscious strands. Packer went to reach for his .357 but was blocked by Angel's men.

"Fuck y'all gonna do!" Packer barked. "I'll—"

"Just chill. I'm all right," Lucky called out. She was staring directly into Angel's eyes as she spoke to Packer. She needed to interject and save him before he said something that would end his life. Packer acquiesced at his boss's request. He was outnumbered and outgunned, but it didn't stop him from acting a fool. Packer was a goon, dragged up in the concrete jungle always on his ignorant shit. If Lucky gave the command, he would have set it off up in that hospital, not giving a fuck if they were cartel. Seething, his nostrils flared wide as Packer blew hard, trying to release his negative energy. He was amped up, hoping to pop off to prove he was the young thug Lucky had entrusted with her safety.

Lucky could feel her hair removing from her follicles as Angel continued to pull, not loosening his grip. A lone tear slid down her cheek as the pain grew to an almost unbearable level.

"Don't ever question me again, puta," he spat. "And don't ever fuckin' keep me waiting or I will chop you up into tiny pieces and feed you to my iguana." Angel was effeminate, with a slight body frame, but he was far from fragile. He was one of the deadliest men in the world, and Lucky was treading in deep water.

Angel was here for one task: infant verification. Finally, she was released. "Go." His command was succinct yet straightforward.

Both walked toward the elevators. As the doors closed, Angel used his right hand to make a gun, pointed it at Packer, and pulled the trigger. The gesture spoke loudly, but Lucky remained silent to the threat. The two rode up several stories, alone. Lucky snaked through the long corridor, through a couple nurses' stations, passing NICU before stopping at the maternity wing. There, twenty newborns were sleeping comfortably in their stainless steel, padded bassinets. Her eyes scanned the room, looking for her child. When she read: Lucchese West, she exhaled. Within seconds, Nurse Pattie appeared.

"Ms. West, we didn't expect you back so soon. Visiting hours are over."

"I want to see my son," Angel demanded in a less than friendly tone. "Now!"

Pattie looked to Lucky, just as they had rehearsed over the phone. Lucky asked, "Would it be okay just for a few minutes. His father hasn't met him yet."

Pattie noisily exhaled. "Okay, Ms. West. But just for five minutes in the nursery. I'll get your son and bring him to you."

Lucky led Angel into the nursery's sitting area. The walls were painted yellow with mint green, baby blue, and pink stuffed animals decorating the space. The chairs were large, with thick cushions and high backs. Changing stations were there, which left a stale stench of urine and defecation lingering in the air. Angel wanted to move this along.

The little bundle of joy was brought into the bright room, and he immediately got cranky. He was awoken from his comfortable nap to participate in this hoax, his real parents unaware of the shenanigans taking place.

The healthy, robust baby was placed in Lucky's arms, and Nurse Pattie quickly left. Lucky looked down into the eyes of a stranger and pretended to care. "Hi, handsome," she cooed.

"Mama's here."

Angel eyed the newborn skeptically.

"You can see that my son is full term," she began as she bounced him up and down, trying to get him to stop crying. This child was nearly ten pounds of baby weight. "As I said, we call him Lou, and he is not your child unless my name is Mary, and you're a god and impregnated me two months before we had sex."

Angel looked down at the child and studied him intently. He was light brown, but his ears said he would get a couple shades darker. His hair was jet-black and curly, but that wasn't a telltale sign of any race with African American children. He looked at the baby's broad nose and puffy, full lips, and knew this wasn't his DNA.

"Why you have a baby with such an ugly man?"

Lucky looked up and tried to act offended. "Lou's father is handsome, and so is my son. I only fuck the best." She thought about the eye candy waiting for her in the lobby. Packer was handsome by anyone's standard. He sported a dark goatee that framed his mouth, accented by his light skin. His dark curly hair softened the eyes of a killer, and she loved grabbing his hair when they sexed missionary style. He had that swag you couldn't buy.

Angel laughed his disagreement. "You crazy," he continued. "You should run and leave him here, give him to the state and start over."

"That's enough, Angel. You've made your point. He's not your child, even though I already told you so."

Angel shrugged.

"Are we done?" she asked.

"Not yet."

Angel reached into his coat pocket and pulled out a clear plastic bag with writing on it. Two giant Q-tips were inside.

"What are you doing?"

Angel roughly grabbed the cheeks of the baby and swabbed

the inside of his mouth, saturating the Q-tips with his DNA before sealing up the medical bag.

"Trust but verify."

Lucky felt lucky to had found a nurse to help her pull off this caper. It would cost her thirty large, but you can't place a price tag on your life. She was now grateful that Angel was who he was and came through early to do his popup. His sneak attack worked in her favor, so now she and Lucchese could relax. And with Angel, they could resume business as usual.

"You should get a DNA test too. These hospitals in America switch up babies all the time."

Lucky rolled her eyes. "I'm good."

Chapter 7

The estranged couple finally agreed to sanction the murders of their firstborn son and daughter. The two had just shared a meal at a popular Harlem dinner spot owned by a business associate of Scott's. As they walked in the brisk night air, Scott was ready to discuss the polarizing, sensitive subject of their younger three. Scott reached into his coat and removed a letter from the inner pocket. He handed it to Layla.

She stared at Scott with uncertainty. "What's this?"

"You need to read it. It's important. You were right."

A cop car flew by with its lights blaring. Scott fixed his eyes on it for a moment and then shifted his attention back to Layla. Her face was in the letter. She was reading it slowly. As she read, he could see the emotions forming in her eyes, the frown on her face, and the tears streamed down her cheeks. He remained silent. He wanted her to read it thoroughly, with no interruptions. They stood on the Harlem street corner, and though surrounded by noise and traffic, it felt like it was only them two. They had more privacy outdoors than inside.

Her eyes were flooded with blinding tears. When she

finished reading the letter, Layla never felt so angry, furious, betrayed, and embarrassed. How could she have been so stupid? What kind of mother was she to leave her children vulnerable to be used as pawns in a twenty-year-old beef? Layla was visibly ill. Her hands got cold and clammy as her heart pounded so loud it felt like her eardrums would burst. *It's my fault*, she thought. *I paid this goon to kill my kids.* Layla's eyes locked with Scott's, and she uttered with contempt, "When do we kill this fuckin' bitch?"

Scott nodded. He understood her hurt and her pain. The letter revealed all that they needed to know—Maxine was the culprit behind everything. She was a mastermind, and they greatly underestimated her.

"It's not that easy," he uttered.

Layla scrunched up her face. "Not that easy?"

"There's Bugsy and the baby," he said.

"And what they got to do wit' it?"

"First, we just beat federal indictments, and there's still unwanted attention on us. We're hot, and we're in the news. We react to this now, and it's gonna look bad on us," Scott said.

Layla seethed. She wanted Maxine dead—more than dead, she wanted the bitch to suffer, to be tortured until there was nothing left of her to torture, and then she wanted the bitch dismembered and her body parts scattered everywhere. Layla dried her tears, and now her heart was on fire with rage.

"She murdered our children, Scott! Our fuckin' babies!" Layla cried out.

"And she will pay, but we need to be patient."

Scott felt her rage. Since Bugsy and Maxine came to visit him while he was incarcerated and told him about their affair, he only thought of the day they would both die by his hands. But Scott couldn't rush to kill anyone—not yet, only when the time was right. And he needed Layla on board to help pull it off.

"I have a plan," said Scott.

Layla was listening. Walking back to where they came from,

they discussed the murders of Bugsy and Lucky like they were at a boardroom table. They had to worry about Meyer, knowing how close he was to his siblings. Would he want to retaliate?

"If we do this, then we need to make the hits appear to come from an enemy. Tear a page from Maxine's playbook. We can't get our hands dirty. For now, we don't mumble a fuckin' thing to anyone…no one! We play things cool and enjoy being home for a moment," Scott explained. "We need to keep those pigs up off of us, because it'll be death by a fed before I do life behind bars."

Layla was listening. She wanted him to keep talking. This was the Scott she fell in love with—smart, violent, and devious.

Her steps were measured, each heavier than its predecessor, as she cautiously approached her SUV. Lucky's hand tightly gripped her .45 as she made her way toward the driver's side of her vehicle. Her neck was on a constant swivel as she scoured the underground parking garage for threats. She could see him; his upper body, his head, in clear view of her lightly tinted window. *How did he get inside of her G-wagon?* She wanted to know. *What was going on?*

Lucky tried to be optimistic and hope that her man could answer all her questions. Eventually, she stood at his eye level and shook her head, exasperated. Her face showed perplexity. Lucky opened her door and saw the tiny bullet hole to his left temple. There was stippling from the close-range entry but no blood. He had been shot elsewhere, and then his body was transferred to her driver's seat. Packer was dead. And her mother was unequivocally behind the hit.

Layla came out swinging first. Packer's murder was a message to just her, not her brothers. It said: You're not protected. You're not safe. You're not untouchable.

And so it begins, she thought. *The start of war.*

Lucky's fingers moved lightning fast as she dialed two of her top triggermen and instructed them to meet her in her buildings' underground parking garage. She hated to do it, but she couldn't stand around gawking at a dead man, nor could she take a chance and leave him there unguarded. Lucky climbed into the passengers' seat and faced him. Her two fingers touched his neck, and he was still warm, recently deceased.

"Damn, Packer," she said emphatically. "How you let them get at you?"

Lucky sat with the corpse and studied his face, the side that hadn't been violated. Packer looked like he had dozed off for a quick nap and would soon wake up. She looked at his clothes. New wheat colored Timbs, red and blue Gucci sweater and matching knitted cap, jeans, and mink jacket. In death, he was fly. Packer always wore every piece of gaudy jewelry he owned and dared a nigga to run up on him. The six platinum and diamond chains hung low, weighted investments that made a statement wherever he went. His iced-out Rolex peaked out from under his sleeve, apparent signs this wasn't a robbery.

Minutes felt like an eternity for the young queenpin. The typical garage sounds could now indicate threats; the elevators opening, footsteps, conversations, and horns all had her on edge. Lucky's head craned as she gripped her .45—counting down the seconds when her men would come to back her up. Finally, Yusef and Opie arrived.

"Yo, who did this," Yusef asked as he opened the drivers' side door. He stared at Packer and felt little remorse. Opie, too, was more surprised than saddened. These men knew that any day could be your last, so they always partnered up to have someone watch his six. But Packer was a lone wolf. He had a serious chip on his shoulder and apparently brought a knife to a gunfight. Someone had punched Packer's clock, and they were clueless as to why. Were they at war?

"Ssssh," Lucky whispered. "Ask questions later. We need to get him the fuck out of here."

Neither man moved. They continued to stare at the dead body. After a long moment of silence, Yusef wondered out loud. "Who put this nigga in here?" He then whistled his disbelief but kept talking. "Whoever did this shit is on some other level."

Everyone paused as the buildings' security drove through the garage, slowing down to observe the two men hovering around the pricey Benz. Thinking quickly, Lucky jumped out and waved his way. Security did a head nod of recognition and kept driving doing his rounds. Lucky was livid, her stomach was doing somersaults. She glared at Yusef. "Get this muthafucka out of here!" Both finally sprang into action. Lucky stood off to the side as the lookout, and Opie grabbed Packer's legs while his upper torso rested on Yusef's chest, their arms intertwined. Packer's dead weight was placed in the backseat where he was belted in. Lucky climbed into the backseat next to him and shuddered. This was a setup? If caught, she would do life in prison. Her paranoia had ballooned, but she wouldn't let her men see her crumble under pressure.

Yusef hopped in the drivers' seat, and Opie sat shotgun. He started the ignition, and before he backed out, he said to Opie, "Yo, get out and make sure the brake lights and signals are working." Opie nodded and jumped out. Lucky made a mental note to give him a bonus for thinking under these circumstances.

While the men made sure there weren't any potential mechanical issues that could get them pulled over, she took another look at Packer. It still hadn't sunken in that he was gone forever.

Finally, Yusef asked, "Where to?"

"Drive to Lincoln's Mortuary in Harlem."

"A'ight."

"Don't speed and obey all traffic laws." Lucky stated what

Yusef already knew. He didn't plan on getting charged for a body he hadn't bodied.

As they peeled out, Lucky braced herself for the chaotic spectacle that only a federal takedown could perpetrate. When nothing happened, she went back to Layla's culpability. She knew in her heart she was behind this murder. Lucky would not let this slide, she would seek and get retribution for her fallen soldier. Lucky would need her brothers to have her back. In battle, casualties were inevitable, but she wondered, had she declared war?

The quiet in the car felt eerie as everyone was in deep thought. Yusef broke the silence with his continuation to his line of questioning.

"You need to be mad careful, boss. Whoever did this was sending a message. They went after your top enforcer, plucked him off, left him gift wrapped at your door. We need to send our own fuckin' message, maybe go kickin' in some muthafuckin' doors until we find out who murdered our comrade. Blow some fuckin' heads off!"

As he drove, he became increasingly animated in the front seat. It was like the totality had sunken in, and he felt violated.

"Keep that same energy, Yusef, and I'm going to bless you. I might have an idea who's behind this hit, but let me do me and speak with Meyer first."

Opie chimed in. "I got your back too. Don't forget 'bout a nigga."

Lucky ignored him as she opened her Chanel bag and sat it on the floor. One by one she removed Packer's chains. The weighty pieces of gaudy bling felt like heavy rocks.

Yusef saw the transaction in the rearview. "Lucky, ma, let me get one of those."

She thought for a moment. The selfishness in her didn't want to share. Lucky felt like a kid on the playground being asked to share the sandbox. She felt entitled to keep it all: chains, watch,

51

rings. Inherently she was territorial, a quality found in predators, but she knew that if you went after lions, you had to keep the tigers happy.

Reluctantly she grabbed the two least expensive pieces. She handed one chain to Yusef, and before Opie could ask, she shoved one in his hand too. The thank you's rolled off their tongues as they immediately draped their necks with what once belonged to Packer. His body wasn't even cold, and he had been violated for a second time.

Thirty minutes later, the Benz drove around back, secured by a privacy gate, and was met by a distinguished gentleman that the neighborhood called Mister Rogers. Rogers had a lucrative business for nearly twenty years disposing of bodies for the underworld. Lucky was introduced to him several years back through her father. Scott had a longstanding relationship with Mister Rogers, and that was the only way Lucky had gotten grandfathered in.

Two men in white lab coats and a gurney came out to retrieve the body as if this was a legit operation. The trio followed Packer into the back crematory and watched with pure fascination as his body went from skin and bones to a pile of dust. She felt bad. Packer deserved a proper funeral, to be mourned by those who loved him, to have a grave marker to prove he had once been here. This action had erased him from history.

But this was the game, and he knew what he had signed up for.

Chapter 8

Had Max planned for the longshot, prepared should Scott and Layla get acquitted, then perhaps she would have spared herself the desperation she now felt. Max was a reasonable thinker making unreasonable choices. Under duress, she was about to take a huge gamble. But her options were limited. She could either wait for Bugsy to realize that he needed to move against his father, or she could take matters into her own hands to survive. Max had chosen to survive.

Max dressed comfortably for the task in front of her. Wearing jeans, a hoodie, goose coat, and sneakers, she strapped her pink handled .22 to an ankle holster and placed a 9mm in her waistband. With no shortage of weaponry around the apartment, Max added a .45 to Dillinger's diaper bag as an additional measure of protection. She was headed into the eye of the storm, the devil's playground. She would be on his territory, with her son, and had witnessed firsthand what he was capable of. But he was what she was looking for. Max needed someone criminal-minded, and you found that character in the hood amongst criminals.

Dillinger was secured in his car seat, but she noticed, to her dismay, that the child safety lock wasn't working. It was yet another thing she would need to handle. Max placed his diaper bag with several bottles of pumped milk on her Benz's backseat. Her son was sleeping peacefully for the moment, she hoped he would sustain that level of peace during their outing.

Her Michelin tires glided on the rugged paved roads of the city as she navigated her way Uptown Manhattan for an unscheduled meeting with an unsavory thug. If you wanted redemption, you went to church. If you wanted revenge, you went to the streets. The familiar landscape brought back memories; nostalgia, fear, exhilaration, and victory were all attached to that night. One of the last times she would see her friend Skip alive. Max drove past the iconic Apollo Theater and continued on 125th Street until she made a few turns heading west, ultimately arriving at Bonita's Beauty Salon on 108th street. It was eleven o'clock in the morning on a weekday, and the establishment was bursting at the seams with customers. From the street view, it looked standing room only. About a dozen beauticians were roller setting, blow-drying, or relaxing black and Dominican hair; arm movements flailing back and forth.

This area was busy. A lot of foot traffic due to the retail stores and local eateries in the neighborhood.

Max sat parked with the car idling for warmth and swiveled in her seat. Her baby was sound asleep, not expected to awake for his feeding for a couple hours. She didn't feel as though this was the worst decision she had made, but it could be in her top three. Max knew it could go either way and prayed that she hadn't placed her son in imminent danger. Currently, she didn't trust Dillinger alone with anyone except his father. Not with Scott and Layla on the loose. As she sat working up the nerve to go inside, Marisol and three henchmen came barreling out of the establishment. Max had only been parked for a few minutes, and she had been spotted as a threat. Max rolled down the window and smirked.

"What's all this?" she asked. Max stared each triggerman eye-to-eye with an unwavering swagger that years in the penitentiary had manifested. Her face was stone cold, her body stiffened, alert—an allegory of readiness. She was down for muthafuckin' whatever.

"You don't belong here!" Marisol shouted, still salty about having to pay for the merchandise during their last encounter. "Leave."

Max ignored her outburst and looked past the insignificant girlfriend. She sized up the three goons and landed on Diego, who was unmistakably one of the henchmen from last year's foiled robbery and double homicide. "Hey, amigo, go get your boss. I came to see Juan-Pablo. Tell 'im it's Max."

"Where he knows you from?" said Diego.

Max turned her head, and up went her passenger's window. If you wanted respect, you had to demand it. Seconds would pass before they back-peddled into the shop. As she waited, Max turned on the radio to a classical station. Mozart played softly in the background, which she used to keep Dillinger lulled asleep. A few taps on her window, and she stared at an unsmiling Juan-Pablo. Max unlocked her door, and he slid in.

He got straight to the point. "You don't know me like that to just be rollin' up on me. You lucky ya man is connected, or you would have problems." Juan-Pablo was fresh in his Yankees fitted, leather shearling, sixty-thousand-dollar watch, and black Uptowns. His light skin was newly inked with an elaborate neck tattoo. Amongst all the colors, vibrant red and yellow and dark blue and black, she saw the insignia and read the words, Murder Inc.

Without permission, Max placed the ignition in drive and peeled out. He barked, "Yo, where the fuck you goin'?"

"Stop yelling!" Max retorted. "My son is in the back."

Juan-Pablo craned his neck to the backseat, saw the sleeping infant, and relaxed. He repeated, his voice on a lower frequency. "Where you goin'?"

"Nowhere," she said. "Anywhere. I'm just driving so we can politick."

Juan-Pablo played along. "About what?"

"Murder."

He snorted. "I plead the fifth. I ain't do shit."

They both chuckled.

Max continued, "Nah, on some real shit. I got a job for you."

"Me?" he quizzed. "That's above my paygrade. I'm a barber, mamí. I only cut hair."

"Stop fucking around," she snapped. "I don't have all day. I came here because after our little run-in, I asked around about you. I know that you're a heavy hitter, the head of Murder Incorporated, and y'all are the best at what you do."

"And?"

"And you know that Scott West and I have history."

He shrugged. "So?"

"He was acquitted."

"That's national news. From New York to Compton—niggas already know he beat that fed case."

Max made a left and then another left, making her way back to the beauty parlor. She said, "Scott and Layla snitched their way to an acquittal. It was all a public spectacle, a magic act, perpetrated by our government meant to distract. Their business associates want them dead."

"Dead?"

Max made a rolling stop in front of Bonita's. "The Garcia cartel wants to outsource this hit to your crew. Will Murder Inc. take the job?"

"And they sent you to broker the deal?"

"It is what it is."

Juan-Pablo whistled his uneasiness. "That's some cold shit." He turned around and peered at her son, thinking it was Scott's child. He weighed the variables. The West's were hot, so much so, their own affiliates wanted them eliminated. However, if they successfully pulled off these hits, the Garcia cartel would become an ally. "We can't take less than one million per body."

Max shrugged. "Done."

"We take half upfront. Balance upon completion of the first contract. I choose who gets hit first, how, and where. No interference."

"When can we expect Scott dead?"

"Put your listening ears on mamí," he said. Juan-Pablo programmed his burner phone into hers and said, "Drop the payment off with Marisol. You and I won't have further contact."

Chapter 9

Lucky had decisions to make, and there wasn't anyone other than Meyer she trusted enough to be her sounding board. He had recuperated; his body slower than usual from drinking in those slugs, but his mind was unaffected.

"Why you think Ma is behind this hit?"

"Meyer, you know how she thinks. I brought him to court as a sign of strength, and that was disrespectful to that megalomaniac. She's a fuckin' lunatic!"

"Lucky, calm down." She was inside his apartment, pacing back and forth and chain-smoking. "Ma's only been home for seventy-two hours. I doubt dude was at the top of her list of retribution. A nigga she don't know."

She stopped dead in her tracks. "So, what you saying?"

Meyer sipped on his drink as he watched his sister near full-blown hysteria. Lucky was animated and angered, but most important, blowing his mellow high. Since his incident, Meyer sipped Lean. Each day he would mix cough syrup, a few Jolly Rancher candies, and Welches grape soda in a glass. The drink did many things for the recovering gunshot victim, but mainly it took his pain away.

"I'm sayin' that Ma couldn't have pulled this off by herself within that timeframe."

"Then, Scott helped her! I think Scott is backing Layla." Lucky was sure of it. Solo, they were a problem; together, they were an indisputable force.

"They don't even fuck wit' each other so teaming up to hit lil' man ain't probable. Besides, you buggin'. Ma hates Pops. All the shit he did to that woman...." His voice trailed off.

"Anything is possible."

"I'm sayin' that you need to think. Scott and Layla don't have no triggermen, no affiliates', no bread—you and Bugsy done took all that. And, they got the FBI on their asses. They even sneeze, and they're doing life," Meyer schooled his sister.

"They don't need triggermen."

Meyer nodded his agreement.

"And they ain't afraid of no FBI."

"Shiit, you crazy, you think that. You can't be a West talking that naïve. The FBI are why you and Bugsy ain't dead yet. They know if anything were to happen to any parties involved in the revolt against them, they're going straight to jail."

Lucky frowned. She was genuinely clueless. "Really?" was all she could say, her voice sounding like that of a child.

"You think they don't know about how Maxine went from father to son? They kick in the door, and Maxine and Pops are all boo'd up. A year later, she comes through with his sons' baby. Oh, they know all that shit, and they're just waiting in the cut for someone to act ignorant and do ignorant shit. And best believe they know about you and Layla's beef. So as I said, the FBI keeping you and Bugsy alive, so don't be a knucklehead. Y'all need to wave the white flag and call a truce. That parlay goes both ways. Should anything happen to them, don't be shocked if your front door gets kicked in." Meyer took another sip.

Lucky was still defiant. "Well, whether they did it or not, I came here to discuss our future. You know how much I love you even though we've had our issues. You and me, we see eye to eye on most things. We have our business to protect. And we both know that our place as the heads of our organization is now threatened with Layla home."

"And?"

"Don't act stupid, Meyer. If you want me to say it, then I will."

The codeine had taken effect. Meyer was feeling nice and wanted to chill. "Say what?"

"Layla's got to go, Meyer. Each day she breathes our lives are in danger."

Meyer was rolling up a tight blunt with some premium weed. His tongue ran alongside the Black & Mild paper, wetting the edges and tip. His fingers curled the narcotic in the brown paper until he formed a smokable cigarette. Meyer sparked up his blunt and took a deep pull, he inhaled for a few seconds before exhaling a billow of smoke. He finally spoke. "I'ma act like I ain't hear that shit. I told you that Pops and Ma ain't have shit to do wit' that dumb nigga getting rocked to sleep."

Lucky wanted to believe it was her archenemies, those formerly known as parents. She asked the question, "If not them, then who?" And simultaneously, they both answered, "Angel."

Meyer continued, "Hell, yeah, it was him. Probably on some jealous shit. I told you that I don't trust him. We should move against *him*. He's the nigga that's got to go."

She panicked. "Meyer, no! We can't. He's too powerful and without—"

Meyer's brows connected in anger. "Without who?"

"Without Bugsy and the full force of an army. All of us, as one unit, and that's still a longshot. I'm just keeping it one hundred. We can't win, *you* can't go up against Angel. He's too powerful."

"You still don't believe in me!"

"That's a lie!"

"Then let me go after that bitch-ass nigga!" He coughed violently as the smoke from his blunt went down the wrong windpipe. Once he got himself together, he continued. "And I'ma talk to Scott and Layla and set this shit straight wit' all y'all."

Lucky exhaled. "Meyer, I appreciate your tenacity. I do. And you're one of the bravest men I know. But Angel is way out of your league. And not to hurt your feelings, but Scott and Layla don't respect you like they do Bugsy, so talking to them means nothing. I came here to go after something achievable, and that was making sure that Layla could never hurt us again. I have a child to think about. Lulu is innocent in all this, and if Layla finds out about her, who her father is, then Lucchese will be in imminent danger. And as her uncle, I thought you'd see things my way."

Suddenly, Meyer wanted her gone. It was all too convoluted. His brother and sister had made moves that affected him. They had attributed to the division of their family and had no way to fix it. Things were splintered, and she had just told him to his face; he wasn't strong enough to be the glue that could keep their organization moving forward.

"I'm tired, I need to chill."

"Oh," she said, offended that she was being dismissed. "You want me to get you anything?"

"Nah, I'm good. I just want you to get the fuck out. And don't slam my door behind you."

Chapter 10

It was a long ride to Plainfield, New Jersey, from Manhattan. Bugsy sat in the backseat of the Escalade as it sped through the Holland Tunnel and came out at the New Jersey end. Bugsy had been on his cellphone since he left home, conducting business and contacting everyone on his payroll to attend an emergency meeting. Nearly sixty of his men—soldiers and lieutenants were summoned to a newly acquired location, a preemptive strike from Bugsy.

His cellphone vibrated, and it was Maxine. Bugsy hesitated momentarily to contemplate whether he should answer. He had a lot on his mind and wanted to focus on business, but he knew if he sent her to voicemail, he would have to hear her mouth later. He answered, "Hey, babe. Can I call you back after my meeting?"

Maxine snapped, "No, Bugsy. I've asked you a hundred times to take my car to Mercedes to get the child safety lock fixed. You can't do that, but you got time for business?"

"I will tomorrow. I promise."

"You said that yesterday."

Bugsy looked at his watch. Now wasn't the time for his Honey-Do list. He replied with, "Why can't you drive the Beamer?"

"That's Scott's car," she explained. "I shouldn't be driving it, so please, the Benz, get it fixed."

Truthfully, both cars—the pearl white Benz S63 AMG and the snow-white BMW 745i were bought with his father's money so he couldn't distinguish the difference. But this conversation put him on notice that it was time to buy his woman a few things; upgrade her vehicle, bling out her jewelry. Maxine was soaked in his father's wealth, reminders of a time he was ready to forget. Scott had bought Maxine everything; therefore, she didn't ask Bugsy for anything. He kept twenty-million and several loaded firearms in the home safe that he gave her the combination to, but Maxine only dipped into it for household essentials. Maxine could have purchased herself ten cars with his money if she wanted to, but instead, she tried to beef about a broken door latch.

"I will," he repeated. "Love you."

"Love you too."

The SUV came to a stop in the parking lot, and Bugsy climbed out of the vehicle, looking sharp in a long black wool overcoat, tailored suit, and hard bottoms. He always seemed more Wall Street than drug kingpin. Bugsy was about to go into the wolves' den and exert his authority—show the other wolves he was still the alpha male of the pack. Flanked by Chopper, he entered the location and proceeded toward the meeting area where everyone waited for his arrival.

Inside the large room were his soldiers and street lieutenants, all standing around waiting for Bugsy—the head of the organization to give his State of the Union Address. Bugsy entered the room like he was the president—the only nigga wearing an overcoat and suit inside the room. His presence personified the strength of a lion. Only a ruthless, smart, and skilled man like himself could bring together and command the respect of dangerous men, hardhearted killers. Bugsy's face was stone. He was a serious man with some serious business to tackle. He moved through the front of the crowd with a tiger's stride and stepped onto a platform. Bugsy scrutinized the sea of faces before him, each man unsmiling. An anticipatory blanket of curiosity swept throughout the room, each goon waiting for Bugsy to give them guidance and assure them that things would remain the same—that money would continue to flow.

Finally, he spoke. "I know by now y'all heard the news that my father has been found not guilty. And although I'm happy that he's home, I want everyone in this room to know that it doesn't change a fuckin' thing! I run and will continue to run the West empire. Now, this has been a very prosperous year, and we will continue to grow…branch out like we've been doing under my leadership. I'm ready to take this organization to the next level. Remember, I'm a man that's smart enough to run a successful drug operation under the watchful eyes of the FBI and not get caught!"

Bugsy's words echoed through the silent room as he took a jab at his parent's misfortune. He was talking that gangsta shit that goons loved to hear. They all knew that Bugsy was up there telling the truth. That's why they all respected him.

The energy in the room was electric, intoxicating the newly minted boss. Instantly his ego had ballooned to that of a dictator. He ordered, "No one under my umbrella can break bread with my Pops. Scott West is now public enemy number one. He's not to be respected, not to be trusted, not while the FBI still has him on their radar. I don't want to hear about none of y'all contacting him, exchanging numbers…none of that.

And most importantly, keep my business, the moves we make from today forward, under my tutelage, between us! This isn't for his ears. Mums the fuckin' word when it comes to my father. Y'all gotta remember, affiliating with him is bad for business."

Just then, a loud and slow clap resonated inside the room. It came from the rear of the assembly of men. Everyone turned toward the noise that dared disrupt Bugsy's tyrannical rhetoric, and Scott loomed into everyone's view. The original gangsta himself had made an impromptu appearance that shocked attendees, including Bugsy, who was stunned. It showed on his face. Apparently, someone still held allegiance to his father. Bugsy was astonished that Scott would show up to undermine him. He was muthafuckin' livid that one of his men had snitched and gave up the new locale and meeting time. Where was the loyalty?

Scott's gaze was unemotional toward his son as he climbed on the platform—his throne—to speak to his men. Seeing Scott unexpectedly, the men stood with grins and gave him a receptive ovation. The love in the room was palpable. He could have been Christ rising from the dead. That's what it felt like—the man was legendary.

Scott shouted. "Everybody shut the fuck up!"

Quickly, the room was silenced. Scott stood a few feet from his son—the prodigal child, and they locked eyes. Bugsy stood his ground on the platform. He didn't flinch or look worried.

"So you're in charge now, Bugsy," Scott said gruffly. The speech Bugsy gave, it extended the betrayal Scott had experienced while locked in a cage. "What'd you think? I wouldn't find out about this meeting. You got a lot to fuckin' learn, little nigga! You stand up here like you built all this in twenty plus years like I'm not shit, huh?"

Bugsy frowned slightly, but he didn't move. He stood upright in front of everyone with his listening ears on.

"So you the one that went to war with the Barkley brothers back in nine-five for corners in Brooklyn, and it was you that went to war with Frank Nitti and Manny Henchmen, and got your hands bloody, huh? You grew up poor nigga…you from the hood, or did you grow up with a silver spoon in your mouth. You had shit handed down to you from day one!" Scott's eyes bore into his sons with contempt. "So, you're the one that established a solid relationship with the cartel? Did you travel to Mexico to meet with the head narcos and have your life threatened if you failed to produce results? What risks you took when you were young, nigga?

"Over twenty years, I've been in this game, and I've lost good men. I know the streets like the back of my hand. I'm from the gutter muthafucka...grew up in one of the poorest neighborhoods in the country. Is this your legacy or mine? I strategically guided this thing into a multimillion-dollar success. Nepotism got you here, nigga! Almost every soldier in this room can do what you do."

Bugsy was annoyed that he and his authority was belittled.

Scott ended his speech with, "I'm giving everyone in this room a choice, a onetime pardon. It's either you roll with him or me. This will be my last act of kindness to everyone here, and to let y'all know, you go against me, there will be no more mercy."

A decision needed to be made between the men inside the room, and it had to be now. No ambiguity, no indecisiveness— not back and forth. Unfortunately for Bugsy, nearly ninety percent of the room sided with Scott. He had the seniority and the creditability—real talk, he was their leader. The remaining were new recruits hired by Bugsy and didn't care about age and wisdom. Bugsy was their man, and they dared not part with him. The only person from Scott's era to stay with Bugsy was Avery.

In the New Jersey room, the organization had been bifurcated, and a civil war was brewing between both men.

Scott announced, "Y'all muthafuckas listen up. You see this man here," he pointed to Mason standing beside him. "He's my new first-in-command. You need me, you must go through him. Now, meeting's adjourned. Everyone get the fuck out!"

The soldiers scrambled for the exit, leaving Bugsy standing there dumbfounded. He wanted to say, *the meeting didn't start yet, so everyone stays where the fuck they're at.* But Scott took a sledgehammer and shattered all his authority. Bugsy had been overshadowed by the looming, dark figure that was his father.

As the room was clearing out, Scott walked toward Bugsy. His business with his son wasn't done yet.

"You see that boy, now that's fuckin' power…real power and genuine respect." Scott mocked his son.

"Well done," Bugsy remarked coolly.

Scott was face-to-face with his son. The conflict between them was thicker than a brick wall.

"I see you've been really busy since I was locked up; you moved some things around and changed up locales, so now I'm gonna need the new locations to every stash house that's holding *my* muthafuckin' money and coke," Scott demanded.

Bugsy frowned at the strong-arming. "I'm not gonna be able to do that."

"Say what again? You're not able to do what? You better come up off what's mine, Bugsy, before I forget that you're my son."

Scott's glare and his menacing growl were intimidating, but Bugsy didn't scare easily. Yes, his father was an O.G.—a violent and notorious one, but Bugsy helped bring the organization into the twenty-first century. Bugsy became the brains behind the family and helped wash the street money clean. Bugsy established numerous Limited Liability Companies for the West organization and learned the tricks and trades of offshore accounts. Scott wanted to come and take it all away. He wanted to label Bugsy's contributions as inconsequential.

"It ain't happening," Bugsy continued to defy his father. "Possession is nine-tenths of the law, Pop, and I'm that nine-tenth. All that street knowledge didn't teach you that?"

Bugsy openly challenged his father. A blatant sign of disrespect and Scott would not stand for it too much longer. They stared angrily at each other—long ago, they had a beautiful relationship. Now it crumbled faster than the Berlin wall.

"You think your dick's bigger than mine?" said Scott.

Bugsy shrugged. "Ask Maxine."

"You ignorant muthafucka!" Scott uttered and lost his composure. He responded to Bugsy's defiance with a solid fist into Bugsy's gut. It was a swift punch, no one saw it coming. Bugsy folded over from the blow, and before he could lift himself up, Scott punched his son in the face, dropping Bugsy to his knees. Scott had had enough of his son's rebellion. He stood over Bugsy, furious, and exclaimed, "I'm gonna teach you some fuckin' manners!"

It was a sucker punch. Bugsy would not take it lying down. He charged at Scott aggressively and tackled his father like a linebacker for the Giants, entangling his arms around Scott. The two went flying off the platform, crashing down on the floor like a meteoric impact—a loud thump boomed. The sudden fall nearly knocked the wind out of both men. Bugsy quickly found his footing and attacked Scott with a hard right, followed by a quick left to his jaw. Bugsy was fuming. Scott struggled against his son; the melee between them was fierce and frightening. They both went pound for pound. Bugsy was the skilled boxer, and Scott was a skilled brawler. Scott had twenty years on his son, and he wasn't as agile and swift like he used to be. And his body was still mending from the multiple gunshot wounds Scott received from the government. Still, he refused to be beaten.

Swollen knuckles, bruised faces, torn clothing, and a black eye ensued, and both men were breathing hard, refusing to lose against the other. The few men that had lingered behind, they stood and gawked in awe at two kingpins—father and son going for the kingpin crown. It didn't take too long for Bugsy to get the best of him. Multiple punches to his face and body made Scott's body buckle.

Both men were amped, looking to fight to the death as men from both camps looked on. It was almost better than a heavyweight fight at the MGM Grand. Bugsy was poised in a boxing stance, glaring at his father—bare-knuckle brawl; winner takes all, and he was ready to end this. Mason stood on the sideline watching, and when he saw Scott losing in the battle against his son, he was itching to break it up. Mason made his way toward Scott, seeing his friend winded and injured, but Scott shook his head at Mason, warning him to back off. He had this fight. Scott wanted to teach his son a lesson. Scott anticipated his son's movements, and a flurry of two and three-piece combinations landed on Bugsy's gut and ribcage, but the young West wouldn't lie down. He took whatever his father could give and kept advancing forward.

Eventually, Mason stepped between the two men pretending to break it up. Bugsy suddenly found himself held firmly; his arms folded behind his back by Mason's stronghold. Scott rushed forward with this opening and painfully delivered a three-piece combination and uppercut to the jaw that leveled Bugsy to the floor. Finally, he was done. Scott towered over his fallen son, and he berated him.

"You not ready, muthafucka!" he shouted. "You not fuckin' ready! You think you can be me! You think you can fuck my bitch, take my shit, disrespect me and get away with it?" He was irate. "I'll kill you! You hear me? I'll kill you, you ungrateful muthafucka!"

Bugsy lifted himself to one knee with his head hanging low in his hands. He needed a moment to catch his breath and gather his thoughts. His father's baritone voice was cutting through the air, fucking with him. Scott had cheated to get the win; Bugsy was tag teamed, jumped, and in his book, that was a clear violation. Bugsy reached in his waistband and pulled out his .45, his arm outstretched and aimed a loaded gun at Scott's head. The room fell into a panic. Everyone stood nearby on pause, their nerves on edge. However, Scott didn't flinch. He stood there boldly, staring down the barrel of a Glock.

"Do it, muthafucka! Your bitch-ass...do it!" he screamed at Bugsy. His eyes showed no fear. It wasn't the first time someone pointed a gun at him, but it could be the last.

Bugsy seethed. He wanted to badly murder his father in cold blood, in front of everyone, but he knew if he did, then he wouldn't make it out the room alive. Mason was ready to take the boys' life with his 9mm. It was aimed at Bugsy's head. Chopper gradually approached Bugsy and reasoned with him.

"We don't need this right now, Bugsy... just chill bruh." Chopper's voice was leveled and calm.

Bugsy knew his friend was right. Chopper coolly brought him down from the ledge, pulling him back from making the biggest mistake of his life. Things didn't need to get any uglier. Bugsy lowered the gun and walked away, his father made him come out of his character.

"This ain't over," Scott called after him. "Not until I say it's over."

Chapter 11

I t had been seventy-two hours since her release from jail, and Layla was a busy woman. She had a lot to do, things to accomplish, and fucking lives to ruin. Today, she had three appointments. Her first appointment was with her lawyer. Her driver drove her to Midtown Manhattan, where Layla sat relaxing in the backseat of the moving SUV. They were coming closer to her destination and soon came to a stop right in front of the towering, modern glass building with a glass-and-bronze entrance on Madison Avenue. The sprawling law office was on the 44th floor. Their logo in raised bronze lettering spelled out, *Spencer, Donnelly, & Bridges*. The place was modern and stylishly decorated with the best money could buy. Layla's driver double-parked on the busy street and opened the door for Layla to climb out of the vehicle wearing a stylish outfit that complimented her figure. In a pair of expensive heels, she marched into the building with purpose and rode up in the elevator with determination.

Layla strutted toward the receptionist and announced her arrival. She stood in front of the young blonde behind the modern curved desk with an attitude, clutching her Hermes bag. The woman pressed the intercom and said, "Mr. Spencer, Layla West is out here to see you."

He replied, "Send her right in."

"Yes, sir."

Her eyes looked up at Layla, but before she could escort her, Layla was already marching by herself, pulling open the mahogany double doors that led into Fitzgerald's corner office. Fitz stood up immediately when he saw Layla.

"It's good to see you again, Layla. Do you want some coffee, tea?"

"I want my money," she sharply replied.

He had extended his hand to her for a handshake, but seeing she wasn't in the sociable mood, he pulled it away. She looked at him intently; almost vehemently, the core of her eyes exemplified a vicious bitch when she needed to be one.

"Have a seat."

"I'd rather stand," she tersely replied.

He sighed. "Okay."

Fitz didn't understand why she had become so hostile toward him. If it wasn't for his legal skills, she would be rotting away in federal prison. Hadn't he proved to her he was worth every penny? After all he had accomplished, she wanted to find an issue with their payment arrangement. She'd found him through word of mouth from other satisfied clients, and she'd hired him on a retainer—an enormous sum—something that was smart of her to do in her line of work.

Her intense eye contact made Fitz fumble around his desk. He was trying to make small talk, but Layla wasn't having it.

"I understand your grievance with my office," he said.

"Do you?"

"You're here to talk billables, right? Well, let's talk," he said politely.

He handed her a stack of papers on expensive linen paper. Layla kind of snatched the documents from his hand and gawked at them. Her eyebrows pulled down in anger, and she exclaimed,

"What the fuck is this?"

"It's your final bill. I put everything I had into your case, the investigation, the discovery, this office doesn't come cheap, Mrs. West. I hope you understand that," he explained, sounding almost arrogant with it. "It was a lengthy trial."

She quickly flipped through every page until the last, and the figure at the end of it was something she didn't want to see. Fitzgerald claimed his services at an hourly rate, totaled $155,000 over the one-million-dollar retainer. She felt bamboozled by it all, along with feeling disrespected.

"One hundred and fifty-five thousand dollars!" she shouted. "Muthafucka, don't you owe me?"

"You're a liberated woman because of *me*," he repeated, smugly. And then questioned. "How do I owe you? You wanted the best, so you paid for the best. And we are the best in this city, paramount when it comes to litigation."

Layla came to his office to retrieve her money. She needed every dime she could get her hands on. Instead, she was handed a bill and told it needed to be paid while listening to him toot his own horn about doing his job. Layla thought Fitzgerald was highly condescending. He wanted to patronize her with his fancy, big words and his fancy, tailored suit, and his lavish office, but he had another thing coming.

"You tryin' to play me, nigga?" she asked, quickly going from somewhat civil to hood on him in zero seconds.

"I'm trying to make you understand that I'm an asset, Mrs. West. There might come a day when you'll need me again…let's not rock the boat here."

Fitz took a seat behind his large solid wood executive desk in his high back leather chair and kept his blue eyes on his client, who had become agitated.

"You know what, how 'bout you need me," she replied.

The statement confused him. "Pardon me?"

Layla had reached into her Hermes bag without him

noticing. She continued to stand but had inched herself closer to her lawyer and immediately removed the loaded gun. The silver .380 gleamed in her hand. And before Fitz could glean what was happening, she rushed over to his desk, grabbed him by the collar, and mashed the barrel of the gun against his bony cheekbone.

"Now, how 'bout you need me not to blow your fuckin' head off right now!"

"Are you crazy?!" he hollered, his tie and shirt ruffled in her hand.

"I am crazy! I'm crazy enough to go after not just you, but your wife and your pretty children if you don't come up off my fuckin' money."

His fear was bonafide. He trembled. The look in Layla's eyes was deadly. She wouldn't hesitate to kill him. He was dealing with an animal.

"Listen…," he cried out. "There must have been an accounting error. I'll fix it. Let me see the bill again."

She threw it in his face, and the papers cascaded to the ground. Layla loosened her grip around his shirt and tie, and Fitz caught his breath.

"Fix it!" she said.

"I told billing that you're supposed to get a twenty-five percent discount."

She wasn't satisfied. She motioned upward with her gun, meaning more. Fitz corrected himself and said, "Forty percent?"

Layla repeated the same action with her gun. Fitz groaned irately and said, "Fifty percent?"

Layla still wasn't happy. He whined and said, "If I cut the bill anymore, then I basically worked pro bono."

"You tried to fuckin cheat me! You better make it sixty percent. I want a sixty percent return of my money."

Sixty percent return of funds on this high-profile federal case was asinine. It was outrageous. But Layla was holding the gun in her hand, toward his head, with her finger on the trigger.

Fitzgerald was sweating, and he was trying to stall.

"Okay, I can write you a check," he said, reaching for his checkbook by trying to pull open the top drawer of his desk.

Layla was becoming an impatient woman. They had some privacy in his office, but there was no telling who would interrupt them. She grew angrier and suspicious, and before Fitz could open the drawer, she smashed the butt of the gun upside his head. It was a vicious blow. He howled and jerked backward with his hand clutching the side of his face. His eye bled.

"Do you fuckin' think I'm stupid? What you reaching for, huh?"

"I was going for my checkbook," he angrily explained to her.

"I don't need a fuckin' check; I want my money back in cash."

"Cash?"

"Cash!" she repeated.

He seethed. The audacity of one of his clients threatening him and violently attacking him. He was a prominent criminal attorney—a wealthy one too. Fitz mistakenly thought that after her ordeal with the FBI and the federal case that Layla would fear any reprisals. *What if he called the police? What if he went to the FBI?* She'd assaulted him with a deadly weapon. It was such brazen disrespect not only to himself but the law. Never in the fifteen years he practiced law had he experienced anything like this. He wanted her to leave. He wanted to throw her out the 44th-floor window and watch her body splatter on the concrete. That quickly, he despised his brilliant work and wished it had been a guilty verdict. She needed to be locked up for life, thrown into the pits of prison and isolated miles and miles away from any civilization—barred from society altogether.

It seemed like Layla read his mind. She thrust the gun further into his face, the barrel of her .380 hovering in front of him. It was so close to him he literally could see the bullet resting in the chamber. It was scary; one squeeze of her finger, and it could be embedded into his skull.

"I muthafuckin' dare you to call the police on me," she exclaimed. The .380 moved from Fitz's face, and the barrel of it pointed down to a picture of his family on his desk—his blonde hot wife and two pretty daughters. She continued with, "They'll be dead by week's end. I swear to you, muthafucka, I don't bluff. Now go get my money."

Fitz wondered what street college Layla had attended because he was convinced, she graduated magna cum laude. She had him paralyzed with fear to do anything but give her the money.

"Layla, it would be best to give you the money in a check, trust me. Would it be okay to write one so we could get this over with," he asked grudgingly.

"Nigga, how you got my money is the way I want it back." She demanded, "Cash."

Fitzgerald stood up, pivoted, and walked to the other end of his office. Layla was right behind him, her gun trained in the middle of his back. She was ready to snap his spine in half with a bullet if he moved wrong in her direction. Fitz stood in front of a large painting hanging in his office. He removed the art from the wall, and behind it was a wall safe. Reluctantly, he pushed in the number combination and opened the safe. Inside, there was an unbelievable amount of cash. It was money he wasn't paying taxes on. It was money he hid from his wife, and his ex-wife, and his partners at the firm.

"Damn, you a baller, huh?" she mocked. "You robbing your firm, nigga? Yeah, you are…all y'all muthafuckas are crooks."

Every ten-thousand-dollar stack he removed from the safe felt like his limbs were being torn apart. He placed six-hundred-thousand-dollars into a large shopping bag. It was Layla's refund. Even after the $600k, he still had plenty left over.

Layla scowled at him and said, "You lucky I don't take it all."

But truthfully, she couldn't take it all if she wanted to. The shopping bag wouldn't be able to hold that much anyway. She could barely conceal the cash in it now.

"Okay, sit back at your desk and chill for a minute. You attempt to do anything stupid…." Layla's voice trailed off.

He did what he was told with a hard frown, still bleeding from his face. He had gotten blood on his $5,000 tailored suit. It was ruined. He sat there enraged as he watched his money walk right out the door.

Layla walked out the lobby quietly and climbed into the backseat of the SUV as it sat there idling.

"Is everything okay, Mrs. West?" he asked her.

She smiled and replied, "Oh, everything's fine. The pieces are coming back together. Now take me to the spa."

Chapter 12

Y ou need a doctor?" Chopper asked Bugsy.

"I don't need a fuckin' doctor; I need to blow his fuckin' head off! You should've let me shoot that muthafucka!" Bugsy heatedly replied.

"It would have been suicide," said Chopper.

Bugsy sat slumped in the passenger's seat of the SUV as Chopper drove him into the city. His tailored, neat appearance was now disheveled and unruly. The right side of his face was bruised, his cheek swelling to an abnormal size. His right eye had blackened, the pupil bloodshot, almost swollen shut. Bugsy's ribs felt fractured, causing his breathing to be labored. He was fucked up. But he tolerated the pain as a gangsta would.

His mind raced, retracing what had just gone down. Scott's words and actions were equally yoked. To his men—Scott was powerful, deliberate, inspiring. His megalomania had mushroomed, erupted, and then infiltrated each mind that only moments earlier Bugsy thought held allegiance to him.

"You supposed to be my righthand man," Bugsy fumed. "You let their bitch asses jump me, and you ain't do shit!" He scowled, his anger palpable. Bugsy continued, "I'ma murder them both. Mason, he's a dead man. Fuckin' dead!" The audacity of his father embarrassing him in front of everyone, and then attacking him out of the blue. It was a sucker move.

"This ain't over," Bugsy promised.

Chopper knew better than to plead his case. It would have fallen on deaf ears. He could only imagine the turmoil that his best friend and boss was going through. Someone with less to lose would have told Bugsy he had placed himself in the position he was in. Chopper would give his right arm to have had a father like Scott West, a man who had placed Bugsy on a pedestal and continually treated him with the utmost respect. And Bugsy shitted on that whole relationship. And for what? A woman? An old broad at that. No fucking way would Chopper have cashed in all his chips for Maxine. But he wasn't Bugsy, so he didn't pretend to understand his actions. But what he would not do was tell his man how he felt. Bugsy had so much pent up anger he could take it out on him.

As Bugsy sulked, he realized that he needed to make sure his business—what was left of it, was still intact. He dialed Javier Garcia, and the telephone number had been changed. Bugsy panicked and went down his contacts list of cartel members. Each telephone number was no longer in service. His father had torn a page out of Bugsy's playbook. Bugsy no longer had a cocaine connection.

"Drive me to Meyer's," Bugsy said, exasperated.

Chopper nodded. Meyer wasn't too far away. Chopper emerged from the Holland Tunnel and into Lower Manhattan. He headed toward Midtown, on the Eastside. Soon Chopper stopped the vehicle outside a towering apartment building.

"You want me to go up wit' you?"

Bugsy didn't respond. He climbed out of the truck and buttoned up his coat. The wind was like a brick to the face—the hawk was out in full force, wings spread, creating a frigid night. He slid into the lobby with a purpose, ignoring the night doorman and headed toward one of the three elevators. He pushed the panel for the lift to open. The shiny elevator doors gave off a hazy reflection of his beaten face, a harsh reminder he and his father were on bad terms. He frowned and made his way to his brother's apartment, the last door on the left.

"Meyer!" Bugsy hollered as he aggressively banged on his brother's door.

Meyer opened the walnut solid wood door and allowed his brother to step inside. Immediately, Meyer noticed the elephant inside the room.

"Yo, what the fuck happened to your face, bruh?"

Bugsy saw the shock in Meyer's eyes and felt insecure. Before Bugsy could answer the question, Lollipop emerged from the bedroom naked, not caring who saw her goodies. She looked at Bugsy and smiled. "Hey Bee, long time no see," she greeted cordially.

He didn't return the warm greeting. Not that he didn't like Lollipop as a person, he just didn't want her for his brother. She looked like she had a disease you couldn't get rid of, and he hoped that Meyer always wrapped up when they were intimate. Bugsy looked to his brother to handle the Lollipop situation. "She needs to go."

Meyer turned toward Lollipop and said, "Get dressed and go. I'll make it up to you soon."

"I thought we were goin' to have a good time. How you gonna tell me to just leave."

"You heard what the fuck my brother said! Don't make me ask you twice."

Lollipop grimaced at Meyer's request. It was rude and uncalled for. "Fine nigga!" she hollered angrily. "Next time you want your dick sucked, don't fuckin' call me!"

She pivoted sharply and stormed into the bedroom. Minutes later, she was sloppily dressed and storming by the brothers cursing and ranting. She slammed the door on her way out. With her gone, Meyer said, "Bruh, this better be important because I was about to have a great time. Now, who did that to your face? Who we gotta body?"

"I had it out with Pop tonight," he explained.

"What?" Meyer was taken aback. "Scott did that?"

Before Bugsy could explain, Meyer's cellphone went off on the living room table. He walked to see who was calling, and once again, it was Layla. She had been blowing up his phone since she was released, but he had yet to answer.

Meyer smirked.

"Who's that?" Bugsy wanted to know.

"That's just Ma, calling," he explained. "I'm not tryin' to hear nothing she got to say."

Layla wasn't Bugsy's concern. He said, "I'm going after him. He crossed that fuckin' line tonight, and he has to go."

Meyer looked concerned by his brother's statement. "You want somethin' to drink."

"Nah," Bugsy said dismissively.

"Nigga, sit down, and have a drink. Beef always gonna be there."

Bugsy sighed, looked around, and reluctantly walked toward the couch. He took off his overcoat and suit jacket and took a seat on Meyer's plush sofa. "You got Macallan 25?"

"You even drink like Pops," Meyer shook his head. "Nigga, I got Henny."

Bugsy ignored his comment.

Meyer fixed himself a tall glass of Lean, Bugsy's Henny, and made his way back into the living room. He tossed his brother an expensive Cuban cigar and treated himself to a tightly rolled spliff. As both men lit up and took sips of their own drinks, Meyer studied his twin. His knuckles were scraped up, his face almost looked Elephant Man distorted, and his pride was shredded. Father and son had exchanged blows, mother and daughter had exchanged words, and now his siblings were contemplating putting their parents on permanent vacations. Things were getting out of hand.

Meyer inhaled the Kush and slowly blew out a stream of smoke that permeated throughout the room. He was already feeling nice. He finally spoke. "You playin' wit' fire, Bee. Pop doesn't have a soul...I'm telling you that man shouldn't be underestimated. You runnin' your mouth talkin' 'bout you want him dead, but you know wit' revenge you gotta dig two graves. You feel me?"

"And?" Bugsy was defiant, he wanted bloodshed. Bugsy took another sip of the brown juice. The cognac stung the cut he had on the inside of his mouth, and he grimaced. All this pain were reminders of war.

"I'm just sayin', let this shit slide before you do something that you'll regret your whole life."

"Who you think you talkin' too? I put thought behind everything I say and do."

"You and Lucky seem to think our parents will be easy to kill. Do we really know what our parents are capable of? Let's not overreact and just think this through. Besides, I don't want them dead. You know Layla's my bitch."

Bugsy glowered at his brother's foul, disrespectful mouth toward their mother but said nothing to check him on it.

Meyer knew he wasn't getting through to his brother. Bugsy was determined to start a civil war with their father. And it was ironic for him to be the voice of reason, the rational one when for so long he'd been the one with a hair-trigger temper. But being shot by his close friend, someone he considered a brother, it calmed him down for the moment. Luna unequivocally had his back, and Meyer had betrayed him just as Bugsy had done to Scott. It felt philosophical to Meyer, or karmic. He needed to show his siblings that if they didn't heed his advice, history would repeat itself. Meyer didn't want to be standing over a hospital bed, or worse, a casket of Bugsy or Lucky.

Bugsy looked at his brother resolutely and said, "You're

either with me or not on this one, Meyer."

"I hear you. But what's this about, disrespect or pussy?"

Bugsy feigned bewilderment. "What are you talking about?"

"You did fuck his bitch and got that bitch pregnant."

Bugsy frowned harder at Meyer's use of the word bitch to describe Maxine. And Meyer quickly picked up on it, saying, "Look at you, nigga... you ready to fight me because I called that bitch a bitch. You let pussy come in between family, nigga...real talk."

"That's the mother of my son, Meyer. Choose your words carefully."

"You got bigger problems than worrying about me calling her a bitch."

"Watch your mouth," Bugsy warned him again.

"She got you fucked up, nigga...pussy got you twisted. Maxine gonna get your wig pushed back. Scott gonna blow a cannon size hole in ya head, so don't say I didn't warn you!"

"Warn me? If I swing you supposed to swing too, Meyer."

Meyer shook his head. "Not on this. You're not reasonable you're whipped. You the one throwing the affair up in his face. Not only did you fuck Maxine while he was locked in a cage, but you gave her a baby and y'all playing house under that man's roof. You didn't even respect Scott enough to move elsewhere. Y'all turned that man's spare bedroom into a nursery. Nigga, you buggin'."

"You talkin' about respect!" Bugsy exploded. "You were ready to murder Pops over Penelope! The fuckin' nanny!"

"But I didn't, though." Meyer reclined farther back in his seat and stuffed his right hand into his sweatpants and fondled his dick with his brother just feet away from him. Between the weed and the Lean, he was feeling nice.

"This ain't just about Maxine," Bugsy explained. "Pops came to a meeting tonight that I held with my men—"

"His men," Meyer corrected.

"And took back his control of the organization right before my eyes!" Bugsy hopped up and became animated. He slammed his fist into the palm of his hand as he paced back and forth. "My pipeline with the Garcia cartel, gone! The inroads, respect that I've built—all gone!"

"You still got his bread?"

Bugsy paused all movements and then nodded.

"Ah, shiit," Meyer grinned. "You lookin' at this all wrong. You still in the driver's seat, bruh. Get down wit' me and Lucky's thing we got goin' wit' the Juarez cartel. And I promise you this, Layla ain't taking over our empire."

Meyer finally understood. While Scott was locked up, Bugsy got a taste of what it felt like to be the head nigga in charge, and he liked it. Power. It was intoxicating. Bugsy needed to go to rehab—go through a twelve-step program to come back down to reality.

Bugsy continued to counter Meyer's attempts at reconciliation. "It wasn't too long ago when you hated the man yourself."

"I still don't have that much love for him, but to war wit' him over some bullshit, nah...Bee. I got better things to do."

"Then you do it, nigga," Bugsy uttered upset.

The two men conflicted with each other. Bugsy thought he would have his brother's full support, but he was wrong. He fumed at Meyer's rejection and unwillingness. He didn't go to his hotheaded brother for advice, he wanted Meyer's wrath. He wanted to hear that his brother would go to war with him against their father. But instead, he received a lecture. It wasn't the Meyer Bugsy knew, a man that not too long ago would jump at the chance to let his trigger finger do what it does.

"Just chill, nigga. Let's call Lucky and figure all this shit out."

Chapter 13

The taste of a good cigar in his mouth once again was like an orgasm to Scott. He puffed on the Cuban cigar, drew in the smoke, held it for a few seconds to taste it, to let the flavor linger, and then let it go—exhaling it into the air. He kept it lit and took a drag or two about once every minute, sitting in the armed leather chair in his hotel suite. Scott was recouping from his fight with Bugsy. His body ached in places he didn't know existed. The brawl had aged him. It made him feel every year he was on this earth. And each battle scar was worth its weight in any precious metal; silver, gold, or platinum—his injuries meant something.

Scott showered and got dressed for his meeting. It was nearing noon. Mason arrived, and the two men got straight to business.

"You think he's gonna make a move on me?" Scott asked Mason.

"If I was in his shoes, I would."

Scott looked at him; his stare was cold, unwavering. Losing Bugsy was like losing what little soul he had left. He taught his children not to trust anybody *but* family. His children taught him not to trust anybody, *including* family.

"He's smart, and he shouldn't be underestimated," said Scott. "So, watch your back."

"I will. I'm watching both our backs."

Scott nodded.

"I know you, Boss. We go back decades, so what's the bottom line here?"

"All you need to know is that I know how the story ends. I've planned this out to the very last detail, and I'll fill you in on a need to know basis."

"I know how you move, but if push comes to shove, are you really willing to take it to the next level with him. Are you ready to kill your own son if needed?" Mason asked him seriously.

Scott stood by the window and contemplated the question. Scott looked intensely at Mason. He replied, "I didn't get this far by being weak. You do what you need to do to survive, right?"

Mason nodded and grinned wickedly. He replied, "Absolutely."

"I'll tell you this. I brought that muthafucka into this world, and I will take him out of it."

Lucky arrived at Meyer's looking like a younger version of Layla. Both brothers noticed her gradual transformation into their mother and didn't like it. She wore her wealth from head to toe. Lucky took off her mink coat, and Packer's diamond and platinum chains were layered on top of her expensive silk blouse. Her tiny wrist now sported a big face Rolex watch and a sleeve of dainty diamond bracelets. Her slim ring finger had a massive diamond engagement ring, and she wasn't engaged. And finally, her earlobes were weighed down with 10-carat diamond earrings. She had that drip on that any nigga would kill for. Lucky looked chic in her boyfriend jeans and Red Bottom leather boots. She was spending Layla's money like it was Monopoly bills.

She looked at Bugsy's face and didn't react. Lucky said, "I can see why y'all called this emergency meeting. We got a lot of shit to discuss. Let's get into it."

The siblings got comfortable in Meyer's living room. Lucky pulled out her Newport, and everyone lit up something—cigarette, cigar, weed, and relaxed. Meyer said, "Let's start with votes. Who's in favor of murdering, Scott?"

Bugsy raised his hand.

"Noted," Meyer said. "Who's in favor of murdering, Layla?"

Lucky raised her hand.

"Noted," Meyer repeated, trying to sound like his brother. "So the murder of our parents is vetoed, outvoted two to one. Now that we're tabling that discussion, we need to really focus on our futures. What does that look like and how Scott and Layla will retaliate toward y'all mutinies. Before y'all speak, y'all need to fuckin' think and take ownership of your actions. That's the only way we can beat them. If we strategize from a place of truth."

The room fell silent. Everyone was in deep thought. Bugsy cleared his mind and allowed himself to be in his father's shoes. He absorbed all the emotions that Scott must have gone through—betrayal and hurt were the two most significant factors. Bugsy spoke first.

"Pops won't act emotionally. He's cerebral and will plan all the way to the end. Scott will want to break me, but he won't kill me," Bugsy admitted. "But, he will murder Maxine if I let him get the chance."

"Then he won't get that chance," Meyer advised. "Put your top men on her twenty-four seven."

Lucky sucked her teeth. She hated that bitch Maxine with her whole being. Lucky crossed her legs and took another pull from her carcinogen. Sometimes she felt like Enron, the smartest one in the room. She said, "Why are y'all so confident that Scott's not already making plans to toss red roses at Bugsy's funeral? We all know that Scott's number one rule is to totally crush your enemy."

"I'm his son."

"You're an *enemy* who happens to be his *son*. Period."

Bugsy didn't like that Lucky wasn't putting the respect and value on his life he felt he had earned. "I'm his firstborn and arguably his favorite."

"He's buried three children, a fourth won't be a stretch of anyone's imagination."

"Let me ask you a question," Bugsy said, speaking directly to Lucky. "If you're so sure that Pop wants me dead, then why didn't you vote to kill him?"

Lucky stood up and went to reach for Meyer's drink for a sip, and he nearly broke her fingers. "Ouch!" she said, and then grabbed Bugsy's. Lucky took a large gulp and let out an unladylike "aaaaaahhh" before responding. "Scott's actions toward me don't rise to the level of murder. But and however, you have my back on Layla, and I'll agree to the murder of Scott. Fair exchange is no robbery."

Bugsy couldn't do it. He couldn't vote to have his own mother murdered because his face and ego were bruised. "My vote stands."

Lucky rolled her eyes. "As does mine!"

Meyer said, "Again. We're past murder. Now we need to strategize. Scott and Layla will want to spank y'all like children for the disrespect—"

"Wait a minute," Lucky screamed, emotionally. "Scott and Layla are two different beings. It's unwise to think Layla will take my disrespect in the same vein as Scott. We all know that she's hotheaded, and no one controls her. Not even our father. That sneaky cunt is coming for me! I can feel it."

"Calm down," Bugsy scolded. "We know that Layla is petty, but you've crippled her. She has no money, no men, and she's lost her ally, and that's Meyer. And since Meyer isn't planning on murdering you—"

"I'm not?" he joked, and Lucky tossed a throw pillow at his head.

Bugsy continued with, "Then, you're safe."

Lucky shrugged. She believed that her mother was planning her demise, and her brothers would not convince her otherwise. Meyer chimed in. "I can tell y'all muthafuckas this. While the feds got them on time out, we need to continue to build our dope empire and wit' Bugsy on our team; we're more durable than ever."

"What you mean, Bugsy on our team?" Lucky wanted to know.

Meyer looked to his brother for an answer. Bugsy spoke, "Meyer asked me to join y'all organization with what men I have left. Scott took back control of his pipeline tonight, but I still have all his drug money."

"We have our own money!" Lucky objected. "And, Meyer, why didn't you consult with me first before making such an offer? You ain't running shit!"

"I wasn't trying to," Meyer returned.

"Just remember, I'm your partner, not Bugsy!"

Lucky could feel her power diminishing right before her eyes. If Bugsy came on board, she could see herself being demoted from first to the second chair, perhaps even third.

"It is what it is," Meyer said.

Bugsy stood up and gave his brother dap. Standing erect, he stuffed both hands in his suit pants pocket and got serious. He stared down upon his siblings; Meyer was mellow, while Lucky was sulking. "Our parents deplore weakness. They'll expose and exploit it. Since the FBI is most likely causing them to bid their time before they make a move against us, I say we strike first. Nothing deadly, just a little warning of what's to come if they fuck with us."

Lucky perked up. "I like how you're thinking, brother. Let's fuck them up real good!"

Chapter 14

L ayla swaggered into the Park Avenue residence like she owned the building, her heels click-clacked against the polished marble flooring, echoing throughout the lobby. The elevator doors opened, and she strutted down the hallway with the carpet muffling her expensive shoes. She knocked—no, Layla banged on her son's front door. Her unexpected visit was long overdue. Layla had been calling Meyer, but he refused to answer, knowing she hated to be ignored.

Meyer answered the door, stunned to be standing face to face with his mother.

"What you doin' here?" he asked.

"You ignoring me now," she barked and pushed past him. Layla barged into his place uninvited. She wasn't about to stand in the hallway. "We need to talk."

Meyer sighed and closed his door. He had company, and Layla quickly saw who she was. Her son was eventuating with some *Thot*, she believed. Layla had never seen her before. She was pretty—stunning, actually. She looked at the girl, and the girl looked back, undaunted by a mother's intense stare. In fact, the girl glared, annoyed at the interruption. Meyer's dining room was set up like they were having Breakfast at Tiffany's—elegant, with beautiful flowers arranged attractively, gleaming silverware to eat with, and a spread of food that could top a White House Correspondent's Dinner. Meyer had hired a chef with a server, and his female company was sitting at the table like Queen Elizabeth was her mother.

"I see you got company," Layla observed. "Shit, you went all out for this heifer, didn't you? How much does this bitch cost me?"

"Excuse me," Zoe responded, feeling slighted by the remark. "You don't know anything about me."

Yeah, bitch, make it that kind of party—a beatdown partay, Layla thought.

"That should concern you," Layla hissed. "That my son doesn't think enough of you to mention you to his mother. You irrelevant little snob." Already, she didn't like her. Layla knew the type. She could spot a gold digger a mile away.

"Come on, Ma. Don't start ya shit!"

Meyer wasn't feeling his mother's timing. He was working extra hard to impress Zoe. Meyer took some time off from the family business to concentrate on making her his. The day Luna shot him, he was supposed to take Zoe to Hawaii for a beautiful vacation and finally have sex with his dream woman after months of waiting. But that came to a halt when his past caught up to him. Now, his Puerto Rican princess had restarted the clock on her celibacy and was once again making him wait a full ninety days until she had sex with him.

And Layla was quickly running interference. He knew his mother had a temper, and he didn't want her to start anything with Zoe. To ease the tension, Meyer saw building between his mother and his woman, Meyer went toward Layla and threw his arms around her, giving her a warm hug—out of his character. While embracing her, he whispered into Layla's ear, "Ma, chill the fuck out. I really like this one. Don't ruin it for me."

He then pulled away from his mother and did a formal introduction. "Ma, this is Zoe, and Zoe, this is my mother."

Layla still didn't warm up to the girl now that she knew her name. The corners of her mouth were still pointed downward, and her stare could freeze an iceberg. "Zoe, what do you do for coins?"

"Pardon me."

"You heard my question." Layla was in no mood to entertain this diva. She continued, "How do you pay your bills?"

Meyer was about to interject, but Zoe silenced him with a quick hand gesture. That action alone made Layla seethe. Proudly, Zoe announced, "I compete in beauty pageants. I'm crowned Miss Puerto Rico."

Layla snorted. "So you broke, huh? You make your money lying on your back like every other stringy-haired ho."

Zoe's naturally tanned skin had turned beet red. She had worked too hard in her industry and too hard abstaining from sex to be reduced into a mere slut by some lowlife thug. But she now needed the woman to see her how her son saw her. Layla had challenged her.

"I'm a good woman, Mrs. West, and I'm sorry that you don't see that, but your son does. I work hard in my career, and I'm respected. And as far as being some ho, I've been with your son for over a year, and we've never had sex!"

Meyer wanted to say 'TMI' and that her depiction of their relationship was a stretch, but he allowed her to have her moment.

Layla chuckled. "My bad. You're a calculating ho!"

Zoe was taken aback by the brash attitude. She didn't sign up for this—she refused to be disrespected and humiliated. It was Meyer's mother, and she wanted to be respectful, but the bitch was making it hard. Zoe now looked at Meyer for any help, for some defense from his mother's vulgar attitude, and she wasn't disappointed. Meyer stepped up heatedly to the plate and swung away with angry words.

"What the fuck is wrong wit' you?" he cursed at Layla. "This is why your kids don't fuck wit' ya crude ass! You have no chill button. Don't ever come into my home again and disrespect my woman!"

"Your home? I bought this fuckin' palace you in here grandstanding in. Now I don't trust this bitch, so she needs to fuckin' go!" Layla hollered. She didn't care if Zoe was standing right there and listening, her mouth was a sewer, a cesspool of insults.

"This is why you're gonna die alone!" he shouted. "You push everybody away."

"Are you threatening me, Meyer?!"

Meyer exhaled, exasperated. Layla could drain him in a nanosecond, push every button he possessed and then push again.

"Ain't nobody threatening you!"

"Everything I did for you and your fuckin' sister and y'all treat me like I don't fuckin' exist. I spent a year inside a jail cell, and not once did you come to visit me! Nor did you come to my trial. That shit hurt. You were always my favorite, Meyer, but I know you let that cunt bitch sister of yours get into your head. Lucky's keeping you away from me…what the fuck is she telling you?"

Meyer was shocked that she accused him of not being there for her. He yelled, "How can I be there for you when I'm in the hospital shot up?!"

"I've been betrayed," Layla hollered and threw her purse across the room in dramatic flair. "You turned your back on me! Just admit it."

They quarreled. Meyer almost forgot that Zoe was standing there, and that's precisely the way his mother liked it—to hoard all his attention.

"That's a lie!"

"You let your sister take everything from me. I gave you fuckin' life, and this is how you do me. Your father was always about Bugsy since y'all were kids, and what did I do? I had your back, and you stab me in mine."

The ambiance in the room went from romantic to ruckus. Zoe stood on the sideline, witnessing the entire thing unfold into one big glob of dysfunction. Meyer's temperament went haywire around his mother, he was losing control. He cursed and screamed, and it wasn't the way he wanted Zoe to see him.

Finally, he turned to Zoe and said, "Babe, can you please leave. I'm sorry for the interruption, but I need to have a serious talk wit' my mother. I'll get wit' you soon. My driver is downstairs and will make sure you get home safely."

Zoe didn't fuss. She replied, "I'll be fine. You work this out and call me later." She collected her things and exited from the apartment, not before smiling sarcastically at Layla. When the door shut, Meyer continued to cut loose on his mother with harsh words that Layla had heard plenty of times before.

As Meyer fussed at his mother, Layla coolly walked toward the spread of food and took a seat at the table. She ate the breakfast intended for Zoe. Layla downed mimosas and ordered the server and chef who had remained hidden in the kitchen around like she had hired them. She didn't care what Meyer said to her. She was hungry, and the food was delicious. Layla was taking full advantage of everything, tasting each dish on the menu. It saddened Layla that her son was living better than her, and it was all off the money Lucky had stolen, but she said nothing.

"You got good taste," she uttered.

"Enjoy it," he replied bitterly. "I know you miss it."

"Oh, I definitely will…and yes, I did."

She drank more mimosas, and she devoured the bacon gravy, and the hash brown casserole like it would be her last, and the Cajun shrimp and cheesy grits were to die for. The chef did a fantastic job on a creamy bread pudding that melted in her mouth.

"So, where did you meet that bitch?" she finally asked Meyer out the blue.

"That's none of your business."

"I don't like her, Meyer. She seems shady to me, I can see it in her eyes, she's up to no good. She's a snob."

He sardonically countered with, "I guess it takes one to know one, huh."

"I'm your mother, boy. I'm gonna always watch your back, despite what problems we may have."

"It doesn't feel like it."

"I brought you this far in life, didn't I? Why would I want to tear my own son down and bare false witness against someone he's into? I'm tellin' you she's not the one."

"Because you're a West, and that's what we do, right? Put ourselves first over each other."

"You need to have that type of attitude toward your sister because that's the bitch you shouldn't trust and who's out to destroy me...and you, if you're not careful around her," she advised him.

Finally, Layla stopped stuffing her face with first-class food. She finished the mimosas, and her belly was satiated. Now, it was back to business. She wanted to have a serious talk with her son. She looked at Meyer and said, "I'm down, Meyer. Fucked up, and I need your help. Whatever issues you have wit' me, let it go, and let's start something new. Let bygones be bygones, and you and I, we can rebuild again. And I promise you, it will be different from now on."

"Nah, Ma. I'm done taking orders from you. Working wit' you almost got me killed."

It was becoming harder for her to persuade him. There was some bad blood between them she'd admit.

"I know you're still pissed wit' me and I'ma give you your space. But in the meantime, I need your help. Where did your sister stash my money?"

"What? Is that why you're here? Not to win me back but to get your grimy hands on that money?"

"I'm broke, Meyer! Living in a fucking rented room! What else am I supposed to do?"

Meyer shook his head. "Look, I don't know. I honestly don't fuckin' know where she stashed it. She won't tell me."

Layla believed him. Lucky probably wouldn't tell him anything because she couldn't trust her own brother to not compromise her cash flow. Meyer wasn't the sharpest knife in the drawer.

"When are you gonna step up to the plate? Huh? How did you allow Lucky to outrank you? Why is your younger sister still in control, while you sit here playing house wit' dumb ho's?"

Layla waited for his reaction. She sat there and studied him. How would he reply? She needed to rattle his cage, motivate him to go against his sister. Divide and conquer was the name of her game. She continued with, "Men should be answering to you, not Lucky. How much work did you put into these streets, only to allow someone not as experienced as yourself to run the show? Without you, there would be no her, and she needs to know that, Meyer. How long you've been home, it's time you made yourself known again…become a man again."

"I am a man," he growled back.

"Not wit' Lucky in charge of things," she said. "She's making all the moves with the Juarez cartel, calling the shots. How many meetings have you had with Angel?"

"Fuck, Angel!" Meyer barked.

"Just as I thought. Zero."

Gradually, Layla was sinking her claws back into her son; her tale of betrayal, deceit, and greed, along with manipulating his ego, she wooed Meyer.

"Lucky ain't trying to outrank me or call no shots! She got too much on her plate right now. As soon as I get fully back in the game, it's gonna be me meeting wit' Angel."

"Too much on her plate?" Layla snorted. "What's more important than getting money?"

Meyer knew it wasn't his place to tell his sister's secret, but he did anyway. "Lucky's a mom now. She had a little girl, so that's what's more important."

Layla feigned shock. "A baby? Who's the father?"

"Some underling named Packer," he lied. "He's dead, though."

"So your father and I got a granddaughter and mums the fucking word from your sister. Just as I said, she's trifling. I should call that bitch right now and curse her ass out."

"No!" Meyer yelled. "I wasn't supposed to tell you. Keep this between us until she tells you herself."

Layla sighed. "Well, I'm not keeping this secret from your father, but other than that, we won't say anything. And that's on the strength of you and only you."

Meyer finally smiled. He hadn't smiled at his mother for a long time; he was putty in her hands.

Chapter 15

Max pulled up to the familiar building in Harlem with the beauty salon below and prepared herself for the impending drama she would encounter. Today she was alone, having no choice but to leave Dillinger with Lucky's nanny because it was easier to slip past the new security detail that Bugsy had assigned to her. Bugsy meant well—he tried to assuage her fears by tethering her to two triggermen when he had only to handle Scott and be done with this unnecessary spectacle.

Max rang the doorbell, announced herself, and was rang in. She expected to be met by Marisol's mother, Anna, a mean-faced old woman who was less than hospitable the last time Max had entered her home. However, the welcoming was lighthearted and warm.

"Hola, Max." Anna embraced her in a bear hug and then planted a wet kiss on each cheek. Max was flabbergasted by the overly sentimental display of affection but said nothing. Anna led her into the living room where the white, pink, and red figurines, crosses, several shrines, lace doilies, and gaudy statues were still an exhibition. The memorial of fallen soldiers had increased, and pictures of young Latino men in caskets taped above numerous lit candles was eerie to Max.

She looked around and said, "Where's Marisol?"

"Mari," her mother called. Anna faced Max and replied, "She soon comes."

Max simply nodded and took a seat on the plastic-covered couch that made noise with each movement.

"You want something to drink?"

"What you got?" Max said, loosening up.

"I'm drinking a Bellini," said Marisol, answering for her mother. Her grin stretched across her pretty face, and her usually unfriendly disposition and hard scowl had dissipated. Marisol came out of the backroom dressed on-trend in the latest Balmain jumper ripped directly from the runway. Whatever Marisol wanted, she got. She asked, "You want one? A Bellini?"

Max knew she should limit her drinking because she was breastfeeding, but you only live once. "I'm here for it."

The two women sat inside the dated living room talking and cackling like old friends. When her needs were met, Marisol was actually cool. And with these two-million-dollar deals that Juan-Pablo had brokered for two measly murders, Marisol was in the best of moods.

Max tossed Marisol, the Louis Vuitton knapsack that held the payout for her to count. Which she did. Marisol thought that the Garcia cartel was muthafuckin' fools to pay so much for a hit, but she also knew these cartels had disposable income and with the feds possibly working with Scott and Layla, her man was smart to inflate his fee. Murder Inc. did hits for a hundred grand, the additional money was gravy over biscuits, just that extra sauce to make things that much better.

Max had reasons to smile too. When she and Scott got engaged, he allowed her to take out a five-million-dollar insurance policy on him. Max wanted one just in case Layla had her husband murdered. The plan paid out double indemnity should

Scott West get killed or died in an accident. Her one-million-dollar contract on Scott's life would payout ten times her investment. And that, coupled with the alcohol she had just drunk, made her grin wide.

Once the money was confirmed, the ladies knew that they would meet again for the balance.

Lucky climbed out of her G-wagon on 155th Street and strolled toward a six-story tenement building. Soundview in the Bronx was a dangerous neighborhood, but it was lucrative for the drug trade. The building was a newly acquired asset she had bought in a public auction for pennies on the dollar. The City of New York held these auctions to get rid of real estate that former owners could no longer afford, which had racked up too many violations and were worthless to most. Lucky had big plans and already had her construction team working on renovating the sixteen apartments. But meanwhile, the abandoned apartments were ideal fronts as a trap house.

She strolled confidently through the uncleaned, grubby looking lobby—littered with cigarette butts, empty beer cans, and candy wrappers. Vagrants were coming in at night to find shelter from the harsh New York winter. She would speak to her men to put a stop to the homelessness problem spilling into the building. Lucky stepped carefully into the elevator, mindful not to step into a puddle of piss. Using her thumb and index finger, she pinched her nose to shut off the putrid smell that had assaulted her nostrils as she ascended to the top floor. Lucky exited and knocked on door 6C. The round slot in the door quickly slid open for the occupant to see who was there. The reinforced steel door flung open, and Lucky walked inside.

Yusef smiled at his boss. He noticed that since Packer's

demise, Lucky was relying on him more, calling him to handle the most critical issues, and he didn't want to let her down. Yusef wanted to be promoted to first-in-command. He wanted to fill Packer's shoes in all areas of Lucky's life, including the bedroom. She was the flyest bitch he had ever met, but he knew that she didn't see him like that, in a romantic way. He felt he had only to prove himself to be smart, reliable, and loyal to her—just as Packer had done, and he'd be promoted in more ways than one.

"Just in time," said Yusef. "It's frosty in here."

The snow had arrived—twenty kilos of that pure white cocaine was purchased from the Juarez cartel without her brothers' knowledge.

Lucky looked around at her newly minted workers in the trap house and said, "What y'all waitin' on? Get this coke street-ready."

Lucky's workers jumped into action, processing the cocaine into cooked crack rocks. The apartment was set up like a lab with steelwork tables placed parallel of each other. Each work area had a triple beam scale, N95 respirator masks, razor blades for cutting the crack rocks and vials. Giant fans were bought to help with circulation, and the windows were opened for ventilation. No one wanted to get a contact high off the addictive product.

Lucky had started her own side hustle right under the noses of her brothers. Yusef and Opie had hired a team of block huggers to infiltrate the side blocks throughout the boroughs of New York, so besides their wholesale business, she was making a killing selling retail. Her brothers thought she was spending her days and nights up in some new niggas face, but she wasn't.

Lucky lit a Newport and inhaled, enjoying the sudden rush of nicotine as it entered her system. Lucky and her lieutenants walked out of the kitchen, allowing the workers to do what they did best—cook coke and bag up crack vials. They went into the next room to politick.

Yusef said, "Meyer called."

Lucky smirked. "Meyer? For what?"

"He said he wanted to meet…he wants me to come through and politick, see what's what, what I'm about."

She shook her head rapidly. Meyer was the muscle, and she was the brain. Her men answered to her, and she didn't want them to get too familiar with her brother. Lucky said, "Let me handle my brother. Next time he calls, don't answer."

"Just ignore dude?"

"That's what I said," she snapped.

"A'ight. But there's another problem." In the drug game, there was always opposition.

Opie couldn't wait to talk beef. He was ready to set it off. "We wanted to pull your coat to a possible threat. This isn't our territory, and some of our soldiers are exchanging words wit' the Bronx Blood niggas up in Co-op City. They ain't puttin' in the work we 'bout to do. They're low-level dirty niggas."

Lucky grimaced. She knew them. It wasn't long ago that she was affiliated with the deadly gang. For years they copped from the West organization, Scott was their supplier, and they held allegiance to him. Now that Lucky had switched sides, and had ties to the Juarez cartel, the Bronx Bloods were now her enemy.

"Those are Scott's peoples, which means they're our competitors. If anyone of our men feels threatened, if those Blood niggas stare too long, lay 'em down quickly without hesitation. They're dangerous—"

"So are we!" said Yusef.

"Prove it."

Chapter 16

W ho fucked you up?" Layla asked as Scott stood in his hotel room's doorway. It was late, nearly midnight—creeping hours for some. Scott opened the door wider and stepped aside, allowing her entry.

"I had to remind Bugsy that he'll never be me."

"Did he listen?" Layla chuckled, amused at Scott's face. "I don't know why you went after that boy. You know the twins been boxin' since grade school."

"How did you find me?" Scott asked.

"No, nigga! The question is, why did I have to find you," Layla snapped. "You up here livin' in the lap of luxury, Scott. A fuckin' suite—with a private balcony overlooking Central Park while I'm several floors down like some basic bitch."

Scott laughed at his shadiness. "I was gonna tell you."

"Um-hmm…well, I saved you the trouble."

The subject was immediately changed to business. Scott asked, "Did you meet with Meyer?"

"I did. We talked, and I planted the seed just as I said I would."

Scott grinned. "Good. You want a drink?"

"I can use one," she said.

Scott walked to where he had a few bottles of top-shelf liquor on the table. He was shirtless, wearing a pair of pants, barefoot and handsome. He was a man in his forties that looked half his age. Layla stared at him, she wanted him. She had no one else to go to, but she didn't want to look desperate. She had to keep her game face on.

Scott fixed her a white Russian and handed Layla her glass. She downed half the drink, Scott did too. He asked her, "What brings you to my room at this hour?"

"I just wanted to talk."

"You could have called me."

"I wanted to see you in person," she said.

He smiled and took another sip from his drink. Scott easily read her. He looked at her, and she was still beautiful, the mother of his kids, the woman that had his back for over twenty-something years—she was heaven and hell simultaneously. But she was always a real one, a grown woman who spoke her mind when it mattered. And Layla was many things, some things he didn't like, but the one thing she would always be to him was his partner in crime. *Shit,* they beat a federal case together, and if that wasn't impressive, then what was?

"Have a seat, let's talk," he said.

Layla took a seat in an armed leather chair, sat back and crossed her legs. Scott sat near her and said, "I'm going to add you to a few accounts so you can have some cash flow."

She nodded. "I went to see Fitz, and I was able to retrieve six-hundred-thousand-dollars from him. He had to learn the hard way not to fuck wit' me."

"You want him gone?" Scott asked her. "I already got Mason on the Arnold Meade hit. He's a dead man, and he doesn't even know it."

Layla looked at him skeptically; she was worried about talking about a murder in his hotel room. Scott noticed her incredulous look and quickly explained to her why it was safe to speak. "The room was swept for any bugs a few hours ago, we're good."

"Smart." She took another sip from her white Russian and said, "But, nah, it ain't that serious wit' Fitz. Besides, we shouldn't kill both top New York defense lawyers. We might need Fitz again for someone on our team."

Scott agreed.

They continued to talk and plot, they were determined to rise back up to their rightful positions in their empire. They realized that they worked better together than against each other. Separate, they allowed Maxine to infiltrate them, the same bitch that'd killed their children. Separate, Lucky and Bugsy took over their money. Separate, they lost their criminal organizations, but together, they built an empire. Together, they won back their freedom. And together, they would get revenge. They both felt disrespected, and it was a mission for them to get their respect back. Scott knew that if he didn't rectify what Bugsy and Lucky did to them, then any day now, another man, an enemy, or supposed friend will think that they could take what Scott had built. It infuriated Scott he had to use his legitimate earnings to fund his drug empire when it used to be the other way around.

"What's up?" Scott asked. "Talk to me. You still look worried?"

"All this plotting and planning just ain't me! I'm ready to blow that bitches head off," Layla said irately. "Each day Maxine breathes is an insult to our babies."

"I know. And I'm gonna make that right if you just trust me."

"It will never be right," Layla replied. Unless Scott had the power of God and could bring back the dead, heartbreak would stay with Layla until the day she died.

The two downed more vodka and shared more conversation. In fact, they shared a few laughs. Who would have thought, Scott and Layla in the same room laughing after everything they'd been through?

Scott smiled and genuinely said, "You're still a gorgeous woman…rough around the edges, but beautiful."

His unpredicted compliment made Layla blush, something she hadn't done in a long time.

"You want another drink?" he offered, seeing she had emptied her glass.

"Yes…thanks."

Scott removed the glass from her hand and turned to replenish the drink. Her eyes studied his every movement, and Layla felt some stirring between her legs. They had been talking for over an hour.

Layla wanted to stay the night with him. She wanted to be pleased entirely.

"I miss you," she blurted out—the statement caught her off guard. It just came out of her mouth, like air. Suddenly she felt weak and vulnerable.

Scott stared at her, his gaze solid. She had no idea what he was thinking. Was it a mistake to express her feelings like that? Did she suddenly ruin the night? For a few seconds, Scott stood in front of her in silence. He continued to sip his drink and didn't react to her statement.

His silence made her insecurities rise to the surface. He had rejected her once; this must be part two. Layla felt like an idiot. How could she so readily forget everything he'd done to her—the bitches he fucked, including Maxine and Penelope? Scott had become very disrespectful to her over the years, and now she was ready to submit to him sexually—to forgive that easily?

It had to be the alcohol—it was making her say things during the night she would never have said.

Layla watched Scott set his glass down on the end table in the room, and he approached her coolly. The look in his eyes was powerful. Layla took a deep breath. He reached for her hands and pulled her forcefully from her seat and into his arms. And then, just like that, he kissed her passionately. She didn't resist. Their tongues wrestled, and their hearts raced.

"I fuckin' want you," he announced fervently.

Layla stood before her estranged husband and peeled off her clothes. She wanted him, Layla had always wanted Scott. He had been and still was the love of her life. Scott wanted to help undress her—he wanted that control, but Layla wasn't having it. She took two steps back and continued to unbutton her shirt to reveal a sheer bra and a flat stomach. Slowly, she unzipped her pants and stepped out of them. Layla stood before him in her bra, lace panties, and stilettos. Her French-vanilla colored body was grown woman curvy and in need.

Scott was turned on with her striptease. He wanted more. "Take off your panties and bra and come sit on my face," he whispered.

She complied. Scott undressed quickly, his manhood rock-solid, hanging low. Layla crawled onto the bed and climbed on her husband as he was lying on his back.

Scott sucked on her pussy, gliding his tongue against Layla's phat clit, enjoying the way she tasted.

Layla wrapped her thick thighs around him, her hips grinding, expressing her pleasure. "Ooooh, fuck," she moaned, biting her bottom lip.

Scott's tongue slid deep inside her wet cave, causing waves of pleasure to wash over her. He nibbled, licked, and sucked on her sensitive button and felt her body shudder, her soft moans turning him on. Scott slid his fingers inside her wet hole, opening her up, causing her body to buck. He used his lips and tongue on her wet clit as her body moved to its own rhythm. Scott wanted Layla to come in his mouth. He wanted to please her.

"Aaaaah, ummm, please, don't stop. Ummm, hmmm. Ooooh shit, don't stop. Right fuckin' there." Layla exploded; her wetness dripped on his tongue as he continued to taste her juices.

"You like that?" Scott asked, and she moaned her approval. Scott flipped her over and moved north with soft, passionate kisses on her stomach, making his way to her breasts. His tongue flickered on her dime-sized nipples until they were both erect. Scott was ready to enter her and see if they still had a physical connection. He pushed the mushroom tip of his hard dick in her pussy, and they both cried out. Layla's eyes closed, and she ground her hips as he slowly inched his way inside. Her pussy gripped his thick dick as her nails dug into his skin.

"Oh, shit," she purred.

"You miss me?" he whispered.

Layla nodded.

"Say it," he coaxed. "Say you miss me."

"Fuck, Scott," Layla murmured. "I miss you...."

Scott moved in a slow and steady rhythm, opening her tight, deep cave with his girth. Scott's movements were intentional—soft and slow, and deep. Layla purred her approval of his lovemaking, as her legs tightened around his waist. But she wanted more. Layla whispered, "Now fuck me."

Scott pulled out and placed his wife on all fours, doggy style. He thrust himself between her open legs, allowing his full length to hit the back of her cervix repeatedly while slapping her phat, plump ass. Layla liked it rough, and Scott knew how to please her. With each deep penetration, Scott felt his orgasm brewing, ready to be released. Layla cooed behind him, her pussy pulsing nonstop around his thick dick. She, too, felt her orgasm peaking.

The couple came simultaneously before collapsing, spent. Both dozed off, and an hour later, Scott was ready for round two.

Scott affectionately kissed the side of Layla's neck, hungrily touching her breasts. The muscles in his chest flexed against Layla's back as she stirred awake. From behind, Scott gently wrapped his strong arm around her slim waist and pulled her into his naked frame.

"Damn, I missed you," he whispered into her ear.

Scott nibbled on her ear and continued kissing the side of her long, dainty neck and softly touching her erogenous zones. He inhaled her skin; her familiar scent was floral and feminine. She smelled like vanilla with a hint of bergamot. "Fuck, you're so sexy," he murmured.

He continued loving on her. Scott couldn't take his eyes off Layla, her pleasure faces made him fall in love all over again. Everything about her felt like home.

They kissed passionately—deep and slow. Their tongues twirling around, exploring one another. Layla got lost in the moment, his kisses, his touch. He was making her forget his repeated betrayals—the abuse, the other women, the lies.

Scott pulled Layla into his strong arms, and she straddled him. He cupped her butt and guided her hips as she aggressively rode him.

They switched positions, and she buried her sweet box in her husband's face and leaned forward to sixty-nine. Layla eagerly sucked her juices off his mushroom tip while her small hands ran up and down his long shaft. She lathered up his magic stick with her saliva as Layla deep-throated his manhood, her hips grinding on his face as Scott's tongue licked and sucked her juices.

"Oh, shit," he murmured, unable to control the nut peaking. "I'm about to come."

Layla was about to come too. They both exploded, swimming in pleasure and a heightened sense of eroticism as they both shared a deep, emotional connection. Layla turned around to face Scott. She wanted more. She lowered herself on top of him, a slow grind was how he liked it. Layla's nails dug into his chest; she bit her bottom lip as the strong feelings intensified.

"Oh shit, Layla, your pussy feels so good," Scott moaned as he pushed deeper and deeper into her. "Oh shit! Damn, Layla!"

Layla arched her back as waves of blissful pleasure washed over her.

"Fuck me!" she cried out.

The couple twisted into multiple positions—enjoying every inch, and every second, of their lovemaking. Layla wanted this forever.

"Come for me, Daddy."

"I'm gonna come in your tight pussy," Scott said breathlessly.

And when he came, she came—their bodies connecting on so many emotional levels.

"Damn, Layla, I love you."

They both drifted off into a deep, needed sleep. When Layla woke up the next morning, Scott was already up, showered, and dressed. She felt uncomfortable. Was this a booty call?

"You should have woken me up so I could get dressed and go."

Scott shook his head. "You don't have to go. Stay…I'll only be out for a few hours. Maybe we can have lunch later."

She smiled. It felt like she was dating her husband. "I'd like that very much."

Scott had a thought and wasn't sure how to broach the subject, but he knew he had to. "Listen, I've been thinking about something. It's about our children…I'm thinking we give them a one-time pardon."

"Say what now?" Layla asked, and sat straight up in the bed. She wanted clarity. "Repeat that."

"My fight with Bugsy shows he's hardly a challenge. He went up against me and lost. I took back my organization, my pipeline, and it won't be long before I find all his stash houses and take back my bread. And I'll help you with Lucky too. She's gonna come up off your fifty million."

"No, Scott. Muthafuckin' no! Let's stick to the plan."

"I saw it in his eyes that Bugsy was afraid…he pulled a gun on me and didn't use it!"

"Scott, this isn't like you...to not follow through on something once you've made up your mind. If anyone else on earth had done to you what your son did, they would be dead."

"But he is my son," Scott wasn't budging.

"He doesn't act like it."

"If I would have offered him a spot back on my team, he would have taken it. That boys nothing without me. It won't be long before he wants to come home. Trust me, he's defeated, he's surrendered without saying the words."

"So now that you've got your happy ending, you want to shut me down? You're underestimating them...you're underestimating Bugsy. You've always had a soft spot for him, and you'll learn the hard way that he doesn't feel the same about you!"

"This isn't a debate, Layla." Scott checked his wife. "End of discussion. My children live."

She nodded. "Okay, Scott. Let's see how long you will."

Chapter 17

$$\underline{\overline{}}\hspace{-0.5em}\triangle\hspace{-0.3em}|\hspace{-0.3em}\triangle$$

It was a smooth flight from Guadalajara, Mexico, for Raffa, Arturo, Félix, and Pedro. The four men were sicarios—Mexican assassins hired by the young West's. The men glided through the airport with familiarity, unchallenged by Customs and Immigration as they'd been traveling to the states for decades. These hired killers were internationally known by the underworld, were military trained, and were alleged to have been responsible for a combined three thousand murders.

Raffa was a former Sinaloa president, Félix is the head of a Mexico City militia group, Pedro works as a Federales in Tijuana, and Arturo was a skilled lawyer who represented some clients he killed for. These men were respected, had generated wealth, and could retire if they so choose to. However, they believed in an oath, to keep and restore order amongst criminals—those traffickers who crossed that fine line of noncompliance.

The sicarios moved with impunity to the Taxi and Limousine area of JFK airport, where a driver held up a sign that read: Haven LLC, it was one of Bugsy's shell corporations he had created since taking over his father's organization last year. Arturo alerted the driver, and within a few short minutes, the foursome was whisked away from the airport to their first meeting place at an undisclosed location.

The barbershop in Spanish Harlem was a good place to hold court. Everyone would blend into the fabric of the neighborhood, and things could go unnoticed. Bugsy, Meyer, and Lucky were waiting for their guests. They sat in barber chairs, looking out the huge, picturesque window just talking shit. They all watched in wonderment as the four men that ranged from their late thirties to mid-forties exited the town car in leather jackets, jeans, and crocodile cowboy boots. Their jet-black hair was slicked back, and their skin looked tanned and weathered.

There wasn't any mistaking the air of professionalism as they entered the establishment. A dark cloud hovered around these men, and Bugsy didn't want to know how it would feel to be on the wrong end of any of their guns. Each man had cold, dead eyes—almost inhuman. Bugsy stood up first and made the introductions.

"I'm Bugsy West, this is my brother, Meyer, and my sister, Lucky." Handshakes were exchanged.

And then Félix, who spoke fluent English, did the talking. He said, "I am Félix, this is Arturo, Pedro, and Raffa."

"Please, have a seat." Bugsy walked and pulled down the shades on each window so they could have complete privacy. He then began the meeting.

"So, as I've explained, we're having issues with our parents— a power struggle, and we needed to outsource this job so that our men's lives aren't placed in danger."

Félix nodded. "But what about your lives. Will they not be in danger if you go this route?"

Meyer shifted in his seat. "Let us worry about us."

"I'll tell you the truth, Don Meyer. In my country, if any of our children disrespected us in this way, if my son hired a sicario, I would personally cut his head off with a dull blade. But not before castrating the cabrón, shoving his manhood down his throat to muffle his cries and leave his body to rot in the Sinaloa desert. I would no longer be his father, he, no longer my son. Are you sure that is what you want?"

"We wouldn't have hired you if we had reservations." Lucky added her two cents. She stood up and dropped two duffel bags filled with one million in American dollars in front of Raffa.

Félix stared into each of their eyes before he spoke again. "We're professionals and will handle our end as you please. But we offer a small… poquito," he placed his index and thumb a quarter of an inch apart and continued, "piece of advice which is, do not leave any survivors. Just handle your business and move on with your lives. We can make the killings quick…they won't feel a thing. You make this linger, and you will have problems."

"Sí, sí," Raffa agreed. "Quick!"

Meyer spoke. "Look, y'all not hearing us! Ain't nobody getting killed—quick or not. So if y'all can't handle the job, just say the word and move on."

Félix said, "As you wish."

Bugsy stood up to signal that the meeting was over. He extended his hand to Félix, and the two men exchanged a firm handshake. "Call me once it's done."

Lucky stared down at Lulu, sleeping peacefully in her crib, swaddled snuggly in her receiving blanket. Lucchese finally was discharged from the NICU as her health had greatly improved. She was steadily gaining weight—nearing five pounds, able to maintain her body's temperature in her crib without an incubator, and Lulu was now fed by a bottle and not through a tube.

Lucky had hired only the best nannies for her daughter, twenty-four-hour attention for the working mom was a luxury that most new mothers couldn't afford. Maria was the day nanny working a twelve-hour shift. She was in her mid-fifties, Puerto Rican, and had a lot of certifications in life-saving procedures such as First Aid, CPR and was National Child Passenger Safety certified. The night nanny was Gloria, who was from the Dominican Republic. She was forty-three years old and had been taking care of kids for over two decades. Gloria came to the United States twenty-five years ago, and her resume was also impressive. She had three grown children of her own and fifteen grandchildren. Lucky used the top employment agency to hire her nannies who vetted the women. Neither had any criminal records, not even a parking ticket in their names.

Lucky continued to stand over her sleeping baby until Lulu stirred awake. Her little eyes opened, and then her small mouth opened too. Her face pulled into a frown as she puckered her tiny lips. Lucky knew what was to come next. Lulu's mouth opened wide, and at first, no sound came out. Soon she cried—a low-level noise that escalated to a high-pitched, throaty holler. Lucky marveled at the lungs, her tiny bundle of joy had on her. Lucchese Lily West would not be ignored. Within seconds, Maria came in with a warm bottle of milk already prepared. She flicked a few drops on her wrist to make sure it was room temperature, before reaching down and scooping up baby Lulu.

Lucky stood to the side, watching. She opted to not breastfeed—too much drama and responsibility for her lifestyle, and she didn't care to be judged on her choices. Maria sat in the rocking chair and hummed a nursery rhyme while Lulu stared deeply into her eyes. Lucky watched, satisfied that she had hired the right people. Being a young mother was a scary thing, and without help and money, Lucky had no idea how she would've handled it alone. She watched Maria feed her baby like a mother should.

"You're good with her, Maria…thank you."

She smiled at Lucky and replied, "I love taking care of these precious babies. Lulu is an angel. So beautiful, just like her mother."

"Thank you," Lucky absorbed the compliment. "She's going to be a beauty."

"If you have time today, I could show you how to feed and burp her?"

Lucky frowned. Maria would teach Lucky the tricks of motherhood, but Lucky had become too busy with her empire that most times, she put motherhood on pause. And with Lulu in good hands with Maria and Gloria, her priorities had shifted.

"Soon, but not today. Today my schedule is tight. Take care of my baby girl while I'm gone." Lucky turned and left the nursery without a second glance.

Lucky had just made it safely inside her driver's seat when her cellphone rang. She sucked her teeth, rolled her eyes, and wanted to hit: IGNORE. However, she knew she couldn't. *This nigga is a bugaboo,* she thought.

In her cheeriest voice, she answered. "Hey, Angel. What's up?"

"How are you?"

"I'm well, thanks for asking." Lucky was using her corporate voice meant to keep a distance between the two. What happened last year, the brief affair was a mistake. And she never wanted to mix business with pleasure again. Her two main priorities were to keep the kilos from the Juarez cartel coming in and keeping her daughter off Angel's radar. She continued, "So you're calling me. Why? We're not expecting a package."

"I've called to personally tell you that I got the DNA test result back, and I'm not the father."

Lucky exhaled. "You didn't have to call to tell me something that I already know. Can we finally put this issue to bed?"

"We cannot."

"Excuse me?"

"You are *not* excused."

Lucky's voice elevated slightly as her body began to involuntarily tremble. A blanket of fear had washed over her, and Angel hadn't even threatened her. "What's going on?"

"Tonight, I want you and your son to get on a flight and meet me in Miami so—"

"You know I can't do that!"

His voice turned gruff. He was using a register lower than Lucky was used to hearing. "This isn't negotiable. The child isn't mine, but we will do a DNA test to make sure that the infant I saw is indeed yours."

Lucky closed her eyes and wanted to die. Why wouldn't Angel just let this go? Practically overnight, he turned into Einstein, some fuckin' Sherlock Holmes enthusiast. "You sound crazy."

"I am that, too, along with a man who doesn't trust you."

The night Angel left the hospital, something in the pit of his stomach told him he didn't see the full picture. Something was off, not right, but he couldn't put his finger on it. When the DNA came back, Angel was 99.9%, not the father, but for some reason, he wasn't relieved. He asked himself if he were in Lucky's shoes would he take the chance to try and pass off a baby to the head of the Juarez cartel as his if she knew that the baby wasn't. Any woman in her position would know that he would ask for a DNA test, and the results would mean either life or death for all parties involved in the charade. Lucky was born into a family of Mafioso's, so she was accustomed to traditions—consequences and repercussions. Although she didn't know about the Juarez cartel rule, she would know that a lie of this magnitude wouldn't go unchecked. And then once he told her about the rule, the baby was miraculously conceived months earlier?

Angel convinced himself that the baby he saw at the hospital wasn't Lucky's. Now he needed to know was she ever pregnant?

At the end of the day, he would get answers to this little mystery the easy or hard way. It would be her choice on how she wanted this to play out.

Lucky cleared her throat. "Okay, Angel. It's not an issue to come to Miami with Lou. I just can't come tonight. Give me a few weeks, and we'll be there."

"You have one week," he agreed. "And Lucky, if I have to get on a flight to New York, just note that I am not coming for test results."

Lucky understood the unspoken threat. She planned to take it seriously.

Chapter 18

🜨

Lucky was a nervous wreck as she waited for her brothers to arrive, it was critical. She sat at her kitchen's island, chain-smoking, plotting, and trying to see a way out of her dire situation. Meyer was the first to show up, he came alone. Lucky smiled and greeted him with a warm hug. He was looking better every day, growing healthier and gaining his weight back.

"What's goin' on?"

"I wanna wait for Bugsy," she said.

"Where's Lulu?"

"She's in the nursery with her nanny."

While they were waiting for Bugsy to show up, Meyer went into the nursery to see his niece. Lucky made herself a drink, and then she looked into the nursery to see a side of Meyer she never saw. He was smiling, laughing, and acting silly—making faces and sounds, hoping to get the baby to respond. Lulu meant the world to him, and already, her daughter was bringing out his fatherly side, so she knew what she had to say to him would be easy. He would have her back against the cartel—to protect Lulu.

Half-hour later, Bugsy was at her door, he came upstairs

alone and had Avery and Chopper wait in the SUV. Lulu's birth was still a secret, and the only other outsider who knew about her birth was Packer, and he was dead.

"How's the baby?" she asked him.

"Dillinger's fine," he responded. "He's growing bigger by the minute. He's solid and strong already." The proud father beamed.

With Bugsy there, now she needed to come clean to her brothers and tell them her situation with Angel. They needed to know. She was terrified inside, though she didn't show it. She and her brothers went into a different room, where she closed the door so Gloria wouldn't hear this intense discussion. She said, "I have a problem."

"A problem? A problem wit' who?" Meyer immediately asked.

"It's with Angel," she admitted.

Immediately, Meyer was ready to fly off the handle and go ape shit. Hearing Angel's name instantly provoked him.

"Did he find out that Lucchese is his?" Meyer asked.

Lucky explained everything to them, about her meeting with Angel at the hospital, the switched baby—leaving out she used an infant boy, the DNA test, and what he said, or, didn't say should the fake baby end up not being hers. She spared no details; she relayed it to Bugsy and Meyer precisely the way it was told to her.

"Why won't he believe that the baby's not his," Bugsy was stunned. To him, Lucky had executed the perfect plan. He couldn't have thought of a better one. "You gave birth two months early and said you went full term…mathematically he can't be the father."

Lucky exhaled. She was baffled. "Angel's like a Pitbull. He's latched on and won't let go."

The looks on her brothers' faces were distinct, they were furious, especially Meyer—to hear Angel was back to threatening his beautiful niece, it made his blood boil hotter than lava. He exclaimed, "I'ma kill that muthafucka! Where he at?"

"Miami," Lucky said. "In his fortress with an army."

"Lucky, he threatened to kill and torture my niece, that fuckin' shit can't slide. You hear me…we gonna find that muthafucka and kill him!" Meyer shouted heatedly.

Bugsy was upset, too, but he didn't shout and scream and openly threaten to kill Angel like Meyer. Lucky had put herself in a dangerous predicament, and he understood that the cartels were not just deadly but equally powerful. Going to war against them was suicide. But he couldn't sit back and allow Angel to harm his family. He agreed with Meyer, something had to be done, but not with guns blazing and charging into battle like some fool ready to die. He had his son to think about.

Meyer marched around the room, fuming. Just like that, he seemed back to his old self, ready to go to war with the world and shoot anything moving.

"They're all dead!" he shouted.

"Chill Meyer," said Bugsy.

"What the fuck you mean, chill? That muthafucka threatened to kill our niece, and you wanna fuckin' chill! She's a baby, nigga. Who the fuck kills kids?! We need to put a contract out on his fuckin' head…that muthafucka need to get got! I'll go and do it my fuckin' self!"

"It's not that easy," Bugsy replied.

"Why not? He a fuckin' man, Bee…and he breathes, and bleed just like us. He ain't a fuckin' god. Best believe I'm gonna find that nigga!"

"You take on Angel, then you take on the whole Juarez cartel," said Bugsy.

"So be it then…fuck 'em!" Meyer yelled recklessly.

Lucky felt terrible that she was putting her family into a dire situation. She wished that night in Miami never happened, but then she wouldn't have had Lulu. The only good feeling she had was that Meyer and Bugsy were there for her, no matter what. She could see the wheel in Bugsy's head-turning, trying to come up with a solution to her problem, one that wouldn't get them all killed, while Meyer was ranting and raving about killing this one and killing that one.

"You should keep a low profile, don't meet with him again," Bugsy suggested. "And don't answer his calls."

"Even if I could postpone the Miami meet, he's still my connect," she said. "What about business?"

Bugsy exhaled. For once, he was stumped to come up with a quick solution, no answers at the ready to make everyone feel secure. "I need some time to think this through, just delay the meeting until I come up with something."

"Yo, y'all need to wake the fuck up!" Meyer hollered. "All these threats being tossed around and comin' our way needs to be handled," he exclaimed. "Damn, I been out the fuckin' loop too long. Y'all done got soft since I got shot."

He continued to march around the room angrily and irately knocked over a large vase, which tumbled to the ground and shattered in pieces. He wanted to shoot his gun, but the vase was a convenient substitute. He seethed. He wanted to make sure his niece was protected. His family went through enough, suffered too many losses—Gotti, Bonnie, and Clyde—enough was enough! If they couldn't protect their own children, then how were they going to protect an empire?

"We haven't gone soft, Meyer. We just can't take on an army alone," Bugsy answered.

"We could if we called Scott for help."

"Scott?!" Bugsy and Lucky both said.

"Yeah, our father. Y'all remember him. He could help us protect Lucchese."

Lucky was beside herself. "He doesn't know about my child, Meyer."

"They know. I told Layla, and she told Scott."

"What!" Lucky was incredulous. "You've killed your own

niece!"

"Relax, I told her that Packer was the father, and she believed that. She doesn't know about Angel. And to keep it one hundred, it's better that I told her than for them to find out. If they felt that you were keeping Lulu a secret, it might make them dig and find the truth." Meyer explained his treason. "Y'all need to go to our parents and make peace. We call off the sicarios, give Scott and Layla back their bread, and put our family back together. We go to Scott and tell him we need his help with Angel and that we're warring with him over some product. With Scott on board, we blow Angel's fuckin' head off!"

Bugsy stubbornly replied, "I ain't giving back shit."

"Me neither," Lucky concurred. "And we ain't calling off what's already in motion."

"Then I guess it'll be up to me to murder your baby daddy."

"Before we hold court on the streets, Meyer, I think I have a quick solution. A band-aid until we come up with something more permanent." Lucky looked at Bugsy. "Can we move in with you?"

"Move in?" Meyer uttered.

Bugsy repeated, "Move in with me?"

"Think about it, we're stronger if we stay together than if we're apart. And we can keep a better eye on Lulu together."

Bugsy looked skeptical. He uttered, "And what about Maxine? You're not fond of her, Lucky… and I know the two of y'all getting along won't happen overnight, or even at all. You hate her. And I don't want any kind of drama at my place and around my son."

Looking at Bugsy, she sincerely replied, "For the sake of our family and my child, my issues with her are no more. I promise you; I won't bother that woman. I'm willing to overlook our issues and get my grown woman on. I've changed…after having Lucchese, my priorities have shifted."

"I'd need to speak with Maxine, but I'm sure I can convince her it's best and we really don't have a choice," Bugsy said.

Lucky nodded, agreeing with him.

Meyer said what he had been repeating for weeks. "So y'all gonna keep getting comfortable in Scott's crib? Now Lucky moving in too?"

"If Scott wanted us gone, he would have said something by now," Bugsy concluded.

"He shouldn't have too!"

"Okayyy," Lucky sang. "Meeting adjourned."

Meyer had taken the conversation left.

The swift uppercut to Scott's rib nearly toppled him over. Before he could react, a black hood was thrown over his head, and an electric shock from 50,000 volts of a taser gun shot through his whole being. The voltage nearly sucked the life out of him as his body involuntarily shuddered and then went limp. The zip ties were quickly and expertly applied to his wrists, and it all happened in under a minute. Scott was tossed in the back of an SUV, and a Glock was pressed to his temple. A reminder of who was in control.

From the floor of the vehicle, Scott seethed. How the fuck did he allow himself to get put in this position? Several minutes would pass before Scott spoke. He began with, "Look, y'all obviously know who the fuck I am. Whoever's paying for this hit, I could triple your fee. Just let me make one phone call, and I'll have my lieutenant drop off the—"

The wing-tipped cowboy boot slammed into Scott's ribcage mercilessly. It felt like it had nipped his spleen, he yelped from the intense pain.

"*Cállate, cabrón!*" Arturo screamed. And then slammed the butt of his Beretta up the side of Scott's head.

"Fuck you!" Scott challenged. If he was going out, then he was going out like a gangsta. "That's all you got! That's all you fuckin' got!"

Chapter 19

Federal agents Randall and Devonsky couldn't believe their eyes when they saw Scott West being assaulted and kidnapped in broad daylight. They watched in stunned disbelief when he was hooded and thrown into the back of an SUV by what appeared to be cartel members. Devonsky reached for the radio and was about to call in backup when his superior, Agent Randall, stopped him.

"What are you doing?"

Devonsky was perplexed. "I'm calling it in. Aren't you going to pursue the vehicle?"

Agent Randall shrugged. "Why should we?"

"Because we have a duty, we swore an oath."

"Not for that piece of shit," he countered. "Look, we put years into investigating that lowlife, even had an eyewitness to corroborate our evidence, and a jury of his peers didn't feel he should atone for his sins."

"And?"

"And one less drug kingpin on the streets is our goal. However, that's achieved is the cost of being the boss."

"Randall, are you sure about this?" Devonsky knew the

answer before he asked. Besides, the SUV was long gone.

"I am. And there's still a long line of West's for us to prosecute. As they say, 'one monkey doesn't stop the show.'"

Devonsky chuckled. "Good fucking riddance!"

It didn't take long for Lucky and Lulu to move into her father's former palace. It was a mansion in the sky—thirty stories up with round-the-clock building security. The place had a 180-degree view of Manhattan through floor-to-ceiling windows, silk wallpaper with a large Jacuzzi tub, a gourmet kitchen, and a grand piano. The place was 4,000 square feet of immaculate luxury. The board was still fighting to evict them, but Arnold Meade was close to getting the case dismissed, especially now that Scott had been acquitted.

"Thank you, Bugsy," she announced to her brother.

Lucky moved into an extra room, and Dillinger's nursery was now shared with his cousin Lulu. There were cameras situated everywhere, and no one could come up in the private elevator without having a key or knowing the passcode. They had their separate areas, and the children's nursery was directly between the two. Dillinger and Lulu growing up together, that pleased Lucky. But the one thing that didn't please Lucky was seeing Maxine walk into the place. The two women locked eyes, and an uncomfortable silence was between them. Maxine had just returned from shopping for her son with her brother's money, and Lucky eyed her suspiciously. Lucky had promised Bugsy she would behave herself. But seeing Maxine, with her smug stare and her old, aging ass, was irksome. She knew it would be harder than she thought. Lucky had to pivot and walk away from Maxine before something foul came flying out of her mouth.

For now, she had to play nice.

Scott couldn't see, but he could feel the man above him, seated. Scott kicked, and one swift kick landed on Arturo's mouth—his head hit the window, busting his lip wide open, catching him off guard. The blood splattered across the seat, and the men tussled. Félix was driving and saw the action through the rearview mirror. This brawl was titillating to him, it excited all his senses. His maniacal laugh bellowed throughout the car, and he kept saying, "He's crazy! Him loco…him locooo…."

But Arturo didn't find Scott's defiance funny. If he weren't a true professional, he would have put Scott's lights out. For now, he had to settle for a massive beatdown. Arturo swung with the butt of his gun, landing numerous blows to Scott's upper and lower body, anywhere there was flesh, he attacked until the mafioso boss had stopped kicking. Sweat trickled down the sicario's face, under his arms, and down his back. It was winter in New York, but Arturo's temperature had risen and nearly boiled over. He was exhausted, winded, and blind with rage. When they finally pulled up to the arranged destination, he was more than ready to finish what they had started.

By his collar, Scott was dragged out of the SUV by both Félix and Arturo, still fighting to survive. His body felt like a bag of boulders as they pulled the drug lord, his expensive tailored suit pants tore, his knees were scraped up, as was his elbows and six-pack abs. A layer of skin was shaved off on the rugged road as his flesh met gravel, broken glass, and dirt. Finally, he was yanked to his feet, his hood was ripped off, and it took several moments for his eyes to adjust to his surroundings. Under the moonlight, Scott could see what he felt would be his final resting spot. And unmarked, pre-dug grave in the middle of nowhere.

Scott steeled himself for the inevitable. "Do it,

muthafuckas!"

Arturo lifted his crocodile boot in the air, and with a swift kick, it met the center of Scott's back, propelling him forward. Scott landed face-first into a pile of dirt. He turned himself over so he could see the faces of the men who were now his judge and executioners. The Mexican faces were unfamiliar, but Scott could only assume that Javier Garcia wanted him dead. And then he heard, "Bugsy said to tell you that you're not untouchable! Come at him again, and you're dead puta! Adiós pendejo!"

A barrage of bullets from high-powered assault rifles came next as the hitmen emptied their clips in Scott's direction. Miraculously when the smoke cleared, Scott West was still alive. It took tremendous skill to handle those high-powered weapons the way they did, spraying unlimited rounds of ammunition, and not one bullet hit Scott. It was a calculated chess move.

Scott watched as the hitmen walked back to the SUV. He remained silent as they pulled away. And then he said, "Bugsy, you done fucked up now...."

His son had taken this to the next level. This was psychological warfare.

Chapter 20

Meyer showed up at his father's former residence unannounced. He walked in to find an apartment almost full. Meyer knew that Bugsy wasn't home, he was handling business, but neither was Lucky. His niece was bottle-fed by the nanny who hummed while Lulu looked deep into her rent-a-mom's eyes. Meyer relaxed, kicked off his sneakers, and grabbed Lucchese from Gloria. Maxine had finished breastfeeding Dillinger and brought him into the room to spend quality time with his uncle. Before Meyer knew it, he and Maxine were playing like best friends with the children, and he realized that she was a great mom. He still didn't see what his brother saw in her, too long in the tooth for his liking, but she was mad cool if you liked the cougar type.

Impatiently, he looked at his watch. Still no Lucky. Meyer blew out air, and Maxine peeped that he was angry.

"You waiting on your sister to come through and play mommy?" she asked.

"Hell, yeah," he said. "Where the fuck Lucky at?"

Maxine shrugged. "I don't know…but she's never here. She's

usually gone at sunrise and comes in two, three in the morning, sometimes not at all." Maxine didn't care she was snitching. She realized too late that snitching came in handy.

Meyer pulled out his cellphone and dialed Lucky. The first call she let go to voicemail. When he called right back, reluctantly, Lucky answered. "Meyer, what?" she said, annoyed.

"Where the fuck you at?"

"Why?"

He growled. "'cause I'm at your house, and you ain't fuckin' here wit' your daughter!"

"And how is that your business?"

"Because she's my niece!"

Lucky sighed. "Again? How is my daughter any of your fuckin' business, Meyer? Lulu is very well taken care of. She has around the clock nannies and is too young to even know that I'm not there."

"Are you insane!" he exploded, and Lulu and Dillinger cried. Maxine coddled the babies, and Lucky heard her in the background.

"You screaming on me in front of that Maxine bitch?" she hollered, incensed at her brother's betrayal. "You fuckin' snake!"

"Chill wit' all that," he calmly replied. "And bring ya narrow ass home."

"Eat a dick!"

Meyer hung up and helped Maxine calm the babies down. He was getting the hang of this uncle thing, and he liked it.

Layla almost floated out of the beauty salon on E57th Street after a long day of pampering. Her day began with a Swedish massage to knead the kinks and stretch out her tight muscles. She then got a sugar bikini wax, a manicure, and pedicure and ended her day in her hairstylist's chair, who gave her a deep protein treatment, clipped her ends, and styled her hair in long layers. Layla felt renewed. After the lovemaking session with her husband, she wanted to look her best to keep him attracted to her. She had lost him once to another woman, Layla would kill the next bitch—as she had done in the past if they tried to take him away again.

The wind nipped at her face and blew through her hair as she stepped out of the salon. She looked left and then right and didn't see her driver. Layla's good mood quickly evaporated as she seethed at his tardiness. She had told him to be there at eight o'clock sharp. Layla spun on her heels to go back inside for warmth when she was nearly knocked to the ground by someone more desperate to get inside than she was.

"Excuse you!" she snapped.

The stranger turned and faced the diva. "Pardon, ma'am. Excuse me, senóra."

"Ma'am? You look older than me muthaf—"

The large hand from behind with chloroform was placed over Layla's mouth, and within seconds everything went dark.

Layla gradually woke up with a slight headache and a dry mouth. There was a putrid smell, and the questionable lighting was indicative that shit was about to go south. Her eyes scanned the room—an abandoned warehouse and saw the caucus of a dead animal. Mice and rats ran freely around the cement floor, and squirrels ran through the steel raptors. Layla's eyes finally focused on the two Hispanic men who were her captors.

She snarled. "What the fuck y'all want!"

"We want your life," Raffa said in his thick Mexican accent. His delivery was shrouded in the omniscience and hubris of knowing it wouldn't be a hard task. "Today, you will die."

"Now wait a minute," Layla began. "We can work something out. My husband will pay good money for my—"

"Your husband is dead!" Pedro spat.

The news left her stunned. They had gotten to Scott too. Her husband was gone, her other half, her partner in crime was murdered. Layla wailed, "Why! Why are you doing this!"

A burlap bag was placed over Layla's face, and her head was yanked back by Raffa as she struggled against her attackers. Her movements were immobilized as Pedro poured water over the burlap cloth, which caused Layla to experience she was drowning. Waterboarding was the method of torture used for this queenpin.

Each time Layla was brought to the brink of death, they'd halt the water, and she would desperately gasp for air while coughing violently. The intensity of this act had Layla begging for death.

"Just do it," she squeezed out. "Just fuckin' kill me already."

Layla could feel herself losing consciousness. The hard slap across her face from Raffa's large hand jolted her back into reality. She didn't see who slapped her. She didn't care. The men were now shadows, figures moving about as the cloth over her head had obstructed her view.

"Not today puta!" Raffa said as he had rehearsed in English. "Lucky said to let you know that if you ever interfere in her business again, she will kill you!"

Chapter 21

$$\unicode{x2696}$$

Several weeks later...

The Escalade came to a stop in front of Cipriani's on W. Broadway in Downtown, Manhattan. Lucky was in the backseat with Lulu strapped in the car seat, and Zoe rode in the passenger's seat next to her man, dressed conservatively for dinner with Meyers' folks, ready for round two with his mother—and the dysfunctional family she believed they were. Meyer didn't know what to think about his mother's unexpected invitation to the upscale eatery after what they had put their parents through with the sicarios. After both assaults and kidnappings, Scott and Layla went underground. Presumably, to nurse their wounds and heal after their egos were crushed.

Layla had contacted Meyer and didn't specifically mention the incidents. She asked that the whole family meet at the restaurant for dinner—and Scott would be there too. Layla told Meyer she wanted to meet her grandchildren, which was understandable, and she ultimately wanted a truce—no hard feelings. But Meyer felt she had a motive because Layla didn't know how to let shit go. They thought alike. She was him, and he was her—both could be vindictive. His mother explained that being locked up had changed her. It made her reflect on losing three of her children, and if she didn't change, then she would lose the remaining three.

"Please, Meyer," Layla was practically begging. "Bugsy and Lucky will listen to you...convince them that this is the right thing to do. Let's squash this shit for good."

Layla needed her son as a mediator.

"I'll see what's up, but I can't promise you that I can make it happen."

The two siblings lingered in the SUV conversing, parked behind them were four dark SUV's that was filled with armed goons. They rolled there deep, ready for whatever to jump off. For Lucky, her parents waving the white flag was met with skepticism. She couldn't afford to take any risks, even with her parents. She knew first-hand how dangerous, deadly, and deceitful they could be. This dinner with them could be a small ploy to a larger scheme. And if so, Lucky knew that she had to be ready.

They exited the SUV as Lucky carried Lulu in her carrier; her baby girl dressed warmly, snuggled underneath layers of blankets. She instructed the goons to remain vigilant outside as they walked into the cozy and romantic atmosphere of Cipriani's. They were greeted by the maître-d, a young woman happy to assist them. Meyer gave their surname.

"Follow me," the maître-d said.

They walked behind the woman, and Lucky instincts were on high. Her eyes darted everywhere, observing every seated patron and moving staff member. The restaurant had a beautiful décor—a black and silver theme with well-dressed waiters in white and black. Attractive paintings were hanging on the walls, and the lighting was set just right. Lucky and Meyer were led to a sizable backroom isolated from the main dining area. Inside the private room was a large, circular table with white table linen, decorated exquisitely with a classy floral centerpiece, and every piece of fine china, wine glass, and silverware was placed accordingly, and above the room, hung an elegant round crystal chandelier.

Layla and Scott were seated together at the table, having small talk. Scott in a dark grey three-piece suit and Layla in a curve-hugging dress with her cleavage oozing out for all to see. She still had it, and she was again flaunting it. Meyer, Zoe, and Lucky's presence brought forth silence and some tension as eyes locked. Layla and Lucky, in the same room for the first-time months after their explosive argument, had the men on edge. Scott and Meyer—were not on the best terms, but they weren't enemies.

There were no smiles, no hugs, and kisses to the cheeks. No jovial hellos were exchanged as the dinner party skeptically eyed each other. The only innocent and pure thing inside the private dining area was Lulu. She was sleeping. Layla looked at her granddaughter in the carrier, and the corners of her mouth turned upwards. It was the first and maybe only smile that would take place in the room tonight.

Layla stood up and said, "There's my beautiful granddaughter. Can I see her?"

Lucky felt some tightness in her chest and stomach. She looked at her mother with uncertainty. *Can she see her?* It felt like a calculus question to Lucky. Did she want her mother's poison touching her infant girl? Meyer stood beside her, and Zoe looked like a referee for the two ladies.

Lucky's hesitation made Layla respond with, "Lucky, I'm her grandmother, and I've come here to meet my grandbaby."

"Just be gentle…she's sleeping," Lucky replied.

"I had six children, Lucky, I think I can handle another newborn in my arms." Layla carefully picked up Lulu and cradled her into her arms. She smiled while holding her granddaughter. "She's so beautiful and precious."

Lucky didn't respond to her mother's comment. She eyed her father who sat at the table coolly, he too smiled when he looked over at his wife cradling Lucchese.

Meyer spoke. "Zoe, this is my father, Scott, and you've already met my mother."

Zoe smiled politely. "Hello, Mr. West...Mrs. West."

Scott nodded, "Zoe, it's a pleasure to meet you."

Layla looked up from her granddaughter and smiled broadly. "Zoe, I'm glad you're here so that I could personally apologize for my behavior. Baby girl, I was going through a lot when we met. Please don't hold my behavior against my son. I can see that he really cares about you."

Zoe relaxed. "It's water under the bridge."

"Good," Layla grinned. "Isn't she beautiful, Scott? She's a beauty queen."

Scott stared at the Latin beauty and concurred. "That she is. My son has great taste."

Zoe sopped up the compliments like a sponge. This was the reaction she was used to getting when introduced to parents. She moved closer to Meyer and squeezed his hand. He turned to face her and could see she was beaming. Meyer didn't know who these people were masquerading as his parents, but he liked them. Anyone that helped him get closer to his dream girl would get points in his book.

"Where's Bugsy?" Scott asked Meyer.

"He should be on his way," he replied.

Meyer wasn't sure if Bugsy would show up. When they last spoke, Bugsy seemed ambivalent. Meyer and Scott had small talk, but they had nothing in common between them.

The wait staff took everyone's orders—still absent Bugsy and Dillinger. As the champagne was poured, Scott and Layla began doling out apologies as Meyer sat there bewildered. Scott and Layla never apologized to anyone.

"Lucky, I want us to be close again," Layla said. "And, I want to apologize for my unforgivable actions toward you."

Next, it was Scott's turn. "Meyer, I should have been there

for you as your father and had your back when you needed me most. Instead, I treated you like an afterthought and not a priority. On my life, I will never make that same mistake. I love you, son."

What's going on? He thought. While Meyer was still trying to grasp his parents' contradictory actions, the unimaginable happened. This was the ultimate test—the motherload of tests to Layla and Scott's hospitality finally came walking into the room. Bugsy had arrived, and he wasn't alone. He came waltzing in with their son, Dillinger, *and* Maxine.

Maxine came through, and Bugsy had spared no expense on his woman. She was wrapped warmly in a $30,000 fur coat, and a limited-edition crocodile Hermes bag was held by her dainty hand that sported a five-million-dollar diamond engagement ring. This ring was Maxine's *Push Present*, compliments of her baby daddy. When she took off her coat, a Balmain red dress hugged her curves. Against her dark chocolate skin, she was hard to miss. Bugsy was looking sharp too, overdressed, with a black tux and Christian Louboutin hard bottoms. He was polished from head to toe, looking sophisticated and educated, holding his son in a Gucci carrier. Bugsy felt uneasy seeing his father. They hadn't spoken or seen each other since the night they fought one another. Scott, however, he looked unaffected at their arrival.

Layla smiled at Bugsy, Maxine too, but on the inside, she felt such an intense rage, it was shifting her stomach into knots. Maxine wasn't invited, yet she was there. Layla had to play nice with Maxine. Just seeing her standing there next to her son, in her hooker red dress, made her skin crawl.

With her façade grin, she said to the happy couple, "I'm glad y'all could make it. Welcome." She walked their way, kissed, and hugged Bugsy, and to everyone's surprise, she kissed and hugged Maxine too.

"It's good to see you again," Layla said. "And congratulations on the birth of this sweet little bundle of joy. Is this Dillinger?"

Maxine was stunned by the sudden hospitality. Did spending almost a year inside a jail cell make her have a change of heart? Maxine was guarded, but she spoke jovially.

"Yes, this is my little man. Dillinger, meet your *grandmother*." The way she said 'grandmother,' Layla didn't like it. It triggered the emotions she felt when she read that letter while she was incarcerated. Maxine said it as a slight.

"My grandbabies will call me, G-ma. I'm far too young to be a grandmother. Shit, I'm younger than you!" It was accurate, but only by a few weeks. Layla felt her voice harden and knew she had better check herself and quick. When Maxine's lips pursed tightly together, Scott distracted her.

"Maxine, you look lovely tonight. My son brings out the best in you. Please, Bugsy…Maxine, have a seat. Join us. Order something to eat."

With everyone settled at the dinner table, Scott finally stood up from his chair with his glass of champagne in his hand. He wanted to propose a toast. He looked into each of their faces and said, "It's good to see everyone here, and no matter what differences and problems we have with each other, we will always be family, that will never change. So…your mother and I wanted everyone to come together because we have an announcement to make."

Everyone was intently listening. The animosity was placed on paused—maybe the babies in the room made the adults behave themselves because Maxine, Layla, and Lucky and Scott and Bugsy all in the proximity of each other was a disaster waiting to happen.

Scott continued with, "Layla and I have gotten back together, and we plan on renewing our wedding vows soon."

Audible gasps could be heard. It was a shock to everyone in the room. Their faces were in awe. Was their mother going crazy? Lucky especially was disappointed by the news. The things Scott did to her—the cheating, the abuse, the womanizing—how could she excuse that behavior?

"I've always been in love with this woman. She's the best thing that ever happened to me, and somewhere along the way, I forgot what she meant to me. I fucked up. Something I've promised your mother will ever happen again. Layla has always been my ride or die queen from day one, and no one can ever replace her," Scott sincerely said.

Maxine smirked. What about what they had shared? Although she had moved on with Bugsy, she couldn't help but feel some kind of way about the announcement. Scott looked her way, and Maxine smiled wide and did a congratulatory head nod. *Cute,* she thought. She didn't want him anymore, and she could not care less what he did with his life or his wife, but his words still stung.

The mood in the room after the announcement was lukewarm. Everyone lifted their champagne glasses to toast to their parents' renewed love. It was a halfhearted toast. Congratulations were uttered, but who really cared? However, Scott and Layla seemed happy. They hugged and kissed each other, passionately for everyone to see.

"So what's next? A honeymoon, retirement?" Meyer asked them.

"We plan on taking things one day at a time." He hugged Layla tightly. "And yes, Meyer, we are retiring from this shit. Your mother and I have been through a lot and feel now is the time to enjoy the fruits of our labor."

Bugsy and Lucky were most relieved. They could finally stop looking over their shoulders and resume as heads of their usurped organization.

"That's good to hear, Pops," Bugsy said, smiling. He was glad he had shown up.

Lucky gave in too. "If y'all happy, then so are we." She was already thinking of dumping Lucchese off with her parents most weekends so she could continue to expand her side hustle.

Meyer hoped this peace treaty would last.

Dinner was nice, but it was somewhat awkward for everyone, and the following day, Meyer asked to meet with his siblings. He needed to get something off his chest. They gathered at his apartment.

"What's on your mind, Meyer? Why call this meeting?" Bugsy asked him.

"Dinner last night, it didn't seem strange to you?" he said.

"What you mean?" Lucky asked. "You were the one that pushed us to meet with them."

"I know I did," he said. "I want us all to squash this beef, but they seemed too fuckin' nice."

"That's true, but maybe they're tired. We're all tired of the inhouse fighting," Bugsy said. "And I think that spanking we gave them made them see that together we're no fucking joke."

"Nah, Bee, they don't scare that easily." Meyer wasn't convinced. "After we had the sicarios get at them, we doubled up our security teams for weeks, and neither one of them thought about retaliating? Pops ain't even have Mason come through and do what he does best?"

Bugsy thought for a second and then said, "I hear you. I do. But neither one of us knows how it feels to be facing life in prison without the possibility of parole. And that's what they've been through. And then to come home to war with your children?" Bugsy blew out air. "That can take a toll on the most thorough of them all."

"Yeah, but you think they just gonna retire and walk away from everything just like that...our father, that man knows nothing but this game." Meyer's mind was racing. "And how come Layla was so nice to Maxine last night? She's been on our mother's shit list since day one."

"Who cares about Maxine?" Lucky shrugged. "Layla took Scott from Maxine once, and she got her man back again. If I were Layla, my beef with Maxine would be dead too."

Bugsy said, "This dope shit is a young man's game, and Scott and Layla could start to feel that they were living on borrowed time. Whatever moves they want to make, good or bad, I'll be ready for them. But for now, I'm gonna take them at their word and believe they're out and moving on to something else. What the fuck they got left?"

Meyer looked to his sister and asked, "Do you feel the same way?"

"If that bitch comes at me wrong, I'm gonna be ready for her too…but for now, I'm wit' Bugsy. We live our lives, and they live theirs. They want to see their grandkids, I'll allow it, but I'm gonna be careful," she said.

Meyer relaxed. He was now ready for them to leave. He wanted to get buck naked, drink a tall glass of Lean, smoke a blunt, and jerk off to Zoe's Instagram page.

Lucky sat in the nail salon chair and watched the Korean girl work on her feet with precision, applying magic to her toes. Her pedicure was looking phenomenal. At $250 a foot, the design had Swarovski crystals and 14-karat gold flakes on each toe. She sat back, sipping on a glass of prosecco, and made small talk with the other young women seated in the salon with her. They discussed men and music and celebrities and man problems. Though her day job was distribution, Lucky loved these moments of escape where she felt normal. She got to laugh and smile and enjoy some girl time.

Chic Nails was an exclusive establishment by appointment

only, in Soho. It was a trendy shop with some of the most talented and skilled nail technicians in the city where corporate and wealthy women went to be pampered.

"Your pedicure is coming out flawless. I love that design," said one of the ladies seated next to Lucky.

"Thank you."

"Do you have anything special planned tonight?"

Lucky shook her head and replied, "Nothing special, just work."

"Oh, really? What do you do?" The woman turned her upper body toward Lucky and extended her hand for a shake. "My name's Pilar."

Lucky now felt uncomfortable, but she shook her hand. She hadn't come for chitchat; she came to relax and ear hustle on the other conversations. "I'm Lucky, and I'm a real estate developer. I own a few properties. My business is stressful, so that's why I'm here…to escape…and relax…to not think about work."

"That's cool. Where are your properties located?"

Lucky rolled her eyes. "If I wanted to discuss work, I'd be at work."

These pampering sessions were a temporary distraction from worrying about Angel, rival dealers, her siblings, the FBI, and Maxine. The nail salon was supposed to provide short-term relief from everything. But then her cellphone rang, and it was Yusef. She answered his call with, "What?"

"Shit went smooth in the B.X. We fed all the blocks on the low, and everybody up top is happy," he announced, indicating the shipment came and left with the right folks, and the corner drug dealers for her retail business had been supplied with the product. Then he added, "But your brothers are here, and they've called a meeting with everyone without you."

She fumed. "Who the fuck they think they are!"

"I just wanted to let you know, Lucky."

"I'll be there in a minute. You tell my brothers to hold off on that fuckin' meeting until I arrive," she hollered into the phone.

"I'll do what I can."

"No, you do your fuckin' job and stop that meeting from happening until I show up."

"A'ight," he said.

Lucky hung up. Her girl time and the laughter in the nail salon ended for her. One phone call brought her back to reality. The Korean girl working on her toes had another layer of polish to go, but Lucky couldn't wait. She gathered her things, excusing herself, explaining to the woman she had a sudden emergency. Lucky pulled out a wad of hundred-dollar bills and included a hundred-dollar tip. Lucky hurried out of the salon in the frigid air with Gucci flip flops on and climbed into her SUV that sped toward the Bronx. She looked down, and her polish had smeared.

"Fuck!" she said, annoyed at the whole incident.

She arrived at the Bronx warehouse almost an hour later and hurried out of the vehicle. She charged into the area where Meyer and Bugsy were arguing with her lieutenant, Yusef. He was doing what he was told, preventing the meeting from happening until Lucky's arrival. Lucky interrupted the squabbling by shouting out, "What the fuck are y'all doing having meetings without informing me. I'm sick of this shit!"

Bugsy and Meyer looked at their sister, and Meyer replied, "I thought you'd be home wit' your baby, sis."

"So you go behind my back and pull this shit because you thought I was gonna be busy with Lulu? That's bullshit, and you know it!"

"We just talkin', that's all," said Meyer.

"I don't give a fuck if you were just thinking! You let me know about everything that's going on," she hollered. "I run this shit, too! I brought this shit together...not you!" Her attention and eyes glared at Meyer.

Meyer smirked. *Yeah, whatever*, he thought.

Lucky continued to gripe. It wasn't the first time her brothers tried to call the shots and cut her authority. When they had their roundtable gatherings with their trusted lieutenants, sometimes, she wanted to take control and speak on vital issues, but she was vetoed by Bugsy and Meyer.

"Listen, Lucky, calm down," Bugsy spoke.

"Don't tell me to calm down!" she snapped.

Bugsy continued with, "All we wanted to accomplish today was to go over operations—that means are we receiving and distributing the kilos most efficiently. And security—have we hired the top triggermen to guard our organization? And finally, expansion—how can we take our organization to the next level?"

Lucky was incredulous. These were significant issues, and she deserved to have a seat at the table. She was also annoyed. Bugsy had to say only that the meeting would be about operations, distribution, and expansion. Instead, he felt he had to mansplain it to her. Lucky was ready to fight. She pointed her finger in Bugsy's face as Meyer, Yusef, Chopper, Avery, and all the underlings looked on. "You can't be serious right now, Bee. I'm shocked that you're even down with this type of deception."

"That's not what this is," he explained. Bugsy stuffed his hands deep into his suit pants pockets and stared into his sister's angry eyes. She was behaving just as he expected her to, emotionally. And emotions either got you locked up or killed. "Meyer and I felt that you needed a break to spend time with your child and reevaluate the decisions that you've made for this organization, including the unwise choice you made with Angel."

Bugsy had to choose his words wisely because the men still didn't know that Angel was Lucchese's father.

Lucky was now incensed. She yelled, "I was the one that fuckin' put this shit together…me! I got control of the connect, I bust my ass to keep us afloat, and this is the thanks I get," she repeated.

"Layla put this together," Meyer quipped. "You just got

lucky."

"Fuck you, Meyer…fuck you!" Lucky shouted, and she desperately tried to go upside his head with her fist. But Bugsy came between them.

Meyer frowned. "Don't put your fuckin' hands on me, Lucky. I swear."

"Or what, nigga?" she retorted.

"Look, it was just miscommunication, that's all," Bugsy said coolly.

"Miscommunication, Bugsy? Do you think I'm stupid? You don't think I know what the two of y'all are doing?" she shouted.

"Lucky, just relax…." Bugsy continued to bring the volume down, but his sister had no chill button.

"Y'all fuckin' relax!" she screamed at them, becoming more emotional, throwing an epic temper tantrum. She was in her feelings. "I swear, don't fuckin' play wit' me Bugsy, or I'll pull my connect and run my organization solo. I don't fuckin' need y'all!"

"Do it then, Lucky…pull your connect, like we give a fuck! We shouldn't be fuckin' wit' that nigga anyway after all his threats. How we fuckin' look, doing business wit' that fuckin' Mexican?" Meyer barked.

"We look like some niggas getting money, that's how we look," Lucky retorted.

Bugsy had to defuse the situation and keep Meyer and Lucky apart. Once again, they were clashing, and he knew it wouldn't be long until someone broke. The two were like oil and water. Lucky continued to fume, but she was done arguing with them. She made her point—loud and clear.

"Don't let this shit happen again," she warned them.

She pivoted in her flip flops and marched away from her brothers, Yusef and her armed guards followed behind her. Meyer seethed. He had always been there for her, but lately, he felt like he'd picked the shorter straw and was becoming more of an errand boy to his sister than a partner. Meyer knew that Lucky's rise only happened because he'd gotten shot, and he had been out of commission for a long while.

With Lucky finally gone, Meyer turned to his brother and grumbled, "I swear, Bugsy, Lucky is out of control. She better watch her mouth. I ain't her fuckin' bitch."

"Chill, Meyer. You know how she gets."

"She keeps talkin' to me like that, and I'm gonna go ham on that bitch. She needs to stay in her fuckin' lane and recognize who the fuck I am. I ain't some soldier in this shit, I'm a fuckin' partner, too."

"We just gotta keep her occupied to make her feel important, so she doesn't pull her connect...send her on a few errands while we handle the real issues. Business is thriving, so now is not the time for dissension," said Bugsy, keeping his cool and talking sense.

Meyer didn't want to hear it. He continued to seethe. "I'm no fuckin' underling in this shit, Bee. I'm letting you know that, too. I'm a fuckin' equal in this shit...the muthafuckas I done killed for this family, y'all niggas better respect my fuckin' gangsta, and I ain't asking, I'm tellin' y'all how this gonna be!" He exclaimed belligerently.

Bugsy did his best to calm his brother down. He knew that having Meyer on his side was more of an asset than Lucky, and if Bugsy didn't cosign on Meyer's request, chances were his brother would become his rival again. He had come a long way without the watchful, hovering eyes of Scott, and his emancipation felt tremendous so he wouldn't do anything to mess that up.

Meyer stormed away, leaving Bugsy to contemplate his next move.

Chapter 22

Diego and Luis sat outside the 20-story National Historical Landmark—The Plaza Hotel in a black Ford F-150 with tinted windows and an abundance of patience. Their keen eyes scanned the perimeter—up and down the populated block looking for their mark: Scott West. This was a stakeout, and both knew that a lot was on the line. If Scott even got an inkling he was on their radar, he wouldn't hesitate to react violently.

It was early evening, just after six o'clock, and the area was bustling with activity and movements ideal for blending in. Tourists were coming out of the hotel to ride in the highly sought-after horse and carriages through Central Park. Guests were checking in and out, and employees were punching on and off the clock.

Tonight they were collecting intel, doing surveillance, gathering information to successfully pull off this hit. They had arrived fifteen hours earlier and had yet to get a glimpse of the elusive kingpin.

Both passenger doors opened, and Juan-Pablo and Miguel slid in carrying Subway sandwiches, and coffee and donuts. No one complained that it was about thirty degrees inside the vehicle because they couldn't sit with the ignition on for heat. Each man would take turns getting out to stretch their legs, go inside one of the many fast food establishments to use the restroom, and then linger to get warmth. A vehicle sitting in park for hours with the ignition on was a telltale sign of potential danger to an organization such as Scott's. His men would spot the SUV from a distance and react.

"Y'all see that nigga yet?" Juan-Pablo asked as he handed his highly skilled triggermen their food.

"Nah, not yet," Diego replied. "Shit, if I had a room in there, I wouldn't come out either."

All the men nodded as they chowed down on their sandwiches. Just then, Diego saw the dark-colored Escalade steadily approaching in his sideview mirror.

"Get the fuck down," he ordered. "This might be them."

Murder Incorporated got low in their seats as the SUV cruised by them and double-parked in front of the hotel. A few minutes later, Scott—dressed in a full-length wool coat, suit, and hard bottom shoes came walking out, flanked by two goons. They climbed into the SUV and peeled out.

"Y'all ready?" Diego asked.

"Always," said Juan-Pablo. He checked his .45 Glock—one in the chamber and his .380 tucked in his ankle holster—and they followed the vehicle.

Scott sat comfortably in the SUV with Mason at the wheel. Zaire sat shotgun, and Kane was in the back with his boss. They were headed to a long-overdue meeting with Scott's connect, Javier Garcia, and all the key members of the Garcia cartel. Since his acquittal, the cartel needed to be assured that moving forward,

Scott had buttoned up all the holes in his organization. That all snitches and weak links had been handled and that Scott was taking all precautions to elude the federal government.

Javier respected Scott's gangster and his loyalty. He proved to be a trustworthy individual who never folded under pressure.

"We got company," Mason announced.

"Sicarios?" Scott wanted to know.

"Feds," Mason concluded, as he eyed the Crown Vic tailing them.

"Lose those pigs!"

Mason nodded. He made several left turns, repeatedly. Federal agents Randall and Devonsky realized that they had been made, and the unmarked Crown Vic called off their tail. Tomorrow was another day.

"Damn, that nigga spotted us!" Diego yelled after he had made several dizzying left turns. "That muthafucka on point."

"We all knew that getting at Scott West wouldn't be easy. We switch up vehicles, fall farther back next time, and bide our time. Tomorrow's another day. He can't run forever."

Chapter 23

Max tried to push the anxiety she felt about Scott, and Layla hits out of her mind, but negative thoughts kept infiltrating. Why was it taking so long? She hoped that she hadn't made a mistake hiring Murder Inc., but they supposedly were the best. It became a struggle for her to think positively and focus on Dillinger.

Maxine would stare at her son in wonderment as he grew, feeling blessed to have had a child after everything she'd been through and at her age. His chubby cheeks, fat arms, and thighs were getting longer, and his fingers would wrap firmly around her index when she gave it to him. Dillinger wasn't lifting his head on his own yet, but he wanted to. Her heart melted each time he would stare in her eyes or smiled when she cooed at him. He was everything she needed and more.

Lately, Bugsy had been spending less time with his immediate family. He was there for Dillinger's morning feeding and would try to be there to put him down at night. However, during the crucial hours between, Maxine felt like he had abandoned them. Bugsy was already heading out the front door, and Maxine hadn't even showered yet. Recently he was leaving earlier and coming home later. She bickered, "Where are you going this time of the morning?"

He paused in the doorway and said, "I got a lot of things to take care of. You know that."

"You're never home anymore!" Maxine pointed out. "Your son doesn't get a chance to spend quality time with his father. I'm feeling like a single mom."

"But you're not though."

"You got some nerve complaining about Lucky being an absentee mom when you two are cut from the same cloth. You're the pot calling the kettle black."

"It's different."

"Why? Because you're a man?"

Bugsy exhaled. It was too early for arguing. "Look, I'll come home early and make it up to you."

"Don't bother," she dismissed. "And what about my car?"

Bugsy was confused. "What?"

"I've asked you for months to take it in and get the car safety locks fixed."

"Come on, Maxine. Dillinger isn't even old enough to touch the doors yet."

"And? It's still a safety hazard. Anything could happen while my baby is in that backseat. The door could fly open, and he could get tossed out. And I don't want to be worrying about it."

Bugsy realized that Maxine was an older mom, and Dillinger might be her only child. Therefore, she would always be overprotective—a helicopter parent, and he was cool with that. He said, "Okay, I'll take it in next week."

"You said that last week," she snapped. "Yesterday...last month, but it never gets done!"

"Well, you're just gonna have to believe me this time."

Maxine observed the day and night nannies become surrogate mothers to Lulu, who didn't even know who Lucky was. Lucky and Bugsy were like bookends, both choosing the streets over parenthood. Maxine was still too lively to sit around nursing her son and waiting for Bugsy to come and go. She needed some air and wanted to do something, anything to pass the time. Maxine decided to take the babies to a studio to take pictures. Since their births, no one had taken any professional photos, so photographs were well overdue.

Maxine asked Maria to come along.

"I call Ms. Lucky and ask if it's okay."

"It is okay, get Lulu dressed," Maxine sternly ordered.

An expensive Givenchy dress and matching booties were picked out for Lulu, and Maria got her dressed. Lucchese looked like a porcelain doll with her rosy cheeks, long eyelashes, and pink lips. Dillinger was dressed in a Gucci logo coverall with the matching baby hat, his small feet had knitted Gucci booties. His face was fat and round, and no one could resist kissing his cheeks, which he always loved the affection.

With security following closely behind in an SUV, the family got into Maxine's Benz and headed to a Midtown photography studio.

Lucky arrived home only to find it empty, no nanny, no babies, and no Maxine. Where was her baby? Where was Maria? Lucky didn't want to worry, but she was concerned. Lucky had enemies out there, and it crossed her mind that maybe Angel came by unannounced and kidnapped everyone. He had given her a week to show up in Miami, and she had continually postponed the visit citing her child was sick, scheduling conflicts, and last week she claimed she had strep throat, which was contagious.

Angel threatened death if she didn't come soon, but ultimately he seemed to accept the excuses she gave. When she wanted, Lucky could be a very persuasive liar.

Don't panic, she said to herself. The penthouse showed no signs of a scuffle, everything was tidy and still in order. Lucky instructed her nannies to inform her before they left the apartment with Lulu. It was unlike Maria to not tell her of their whereabouts. Lucky closed her eyes and swallowed hard. *This cannot be happening*, she thought. Her baby was gone! Her hands trembled as she pulled out her cellphone to call Meyer. He would know what to do. And then as quickly as the thought came into her mind, it dissipated. She couldn't call Meyer or Bugsy. Lucky would have to handle this situation on her own, like a boss bitch. And bosses didn't overreact or panic. She needed to calm down and not be the emotional female her brothers accused her of being. Lucky paced around the room and called Maria, but the call went straight to her voicemail. She called again, and Maria answered.

"Where the fuck are you? And where's my baby?" Lucky cursed.

"Ma'am, she said it would be okay."

"Who said it would be okay?"

"Ms. Maxine. She said it's okay to take pictures with a professional photographer...they look nice...Lucchese looks so pretty," Maria said.

Lucky fumed. *This fuckin' bitch!* Her rage simmered. "Bring my baby home now!" Lucky sternly demanded.

"Okay, Ms. Lucky. We on our way, I am sorry," Maria said submissively.

"You better hurry up!" Lucky exclaimed angrily.

She ended the call and heatedly clutched the cellphone so tightly in her hand, it could snap in two from the pressure. The audacity of Maxine taking her child out without her permission and getting professional photos taken in her absence. Lucky was done playing nice with that bitch. Maxine had voided Lucky's promise to her brother when she disregarded Lucky as Lulu's mother.

Half-hour later, everyone walked through the front door into the penthouse, and Lucky stood in the center of the foyer, waiting angrily to greet them. The rage that bubbled inside of Lucky couldn't be contained. Maria had Lulu in her arms, and Lucky charged toward the nervous nanny and bitterly said to her, "Take my baby into the nursery and stay there; I'll deal with you later."

Maria nodded timidly, and once again apologized, "I'm so sorry, Ms. Lucky," and she quickly did what she was told. She carried Lulu into the nursery while Lucky was left to deal with Maxine. Maxine stood with her son and smirked. She asked, "What's wrong with you?"

Lucky stood toe-to-toe with her.

"Bitch, you got some fuckin' nerve taking my baby out of here like you're her mother! Who the fuck you think you are?"

"Calm down, Lucky. As usual, you weren't around, so I figured it was a good idea to let Lulu get some air. She's cooped up in here all the time, either staring at these four walls or in the faces of strangers masquerading as her surrogate moms."

"Excuse me?" Lucky was embarrassed.

"Oh, you heard me." Maxine walked past her and walked into the nursery to lay her son in his crib. Dillinger was knocked out from the full day of activities. Lucky was right on her heels. Maxine continued, "I got professional photos of the babies today, something you didn't think about…and they had a good time, especially Lulu. You should have seen her smile in front of the camera," Maxine replied with sarcasm. "It's what mothers do, right?"

Maxine wanted to take shots at Lucky, knowing she had been too preoccupied with drug dealing to be present in her daughter's life.

Lucky retorted with, "You old fuckin' ho!"

155

Maxine had heard it all before and was unmoved by the tantrum and insults. She stared down at her bundle of joy and then over at Lulu—both children were sound asleep. She exited the room, hoping to pour herself a glass of wine and finish binge-watching Luke Cage on Netflix.

However, Lucky refused to let this go. She said, "You hear me talking to you bitch?" —and Maxine was thrust forward as Lucky aggressively pushed her from behind. The impact forced her to take several steps before she got her bearings and stopped the momentum of the shove. Maxine spun around, and cold clocked Lucky in her mouth, causing the girl to stagger, stunned. Before Lucky could regain her footing, Maxine struck her again in the face, her lip burst open. The barrage of uppercuts to Lucky's chin and body shots to her ribcage had the young mom gasping for air. Lucky wanted mercy, but none was given. The fist repeatedly smashing upside her head had Lucky dazed and confused. Her hands went up to block the blows, and she was met with another fierce blow to her cheek. The throbbing pain coursing throughout her body was almost debilitating as she tried to fight back. Dazed, Lucky swung wildly hitting air, as her fists missed their intended target. She locked eyes with Maxine and saw a side of her nemesis that sent chills down Lucky's spine. Maxine's eyes exhibited more than anger and rage—she looked almost inhuman. There was a bloodthirst behind her dark, cruel eyes.

Lucky tried to crawl away, to escape this lunatic, but Maxine grabbed her by her barefoot and calf and dragged her back into the arena. The six-inch Prada boot came crashing down on Lucky's head, the heel of the shoe slicing into her skull. Lucky yelped in pain but was silenced when the boot smashed into her mouth, loosening a few teeth. Lucky was disoriented as blood dripped into her eyes, and pain nearly paralyzed her. Maxine got down low and punched Lucky repeatedly in the face until her hands were bloody.

"H-h-help," Lucky squeezed out. "Help me!"

Maria had heard the commotion; she came tiptoeing out of the room to see the kafuffle but returned into the safety of the nursery. This was above her paygrade.

Maxine took her strong fingers and wrapped them around Lucky's long, soft locks and pulled. She could feel each strand ripping from the roots, and the pain was almost too much for Lucky to bear. "Aaaaaaah!" she screamed. "Aaaaaaaaah!"

No one would rescue her. She wouldn't be saved. If jail taught Maxine anything, that was violence and brutality. Max was ready to teach Lucky to have some respect for her. She was dying to beat down the smart mouth brat for some time now. Bored, cooped up in the apartment all the time with Bugsy running the streets, now guarded by his goons, Maxine felt like a prisoner all over again. She wanted out. She wanted out of the penthouse and felt this would be the only way possible that Bugsy would find them a new place—through violence. She had pent-up energy simmering inside of her for some time now—everyone pushing her, testing her; Scott, Layla, Lucky, Wacka, and Tarsha—all tested her, and now Lucky found herself at the end of an exploding time-bomb.

Maxine stood over her, and gruffly said, "I'll take Lulu wherever the fuck I want!"

Chapter 24

The Hennessey bottle tilted, and the brown liquid spilled into the small glass cup. Meyer poured himself half a glass of Henny and downed it like it was water going down his throat. He poured himself another drink and looked over at Zoe seated on his long couch, looking too sexy in her tight skirt that highlighted her long, crossed legs and a skimpy top that revealed her ample cleavage. She was so stunning that Meyer would continuously find himself staring at her, completely mesmerized by her beauty. What he would do to have her right now—to taste her below and feel her pussy pulse while he was inside of her. They were less than ten days away from Zoe's 90-day no-sex rule—and that expiration date couldn't come fast enough for him. Meyer downed his second glass of Henny and sighed. He was antsy. He stood in his home with his shirt unbuttoned, his scars from his surgery, and street battles displayed as a testament of his violent life, his arm sleeve and hand tattoos peaking out. Meyer was doing everything in his power to impress Zoe, to keep her happy—but still, Zoe wasn't budging from the rule. They had come from having dinner and seeing a movie. It was a beautiful night out, and they went back to his place for a few drinks and conversation. He had Hennessy straight, and Zoe preferred champagne. She was a classy girl, and there was no changing it.

It was a full moon night, and it felt like the perfect evening for intimacy. He approached Zoe and took a seat close to her, placed his arm around her dainty shoulder, and stared deeply into her chestnut-colored eyes. She smiled. He smiled.

"Damn, I want you."

"You do, huh?" she said giggling.

"Fuck yeah!"

Her full lips were succulent, and the scent of her was intoxicating—like fresh roses and a strawberry cake. Everything about Zoe was too tantalizing to resist, bringing out the animal urges in Meyer. He badly wanted to fuck her. It wasn't a secret. The two locked eyes and Meyer could resist no longer. He leaned in closer for a kiss, and soon a sweet kiss turned into a deep and passionate exchange between them. Their lips and tongues entwined fervently, and as they kissed on the sofa, Meyer's hand traveled elsewhere, wandering from her stomach down to her legs and found its way underneath her short skirt. The softness of her lips against his, the touching of her silky soft skin, and the warmth he felt from his hand being between her legs, it showed in his jeans. An erection bulged for her to see and do with whatever she wanted. In under a minute, things became intense. Zoe found herself on her back, her panties removed and tossed to the floor. Almost immediately, Meyer's fingers entered her. Slowly, he fingered her shaved pussy with his index and middle finger, feeling how wet and tight she was. It was the furthest he had gotten with her—but he wanted more.

Meyer went down low, nibbling on her pussy and sliding his tongue against her phat clit, enjoying the way Zoe tasted.

She wrapped her toned thighs around him, grinding her hips, expressing her pleasure. "Ooooh, fuck, Meyer," Zoe moaned, biting her bottom lip.

His tongue slid deeper inside her, causing waves of pleasure to wash over his beauty queen. He nibbled, sucked, and licked on her sensitive button and felt Zoe's body shudder, her moans turning him on. She was ripe, and he knew it. She wanted him. Meyer inched his fingers back inside her wet hole, causing her body to buck. He used his lips and tongue on her swollen clit as her body moved to its own rhythm. He wanted her to explode in his mouth.

"Aaaaah, please, Meyer, don't stop. Ummm, hmmm. Ooooh, don't stop. Right there." Zoe grabbed his head and held it to her neatly waxed mound, restricting his movements to her sweet box. She exploded, her wetness dripping on his tongue as he continued to taste her juices.

"You like that?" he asked, and she moaned her approval. Meyer moved north with soft, wet kisses on her stomach, tasting her skin, making his way to her breasts. His tongue flicked on her dime-sized nipples until they were both erect. "Get undressed," he demanded as he rose and reached in his jeans for a condom. Meyer kicked off his jeans and boxers in a nanosecond and rolled the Magnum back onto his massive length and girth. He noticed that Zoe hadn't moved. She had hesitated.

"I'm not ready...not yet," she said.

"Not ready?" Meyer was incredulous. "Are you serious? What the fuck was all this then? Huh? You gonna make me wait nine fuckin' more days for some pussy."

"It'll be worth it," she said teasingly.

He was horny and agitated—two things that shouldn't mix. Zoe was now sitting upright and putting her panties back on, and Meyer was standing up, naked, dick hard. "Why you playin' this game wit' me, Zoe?"

"I'm not playing any games with you, Meyer. I got rules."

"You make me eat you out, you come in my mouth, got my dick fuckin' hard like rocks, and you wanna just stop?"

"I didn't make you do anything."

"Yo, can you at least suck my dick? Give me some pleasure, so there's a fair exchange."

"What?" Zoe uttered her disapproval. "No!" She was appalled that Meyer would speak to her in such a way.

"Yo, you a fuckin' tease," he said.

"You knew my rule from day one. I didn't sugarcoat anything. It was your choice to pursue me or not, Meyer. You should be happy that I let you get this far; this level of intimacy is reserved for much later in my relationships. Tonight I gave you a part of me that I don't give to just anyone. I connected with you tonight because I like you, Meyer...but don't ever disrespect me again, or I'm gone. For good next time."

Zoe had Meyer fucked up. She made him feel special that she allowed him to eat her pussy and trick on her.

His erection felt like a fifty-pound weight on him. Zoe had gotten him all worked up, but still no action. He didn't push the issue though or curse her out as he would've done to anyone else. Instead, he said, "I apologize for comin' at you like that. Just chill, and I'll be right back."

Zoe watched him disappear into the bathroom, and she soon heard the shower running. Meyer needed to jerk off. He couldn't believe that he was taking this abuse from her. She was selfish and spoiled, but he was head over heels in love with her.

Zoe grinned. Men were so easy to toy with.

She had made the same moves to so many men. She always had them eating out the palm of her hand. Men like Meyer, who thought that every woman was supposed to open their legs for them because they had money and power, always felt challenged with her antics. It didn't hurt she was smart and gorgeous and had a beauty queen title. Zoe knew what men like Meyer were all about. He was an uneducated thug, and men like him were always in search of a trophy wife.

Chapter 25

The embarrassment Lucky felt was insurmountable. How did she allow an old cougar like Maxine to get the best of her? She had a black eye, bruises, lacerations, and her mouth was so damaged that each time she opened it to talk, it felt like someone was slicing it with a razor. And when she thought it couldn't get worst—it did. Her hair, chunks of it had been ripped out, leaving several quarter size bald areas all over her scalp. She was an ugly mess. When she looked in the mirror, it traumatized her. Her face triggered the emotions she felt the day she was kidnapped and left for dead. The day her assailants left her beautiful face permanently disfigured.

Lucky had underestimated the bitch, and now she wanted her revenge. She wanted Maxine to suffer and die slow, but the problem was Bugsy. He would not allow anything to happen to his cougar.

Lucky finally exited her bathroom, her eyes low, ego crushed, self-esteem at an all-time low. There wasn't any way she was leaving her condo looking as she did. She made an emergency appointment with her beautician, Kelly, who was one of the best in the city and the most qualified to treat hair no matter what condition it was in. She preferred Kelly to come to her. Lucky didn't want to go to her shop and have other women see her under these circumstances. She would pay Kelly anything, and Kelly agreed.

Kelly walked into the gigantic penthouse carrying a large bag of equipment and a portable hairdryer. She was immediately impressed by how her client was living. The place was like something in a movie—the lifestyle of the rich and fabulous. She knew Lucky was paid, *but damn*—not this paid. Lucky emerged into the living room in a sweatsuit, and her hair covered under a black headscarf. Kelly looked at her and said nothing about her battered face. "I'm here for you, Lucky. What you need me to do?"

Lucky sighed. "It's bad."

"Girl, it can't be that bad, you always had good hair."

She hesitated to remove her headscarf.

"Lucky, I can't help you if you won't show me what I'm working with," said Kelly.

"I'll pay you whatever, I just need something done to it."

Lucky removed the headscarf, and Kelly finally got a good look at the damage. Even she, after ten years of doing hair, was somewhat shocked. There were several areas of trauma where her scalp was raw and tender, and there was a long laceration that had it been deeper Lucky would have needed stitches. She would be unable to do a lot of styles, not wanting to cause additional damage. It needed to heal. Lucky wouldn't be able to get a relaxer, color, braids, or a weave—not yet, not for a while.

"Okay, where can we sit," she asked, and the two walked into the kitchen, and Lucky sat down in one chair. Gently, Kelly used her fingers to part through her client's hair to get a full scope of the damage. "I think we can do a protective style. I can wash and condition your hair and then make you a custom wig. It'll take me a few days, though."

Lucky rapidly shook her head. "I'm twenty-one years old,

Kelly. I'm not wearing some granny wig."

"Girl, it won't be dated. I slay...you should know this by now. I would never play you. No one will even know that it's a wig."

"I'll know. Besides, wigs fuck up your edges, and a black woman without edges is a hot mess."

Kelly moved closer to her client and thought about the limited options. "Well, we can't do a weave if that's what you want. You'll lose more hair, and it might be permanent. You could run the risk of developing traction alopecia."

Lucky was aggravated and wanted to take out her frustration on the innocent party. What was wrong with Kelly? Didn't she know that the very word alone was enough to spark fear in folks? You don't say *hair* and *alopecia* in the same sentence.

She snapped, "Well, what *can* you do!"

"I have an idea," said Kelly.

"What?"

Kelly sighed and suggested one more thing, "I feel you should go with the big chop, even out all this breakage, and go natural. Once I wash and deep condition your hair and scalp, the natural curl pattern of your hair will camouflage the bald areas. No one should be able to see your scalp."

"What, no!" Lucky was against it.

"Look, you're still a pretty girl, and a lot of women do it all the time, start over and grow it out thicker and healthier than it was before."

Still, Lucky wasn't having it. Never in her life had she had to cut her long, thick, and shiny hair. The money and time she put into her hair, for her to chop it off, it sounded ridiculous. The mentioning of cutting it all off made her seethe even more, and she wanted to throw Maxine off the fuckin' terrace and watch her splatter below.

"It's either that, Lucky, or back to the wig," Kelly said, a few minutes away from losing her patience.

Kelly could only do so much with the little Lucky was working with. And after contemplating the idea and seeing the damage in the mirror, Lucky sighed heavily and said, "Go ahead...just do it. Cut it all off."

"You sure?"

"You suggested it, right?"

Kelly smiled and nodded. "I'm gonna hook you up, Lucky...believe in me."

"I do, that's why I called you."

Lucky readied for her significant change. Kelly removed her tools and products she needed from her bag, and she started cutting away the rest of Lucky's long hair until she got to the new growth. The more she cut, the more Lucky cringed. Moving in together with Bugsy and Maxine didn't feel like such a great idea anymore. She wasn't in any rush to see the end results. Kelly continued to comfort one of her favorite clients with words of encouragement and promised Lucky she would like the finished results. It took two hours for Kelly to cut, style, and deep condition her hair. Lucky's new hairdo—the natural look, a mini curly afro was now complete.

"Well, what do you think? Do you like it?" asked Kelly.

Lucky inspected every area of her hair, and the natural curls camouflaged the bald spots, which made her exhale.

"I like it," Lucky said. "I don't like that I can no longer hide my damaged eye with my hair, but a pair of Chanel shades will suffice until my hair grows back."

"I told you, girl, let me work, and do my thing. I know how to make miracles happen."

Lucky couldn't argue with her. She made a miracle happen, and for that, Lucky paid her handsomely. It was more than Kelly expected, and she was grateful. It was late evening when Kelly left, and Lucky made an appointment for her to come back in a week. The new look on Lucky wouldn't make up for what Maxine had done to her. She couldn't wait for her brother to come home and see just how dangerous his baby mama was.

Lucky had fallen asleep, exhausted from a full day of drama, combat, and transitioning into her new look. She stirred awake when Bugsy tapped on her shoulder just after seven the next morning.

"I heard what happened between you and Maxine," he said. His face didn't register how he felt about her battered face and small afro. "She's sorry about how things went down, and I want y'all to get past this. We got kids to raise, and I don't want any tension between y'all."

Lucky pointed to her face. "Sorry? Are you kidding me? I hope you beat that bitch's ass for this!"

Bugsy sighed. "Lucky, I love you. I do. But I would never put my hands on any woman, and I won't ever put my hands on the mother of my son. I'm not going to repeat myself again. I love Maxine, and no harm will ever come to her by you, Scott, Layla, or Meyer. If anyone even looks like they want to think of injuring her in any way, they will have to deal with me. So, lick your wounds and move on. It was a fight, you lost…get over it."

Bugsy walked out of Lucky's room, leaving her mouth gaping open.

Lucky met with her brothers to discuss moving stash houses and drop points. It was critical for them to always keep things mobile and to stay a few steps ahead of rivals, stick-up crews, and police. Lucky wasn't blind to the changes happening around her in their organization. Several of her lieutenants, including Yusef, were now answering to Meyer and Bugsy—not her. These were men under her wing and leadership, and slyly her brothers had infiltrated what she had built.

How ruthless did she need to be to gain the respect of her people? She had opened Pandora's Box and let her brothers colonize her organization. It was looking like the shoe was on the other foot, and karma was coming back to bite her because of what she did to Layla. Had she still been in business with her mother, her role wouldn't be this diminished.

Lucky had a couple tricks up her sleeve, and she was ready to use them.

Zoe purposely showered with the bathroom door ajar, and her silhouette behind the glass shower door was almost unbearable. Meyer's eyes drank in her curves as he stood in the entryway, gawking at the exquisite sight. He pushed the door open more, and unflinchingly stood there watching Zoe bathe. The way she moved while soaping her sexy body, lathered-up with soap from head to toe before rinsing off, had his dick standing at attention. The way the steaming water cascaded down on her lovely petite frame, it was like watching the sunrise for him. It was sensual. Meyer was turned on. He wanted her so badly that it was hurting all over.

The shower door slid back, and Zoe stepped out naked, dripping wet from head to her perfect toes. She noticed Meyer's lustful eyes and smiled his way.

"You were watching me the entire time?" she said, reaching for a bath towel.

"I couldn't help myself," he said.

"Did you like it?"

"What you think? I wanted to join you."

"You could have." Zoe began drying off, allowing her towel to touch the places that Meyer wanted to explore.

"And continue to torture myself," he said. "You know I wanna fuck."

"You ever heard the saying; the best thing comes to those who wait?"

"I've been waiting for too long now."

She chuckled, and then replied with, "Five more days, baby…and you get to enjoy all of this glory," she said. "And I will be worth the wait."

He grinned, "You better be."

To tease him more, she propped her leg onto the toilet and continued to dry off.

"You staying the night?" he asked her.

"I can't. I have somewhere to be tomorrow morning."

"Where at?"

"I have to meet with my manager."

"You need a ride home?"

"I'll take an Uber."

"It's gettin' late, though," he said. "Let me drive you."

"I'm a grown and independent woman. I think I can get home on my own. But it's cute that you care about me."

"I do."

She grinned. With the towel wrapped around her, she went up to Meyer and kissed him on his lips. It was a tender kiss, and he wanted more of it—and more of her.

"After I'm done, we can go have lunch. You cool with that?" Zoe said.

"Yeah, my schedule is free tomorrow."

"I'll be looking forward to it," she said. "Now, you saw enough of heaven, so let me finish getting dressed in peace. I don't need the devil trying to corrupt me."

"You got jokes," he laughed.

She pushed Meyer out of the bathroom and into the hallway and closed the door on him. He stood there, somewhat amused. He had to shake his head and laugh.

Zoe kissed Meyer goodnight, and she trekked out of his building and climbed into an idling Uber. She sat back and lit a cigarette then asked the driver, "You mind if I smoke?"

"No, go ahead," he said.

Zoe rolled the window down and exhaled while the driver drove her from Manhattan to her new place in Brooklyn. It was a long drive, but it gave her time to think and contemplate her next move. Meyer was spoiling her rotten, and she loved every minute of it. But in five days, she had promised they'd make love, and she wasn't ready—not yet, or maybe not at all. It was amusing teasing him, but men like him were dangerous and had a short shelf life. Any day he could be killed or locked up, and then where would she be? Men like Meyer, you didn't let wife you unless you didn't have other options. Zoe was looking for a surgeon or the CFO of a startup tech company—anything but a thug.

The driver crossed over the Brooklyn Bridge and soon arrived in downtown Brooklyn and came to a stop in front of her charming tenement in Brooklyn Heights. She paid the driver his fare and climbed out of the cab, feeling sexy in her little black dress that hugged her curves. It had been a long day, and Zoe wanted to go inside her apartment and change outfits. For her, the night was still young, and she wanted to call up her girlfriends and see what they were doing—maybe get a drink and flirt with some established men. The street was quiet, and it was late, and her neighbors were most likely asleep. Zoe loved the area because it was prestigious and affluent, and it was right up her alley.

She walked toward the concrete steps to her building, and it didn't dawn on Zoe she was in trouble until it was too late. She was a few feet away from the entrance when two shadowy figures immediately swooped down on her and attacked. They came out of nowhere. The first punch dazed Zoe. The second punch made her stagger like a drunkard and brought blood from a soon-to-be fat lip. And the pretty in Zoe quickly became disfigured as fists punched her repeatedly in the face and body, and she felt herself being pulled to the ground by her long hair only to be stomped and kicked. Immediately she knew it was two girls attacking her. They continued to beat her savagely like she was the slave, and they were the overseer, and then one of them yelled, "Stay the fuck away from my man, slut!"

Her face hit the sidewalk hard, her right cheekbone shattered; it felt like she had glass in her mouth. Her ribs were broken, and she could taste blood. She cried out and shrieked loudly, pleading for someone to help her, but no one came. The pummeling felt like the nightmare would not end.

"If I ever catch you wit' Meyer again, I'll fuckin' end you, bitch!" the attacker yelled. "Stay the fuck away from him, or next time we gonna kill you."

Her petite frame was glued to the sidewalk in agonizing pain. She felt paralyzed. The contents from her purse were scattered everywhere, and one girl stole her cash and I.D. And just like that, they were gone—they disappeared from the scene like two apparitions, to hell they returned, leaving behind a beaten Zoe. Her pageant career was over.

"Someone help me...call 9-1-1!" she desperately cried out. "Aaaaaaaahh!"

The next day, Meyer called Zoe to plan for their afternoon date, but she didn't pick up. At first, he left a couple casual voice messages. When she didn't return his calls, Meyer panicked. After riding to her home a few times, leaving Post-it notes, and not getting any response, he was confused. What game was she playing, fuckin' with his heart like this? Weeks after the 90-day rule had come and gone she called and said to him, "It's just not working out between us, I'm sorry. I can't deal with you anymore."

At first, Meyer exploded, and he cursed her out. He was furious that she cut him off when he was so close to exploring her intimately. And after all the quality time Meyer had invested in their relationship. What had he done wrong?

"Talk to me, Zoe, what the fuck is going on? Why you doin' this to me?" he pleaded with her for an explanation. "Baby, I'll do anything for you. I want you, and only you. There is no one else more important to me."

She remained adamant with her decision and had replied, "I don't see a future with you, Meyer. I need someone in my life that's more stable and intellectual. You're a gangster, and I thought I could do this with you, but I can't."

"Are you fuckin' serious! I waited for you, and you pull this shit! What the fuck is wrong wit' you?" he'd shouted. But in truth, her last remark kicked him in the gut. He wanted to wife her. He wanted Zoe to have his babies. Screaming and yelling and threatening her would not get her back, so he calmed down and changed his tone. "Zoe, look…I miss you, and I'll do anything for you. Just give me a second chance," he pleaded. "What do you want from me? Just ask me, and it's yours…whatever you want or need from me."

"Goodbye, Meyer…."

"No, don't say that…don't you dare say that to me. I'll take you anywhere. Wherever you want to go…Seychelles, Maldives, Greece, anywhere," he proclaimed wholeheartedly, remembering the places she wanted to travel to.

"Goodbye, Meyer," she reiterated. Two unknown girls had beaten the shit out of her, messed her up bad, and they called out Meyer's name. She knew that something like this could happen when you mess with thugs. It was just as much her fault as it was his.

She hung up, and Meyer immediately threw a temper tantrum and destroyed things in his home. He seethed. All the time and money he put into Zoe to only come up empty-handed.

"Fuck that bitch!" he heatedly yelled out.

He was crushed inside. He couldn't stop thinking about Zoe, and he wanted a reason she cut him off. He took out his gun and was ready to shoot holes in his walls to release his anger. He tried to forget about her the only way he knew how. Meyer dialed Lollipops' number and said, "What you doin' right now? I want you to come over."

She grinned, "I was expecting your call."

Chapter 26

I fuckin' love it!" Layla said about their new place in Chelsea.

Layla walked around the deluxe apartment fifty-stories high in the sky in her Manolo Blahnik heels. The luxurious condominium was ideal with all the latest amenities and the security they needed. Layla turned around and smiled at her husband. He looked handsome in his dark grey suit and silver tie, and his dark eyes focused on her. His Cartier watch gleamed around his wrist, and he recently put his wedding band back on, a sign of their renewed commitment.

"You always had good taste in real estate," she said to him.

"I knew you would love it."

"I do," she said.

Scott wanted to do everything in his power to make Layla happy again. He walked closer to her and grabbed her from behind. He placed his arms around her, and together they both stared out the window, admiring the picturesque view. Scott then said, "This city is gonna be ours again."

Layla grinned. He took the words right out of her mouth. He continued to hug her tightly, the closeness with him made her confident they would get it right this time. His masculine arms squeezed her with firmness.

"Talk to me," he said when he noticed that his wife was in deep thought. Her jovial mood only moments ago had dissipated. He could tell something was bugging her.

Layla asked, "We okay?"

"Absolutely," he replied with an unusual hint of excitement in his voice. Scott didn't get as far as he did in the drug game by repeatedly making the same mistakes. When Layla took him to task about continually underestimating their children, he should have listened. To Scott, Bugsy had forfeited his life. His near-death experience with the sicarios had morally bankrupted the generous line of credit he had extended to his son. Scott had to come to terms that Bugsy wasn't who he thought he was. That his favorite, the most beloved son, had put ambition over him. His wife was correct—somewhere they had gone wrong as parents, maybe didn't give their children enough hugs. Whatever caused their bond to be splintered was irrelevant. The fact remained there wasn't any mending their father/son relationship. Too many fuck you's were exchanged to be ignored.

That shit Bugsy and Lucky pulled with the sicarios had blindsided them. If this was a game of chess, Scott and Layla had been backed in a corner and checked. Scott replayed that day he was kidnapped over in his head until it looped in his mind, easily recallable so he could tap into those emotions whenever necessary. Scott had never felt more alive than when he watched the sicarios walk away and leave him to crawl his way out of a ditch. He understood just how close he came to losing his life.

Layla had taken her kidnapping and torture worse than he did. They not only fucked her up, but she also grappled over thinking they had murdered her husband just hours earlier. When Layla was released and then discovered that Scott was alive, she had broken down into an uncontrollable hysteria he had never seen. The vulnerability she displayed had moved him, and he could only hold his wife tightly throughout the night, kissing away her tears.

Scott was still the man with the master plan. But with the feds lurking, it would take longer than Layla liked to exact reprisal. Scott could handle the slow burn of retribution. Revenge could be just as sweet as one of his Cuban cigars—you took your time and enjoyed it.

It took calculation, but every step he made was an important movement in rebuilding something critical. He hated that he had to use his legal money to fund his drug organization, but he knew he would be vindicated. He had to liquidate a few stocks to get things moving, get his men back to work after he snatched them back from his son's control. He'd purchased fifty kilos from his supplier, the Garcia cartel. Fifty kilos was lightweight to him. He was a man used to moving two hundred kilos or more a week. Scott would rebuild his organization brick by brick.

As if on cue, Mason arrived at their new location. He walked into the deluxe high-rise and was immediately impressed by everything.

"This shit is nice," he said.

Scott nodded. Mason was there for one reason only, to discuss business. The trio stepped out onto the terrace to talk; one could never be too careful discussing murder, especially since Scott wasn't able to have his new home raked yet. Outside they were alone with the sun high in the sky. Scott closed the sliding glass door behind him and said to Mason, "I want a fuckin' bloodbath."

Mason nodded. "Just give me addresses, and I'll get it done."

Scott had an informant in Bugsy's organization. He provided Scott with the information he needed to send the message no one would be expecting.

"Be careful, Mason," Layla warned. "We can't lose you. Not when we're this close."

Mason was almost like the third wheel, having been around the couple for decades. He was there through arguments, affairs, childbirth, hostile takeovers, the come up, the knockdowns—the whole gamut. Mason was practically a West. He would never admit it, but he felt some kind of way when Scott made Whistler his first-in-command. A position he thought he deserved. But now, through hard work and loyalty, he was finally promoted. Mason would see this organization restored to its glory days, or he would die trying.

Before Mason exited, Scott made his wishes crystal clear. "Everything needs to be done on Valentine's Day."

Mason nodded. "Understood."

"I want no one left alive."

Mason replied, "I wasn't planning to anyway. I'm on it."

Bugsy was expecting to be woken up by a morning blowjob and then breakfast in bed. He thought his grown woman would feed him strawberries, and they'd drink champagne before Dillinger woke up for his morning's milk. Bugsy and Maxine hadn't had sex since the birth of their son, and he knew that medically they could, but she didn't want to. Her stitches were healed, she had shed her pregnancy weight, and each moment she was around him, he was turned on. Bugsy was horny, but any and every time he would reach for her, she would push him away. He didn't want to cheat, but he was a man. How long did she expect him to be deprived? Today was Valentine's Day and still no loving?

Bugsy had bought Maxine a fully loaded, custom Tesla Roadster in midnight blue. He wanted to surprise her today with the news. It was on backorder, but once it arrived, she would be one of the very few people with the latest model. Bugsy sighed. Maybe she was planning something special this evening. A night of seduction was hopefully in the cards for him. Bugsy showered quickly and dressed. He walked toward the kitchen and slowed down once he heard an unfamiliar male's voice. He gripped his .45 in his shoulder holster and proceeded with caution until he heard Maxine laugh. Bugsy bent the corner and saw an elderly white man in a wrinkled suit, briefcase, and lots of paperwork.

"What's going on?" he asked and was about to have an attitude until he saw the look on Maxine's face. She was pissed again.

"This is Robert Wheeler. I told you about this appointment. He's here for the insurance policies." Maxine's voice and eyes were stern.

Bugsy searched his memory for this discussion and came up blank. He didn't want to say the wrong thing and possibly ruin his chance at a night of lovemaking, so he went along with it. "Oh, yeah, right. Cool. How long will it take?"

"Not long at all," said Wheeler.

Chapter 27

St. Valentine's Day Massacre

I said get the fuck down!" the masked gunman yelled at his victims, aggressively thrusting the sawed-off shotgun into one of the hostage's face. "Y'all think this shit is a fuckin' joke?!"

"Y'all know whose warehouse this is?" one hostage asked with his eyes narrowed in anger at the gunman. "Whose drugs y'all taking?"

"Yeah, muthafucka…we know!" the masked gunman replied with a menacing chuckle, and then he aimed center-mass and fired the shotgun at point-blank range—*Boom!* His victim flew off his feet, flying backward in the air, collapsing dead on the ground with his stomach turned inside out. His blood pooled thickly on the ground like an oil spill.

The other six men being held hostage, including the two Hispanics driving the box truck, were in shock. Somehow four gunmen suddenly burst into the warehouse, and commotion had spread like wildfire. The gunmen came in armed and dangerous after they killed the six henchmen who patrolled the rooftop and perimeter and seized control over everything.

"We came to party, muthafuckas!" another gunman shouted.

"Y'all fuckin' ready to party…huh muthafuckas?"

His mocking question was met with silence. No one dared to reply.

"Y'all don't wanna talk?" He then laughed. Their fear was a game to him, and it was a turn on—to see a coward on his knees, not knowing the next few minutes of his fate.

"Puta, we cartel, and I guarantee you; you kill us, and it will be a mistake," one of the Hispanic men finally spoke out.

"You cartel, nigga?" the man asked aggressively.

"Juarez cartel…," he replied nobly, looking up at the masked man daringly, locking eyes with him.

"Cartel, huh…y'all muthafuckas think y'all invincible, huh? You invincible nigga?"

The Hispanic man didn't reply, but heavily frowned at the gunman, and the intense look in his eyes said it all. If they didn't have weapons, and the shoe would've been on the other foot, he wouldn't show them any mercy.

"Well, let me tell you what I think of you, cartel assholes…matter fact, I'll let my gun do the talking for me," said the gunman, and in the blink of an eye, he plunged the sawed-off shotgun at the man's head and squeezed—*Boom!* He blew half the man's face apart, and the body dropped face down with his blood splattering everywhere.

"Oh shit!" another captive shouted in panic.

"Who else cartel?" he questioned.

The four gunmen's identities were concealed with knitted masks. They wore all black down to their socks. Each man had on a Kevlar vest and combat boots like they were ready for war. Two gunmen were armed with automatic machine guns—high-grade firepower, able to cut a man in half. The third gunmen gripped the sawed-off shotgun, and the fourth came with two Desert Eagles .50 Cal handguns with the triangle barrel. They came for the kilos and the cash but wasn't leaving without body snatching.

"Yo, go get the yayo," said one gunman to the other.

The man nodded. He went into action and dumped the kilos into black duffel bags. It was all spread out on the pallets for easy taking. The room grew tense with extreme nervousness, and the five remaining men were still down on their knees with their fingers interlocked behind their heads. They were edgy, they knew they would die today. Seeing their own stretched out dead on the cold warehouse floor, was devastating. One man panicked and hyperventilated. It seemed like he had a sudden asthma attack.

"What the fuck is wrong wit' you, nigga?" one gunman asked him.

"Please...I can't breathe. Please...Please," the victim begged breathlessly and looked like he was going to keel over and faint.

"You sick or sumthin', nigga?"

"I can't breathe...help me! I don't wanna die!"

The masked man stared at the hostage on his knees. He stood in front of him, towering over the kneeled man and watched him hyperventilate with amusement on his face like it was Showtime at the Apollo. He then said, "You really are fucked up over this shit, ain't you?"

"I-I...can't breathe...help...me. I don't wanna...die," he cried out.

There was no sympathy for him. Instead, the masked man put him out of his misery. He put the *.50 Cal* to his forehead and didn't hesitate to pull the trigger. "Noooo," the man cried out before the bullet slammed into his brain. The room smelled like death, and the remaining few could only accept their fate. They were overcome with sadness and anxiety. They knew that they weren't leaving the place alive. With sixty kilos of cocaine crammed into the duffel bags, the batch of pure white secured for the opposing team, it was time to go. The men with the machine guns opened fire on the remaining hostages, gunning them down in a hail of bullets—and then there was none. For the rival crew, it was one spot down and several others to go.

Rah from Brooklyn had no idea he was being followed as he navigated his dark green Benz from off the BQE expressway and traveled deeper into Brooklyn toward his Bushwick territory. With ten kilos in the trunk of his car, he drove carefully. He didn't want to attract any attention to himself. His seatbelt was fastened, and he did the speed limit. It would be another payday for him. A year in the game and he was becoming a notorious kingpin in his area. Fortunately for him, he left the Bronx warehouse just in time with his merchandise before it became a slaughterhouse. But unfortunately for him, he didn't leave the area undetected. A crew of killers followed him from one borough to the next, and they were eager to take what was his.

He traveled alone, going east on Broadway, then made a few turns onto the side streets and finally came to a stop in front of a four-story walk-up on Quincy Street. The block was relatively quiet this evening. Rah parked his sleek Benz out front and removed his cellphone to make a call. His gun was placed underneath the seat, and his tinted windows were rolled up. He was always cautious, but tonight, he wouldn't see them coming.

Out of the blue, a black Tahoe with tinted windows came to a sudden stop on the block and parallel parked next to Rah's parked Benz. The passenger windows were rolled down, and two Uzi submachine guns concentrated on the driver's side and opened fire—spraying the car with a hail of bullets, shattering windows and fucking shit up—round after round slammed viciously into Rah, making his body violently dance in the front seat of his car until it finally slumped over the steering wheel. He didn't have a chance. A man hurried out of the Tahoe and went directly to the trunk of the Benz. The ten kilos of cocaine were quickly removed before he jumped back into the vehicle, and it sped off, leaving behind a ghastly scene. Neighbors stood around in awe at what just happened, the scene felt so unreal to them. The gunfire was loud, and it was frightening. It sounded like a succession of cherry bombs going off. And when the smoke had cleared, everyone saw that Rah had gotten taken out gangland-style, his body a spectacle on the block.

The next stop for the killer squad of body snatchers was a Yonkers stash house rumored to have at least forty kilos and bundles of cash.

Chapter 28

A very was the one to deliver the bad news. His usual gruff voice and slow cadence were more rushed as he explained the horrific events that had taken place.

"We got hit," he continued. "The Bronx warehouse looks like a slaughterhouse. Thirteen dead, including two of Angel's men."

"Fuck!" Bugsy exclaimed as he paced around his bedroom, worried. "Where's Chopper?"

"I don't know, Bee." Avery exhaled his frustrations. "I been calling dude all morning."

"A'ight, I'll hit him up so we can figure this shit out."

"You think Scott had something to do with this?" Avery questioned. "No disrespect to your Pops, but I had to ask."

His parents were at the top of his list of enemies, but in this game, you couldn't put all your eggs in one basket. The wolves were always lurking, so the list of assailants was comprehensive, including Angel and the Juarez cartel.

"He's supposedly out the game...I forced him into early retirement, but you know anything's possible. But I promise you this, I will find out who's behind this hit, and they will be dealt with."

"There's more," Avery said. "The Yonkers stash house got hit...four dead. And Rah from Brooklyn was gunned down in a drive-by last night. He had just picked up ten kilos from us. His peoples aren't happy and are seeking retribution. We need to assure them that we ain't have nothing to do with his murder."

Bugsy whistled his disbelief. "We need to meet...at the spot." The *spot* was code for an arcade room in Harlem, where they would sometimes discuss business on short notice. He needed to mull over this tragedy. He couldn't sit still, nor could he relax. Things were going well until it went ugly. And just when he thought the day could get no worse, Bugsy saw the footage of his stash house on his local news channel. He quickly turned up the volume.

The Mayor of New York City held a news conference along with the Chief of Police to discuss last night's tragedy. When describing the carnage, the mayor said, *"Last night, on a night that's reserved for love, over a dozen men were brutally killed in a gangland-style attack in a Bronx warehouse. This industrial area is an epicenter for commercial businesses and could have a direct effect on those businesses' economy. The victims were gunned down with high powered assault rifles, each sustaining several gunshot wounds that was clearly overkilling. This incident was undoubtedly meant to be reminiscent of the infamous St. Valentine's Day Massacre. And my only message to the perpetrators is, you will get caught!"*

This was the kind of heat his organization didn't need. With the mayor and the local police, Bugsy could only hope that the federal government didn't join the investigation.

The three locations hit were key spots that only his team were privy too. Bugsy deduced that they had a snitch in their camp. He got on his cellphone to call his twin. Meyer answered his brother's call with, "Yeah, I already heard."

"Meet me at the spot," Bugsy said.

"I'll be there in an hour."

Bugsy ended the call and then went into the nursery to see his sleeping son in the crib and his niece. Dillinger was lying face up with his arms and legs spread wide. The sight of him always melted Bugsy's heart. He then walked to Lucchese, also sleeping peacefully. She had her thumb shoved in her tiny mouth, a habit that the nanny couldn't break her out of. Her beautiful features and the massive amount of jet-black curly hair made her look like a doll. Bugsy smiled. Lulu would break a lot of hearts when she's older. The average man won't stand a chance.

Bugsy was a father now, and that brought more purpose to what he was doing. He wanted to build a future for his son and to pass down to him an empire solely legitimate like the Kennedy's and Rockefellers' had done for their descendants. He wanted to leave his child a legacy. There wasn't any way he would allow Dillinger to get into the drug game as his parents had allowed that life for him and his siblings.

He spent enough quality time with the children, but it was back to business. He reached for his pistol, placing the 9mm into a leather shoulder holster and covered it with his suit jacket, and left the room. He came across Maxine on his way out the door and the two locked eyes. She quickly read him, knowing something was wrong. Bugsy was silent, not willing to share the tragedy with his woman. He knew she had seen her fair share of adversity over the years, and he wanted her only focus to be on raising their son.

"Just come back to me," she said.

"I will." He kissed her passionately and exited from the penthouse. Lucky was an afterthought. She didn't come home last night, and Bugsy didn't feel that her input would be germane. Instead, he called Chopper, who picked up on the second ring.

"What's up, Bee?" Chopper yarned and stretched, waiting for his boss to give him his orders for the day.

Bugsy was annoyed at his cavalier demeanor. "Yo, where you been?"

Chopper looked at the sexy beauty sleeping in his T-shirt and grinned. He had been seeing Natasha for a few weeks, and she had him whipped. He said, "I'm wit' this shorty. Why? What's up? Is there somewhere I needed to be?"

"So you ain't heard that Rah and two of our locales got hit?"

Chopper was stunned. "Nah, I ain't hear shit."

"I'm on my way to the spot. Be there."

Bugsy climbed into his SUV and traveled to Harlem. Meyer, Chopper, and Avery were all there when he arrived. The four men went into a private room in the back, where they could talk. Meyer looked at his brother, and they both were thinking the same.

"Bee, you already know who hit us like this...who had the means and the manpower to come hard at two locations and kill one of ours on his own turf in Brooklyn—Scott, and Layla...they behind this shit," Meyer said.

"It came to my mind," said Bugsy.

"Fuck that talk about their retirement, I told you it was only a ruse to catch us off guard for the sicarios...and all the other shit y'all pulled."

"But how, though? How the fuck they find our trap and stash houses so easily when we constantly moving our shit around?"

Meyer was clueless.

Bugsy answered his own question. "We got a snitch in our camp."

Meyer agreed.

"We need to smoke out whoever it is asap," Chopper chimed in, amped up off the possibility that someone had betrayed them.

The brothers grew quiet. And then Meyer said, "Bruh, we need to talk in private...y'all niggas get the fuck out."

"Y'all good?" Avery asked.

"Yeah, we fuckin' good, muthafucka. I wanna talk to my brother wit' out y'all niggas around," Meyer exclaimed. "A'ight?"

"Yeah, I got you," Avery said.

Avery and Chopper left the room, leaving the twins to discuss the issues alone. The moment the door shut, Meyer wasn't shy about suggesting who he believed the snitch was.

"I'm ready to blow Avery's head off, nigga, I think it's him," he said. "Think about it, he's from our father's clan, and he stayed on wit' us, why?"

"He would have been my first thought too. But think about it, the last stash house in Yonkers, the only people who knew about that location was you, me, Lucky, Chopper and everyone that was killed. Avery didn't know anything about that place, so he ain't the snitch," said Bugsy.

"Are we sure about that?"

"Positive."

"So what about Chopper?" Meyer mentioned with a raised eyebrow.

"He's not our snitch. I can bet my life on that."

"Nah, you can't put that type of trust in no man, Bee."

"I do! I said it ain't Chopper." Bugsy was emphatic with his belief.

"Sometimes, I don't even trust my fuckin' self. But a'ight. We wait, and we watch that nigga."

Bugsy nodded, agreeing with Meyer. With that topic spoken about, Bugsy felt it was time to bring up other issues happening. He squarely looked at Meyer and said, "This thing with Lucky, it's got to stop."

"Fuck her man, she be trippin'. She threatens to cut us off from her connect and you siding wit' that bitch?"

"She's still family Meyer and this tension and conflict y'all got going on with each other is too petty. We got other shit to worry about. And for real, Lucky would never hurt our business.

She always places business above anything. Ask Layla if you disagree."

"You give her too much credit, nigga… fo' real. Lucky thinks she's running shit like she's this mastermind who can outthink us or at least outthink me."

"Just make peace with her, please."

"Whatever nigga. I ain't thinkin' about her right now," Meyer said.

He was done talking. He turned and left the room. Bugsy simply stood there knowing it would get worse before it got better.

Chapter 29

Ⓣhe pure white horse went galloping up Meyer's nose, and he started to quickly feel the effects of the cocaine he snorted. He sniffled and rubbed his nose from the high-quality shit. It was a white stallion—beautiful and sleek. Its legs powerful and ran for miles without exhaustion. It couldn't be contained, as it galloped through the open field like a race car and took Meyer across the grassy plains at top speed.

"I need to do one more line to be sure," he said to the men he was with.

"Our pleasure," Benicio responded.

Meyer leaned closer to the table and put the small straw up his nose and did another long line of blow. "Oh, shit…Now that's some good coke," he said.

"I'm glad you like it," Benicio said, smiling.

"Yeah, I like it…so let's talk business," Meyer said.

"Talk."

"I can take a boatload off your hands, like one hundred kilos at twenty thousand a ki."

"Twenty thousand?" Benicio snorted. He was insulted that the thug would even waste his time. "Our business is concluded." Benicio stood up to leave, and Meyer stood up too.

"Hold up," Meyer said with conviction. "My brother and I are looking for a new connect, and you and your organization have that grade A quality product that we're looking for. We just need you to come down on your numbers so we all can make some bread."

"I understand, but twenty thousand a ki are numbers from the nineties...you know this. Why are you wasting my time? I can do twenty-eight a ki," Benicio negotiated.

"Nah...too steep, twenty-five thousand," Meyer countered.

"Twenty-six five...and that's my final number."

It was lower than what they paid now with the Juarez cartel. Meyer was there to establish a new Bolivian connect, and he wasn't leaving the room without a deal. The men met in a motel room on the outskirts of Hartford, Connecticut. Benicio was a part of a notorious Bolivian organization ran by Kiqué Helguero. The Helguero cartel had begun to slowly gain traction on the east coast because they not only distributed high-quality cocaine, but they also imported Bolivian black tar heroin now highly sought after. Bolivia was becoming one of the world's top cocaine producers, competing with Colombia as the world's number one cocaine manufacturer. The country produced tons of cocaine and heroin, and Meyer wanted to sell every ounce of it. With Lucky drying up their cocaine supplier, Meyer worked overtime to find a replacement. Word of mouth got the two men together.

Meyer desperately wanted to close this deal on his own. He had been walking around with a chip on his shoulders for years, insecurity he allowed to be placed upon him when his family members treated him as subpar, second best, inferior to his brother's book smarts. He wanted to prove that he could do more than just buss his gun.

Two things had prompted Meyer to go hard. When Lucky said there was a drought throughout the tristate and their shipment from Angel had been placed on hold, he knew that she had moved forward with her threat. And second, Angel's men getting murdered on their watch would lead to even more animosity between the clans. Meyer never liked Angel from day one, so this move was not only business, but it was personal.

They sat across from each other in the motel room negotiating. Standing behind Benicio was his righthand man, Carlos, and with Meyer was Avery.

Benicio was a shrewd businessman in his early thirties and highly respected in his cartel. He was an average size man and had naturally tanned skin and sleek, jet-black hair and a salt and pepper mustache and goatee. Dressed impeccably in a tailored suit, his shirt was unbuttoned, exposing the thick hairs on his chest. He was a direct contrast to Meyer's hoodie, jeans, and Timbs. Both men wore expensive watches, but Benicio also wore a custom diamond rosary of St. Jude, the patron saint of lost souls. His boss, Kiqué Helguero, had gifted all his top lieutenants this chain he had blessed by Father José, a high priest in their country as a sign of respect.

"Twenty-six-five a kilo, Benicio...we can't go higher than that, and I'll take one hundred ki's." Meyer said with finality. "Now, let's talk heroin."

The two men continued to negotiate until both deals were struck.

"So when can I expect the first shipment from you?" Meyer asked.

"In about a week."

Meyer and Avery left the motel room and got into his dark-colored SUV. He lit a cigarette and smiled, Meyer had done it. He successfully got them a new connect at competitive prices, and his siblings didn't have shit to do with it. With the supplier secured, he called Lucky.

"Still no coke?" Meyer asked her.

"I told you, there's a drought."

"A drought, huh?"

Lucky was driving uptown to oversee her side hustle and had little time or interest in this conversation. She shot back with, "Yes, a drought. It means that the streets ain't getting fed."

Meyer pursued his line of questioning. "No coke or heroin? You sure? I mean, you gotta do something. You know how much paper we stand to lose?"

"Yeah, well...it is what it is," Lucky said, dismissively.

"A'ight. A drought it is then," Meyer replied and hung up.

The news of the bloodshed, along with two cartel members being killed in her Bronx warehouse, made Lucky uneasy. She had gotten a phone call from Angel, informing her he wasn't too pleased with the mess someone made of his men on her property. He placed her on speaker as he and his top enforcers sat at a roundtable listening to what little explanation she had.

"Why did I have to hear about this incident from one of my New York affiliates'? It is your job to inform me about what goes on in your organization when it pertains to my men or my product. Is it not? Do I have to school you on how to run a drug empire?"

Lucky was annoyed. Bugsy had told her about the incident twenty-four hours after it occurred, and she hadn't gotten around to calling him because she had spent most of the time arguing with her brothers. She said, "You do not, Angel. I was going to call you once I put a few things into play."

"It's been a week. How much time do you need?"

"You're right, and I apologize. This won't happen again."

"How will you handle this?" he asked.

Lucky vowed to the cartel, she would find the culprits responsible behind the savagery and brutally make them pay. "I'm gonna put a hundred guns on the street lookin' for these muthafuckas, I promise," she said.

"And when shall I expect payment?"

She was perplexed. "Payment? We're paid in full for our last shipment. The West organization has a zero balance."

"You're paid up for the yayo...sí, but what about my men?"

His words had her baffled. Why was she confused? "I don't understand. What about your men?"

"My men had families...bills...responsibilities."

"Okay?"

"They brought in ten million each a year to the Juarez cartel."

She repeated, "Okay?"

"So this is what you owe us. And to prove to you that I am a reasonable man, I will take a one-time payment of twenty million. The Juarez cartel has agreed that we won't seek this payment each year because we like our business arrangement with your family."

"Are you crazy!" she hollered.

"I am crazy," Angel said. "I'm fucking loco, señorita. Now you and your hermanos better come up with our money. I want it personally delivered by you. I will send a private plane, and when you step off that flight with our cash, you better have that ugly baby with you! And Lucky..."

"Yes, Angel."

"I won't threaten you. Threats don't seem to sink in your thick skull, but maybe the bullet from a .45 will."

The call suddenly ended. Lucky knew the bloody incident put her in a bad place with the cartel. She already had one serious issue with Angel, now another issue had surfaced, and it came at the wrong time. There wasn't any way she would get Bugsy and Meyer to cosign on paying out that money for two drug runners, but if she didn't, she could foresee a few bodies dropping. And the inevitability that one body would be hers was highly likely.

Although she hated to do it, she still had Layla's money. And though peeling off twenty million would be like removing one of her kidneys with a dull knife, she felt confident that if she paid Angel, she could get back in his good graces.

Lucky sat alone in her private office and stared at the walls, zoning in and out. She was furious that Meyer had established a new cocaine connection. He'd gotten into bed with the Bolivians with high-grade cocaine and heroin, and it made her crumble. Meyer announced his latest business dealings with the Bolivians at their most recent meeting to undermine her and that he did. Lucky will never forget his smug expression as he reveled in his victory. She wanted to smack that smirk off his face so badly, but she just sat there stoically. She had always competed with her brothers, but Meyer was the only one who indulged in the competition.

Lucky thought when she hired two girls to beat down his girlfriend Zoe and force her to dump Meyer, it would have caused him to stay home and self-medicate with his weird drinks and recreational drugs. She knew he was truly in love with the girl—*Meyer in love, imagine that*, she thought—only Meyer didn't nurse his broken heart like she had expected. It looked like he'd gotten over Zoe by throwing himself into his work. Now Lucky had to find another way to clip her brother's wings.

As she sat in her office, plotting, her cellphone rang. It was Avery calling, and he sounded panicky. He frantically yelled, "Lucky, you need to come home now! Something happened!"

"What the fuck happened?" she desperately asked him. "What's going on?"

"Something happened at the penthouse…I was ambushed! Fuckin' ambushed!" Avery shouted hysterically, and then his voice got muffled, and she couldn't hear full sentences. Lucky heard, "Oh shit! Dead…all dead…murdered…."

Chapter 30

He was up at the crack of dawn; it was a routine for him. He believed the adage you sleep when you're dead, and he breathed only to make money. Arnold showered and shaved in his marble bathroom and then stepped into his large, neatly organized walk-in closet. His closet held three hundred tailored suits, all color-coordinated, hundreds of expensive hard bottom shoes, and crisp white shirts that were monogrammed with his initials. His silk ties were conveniently folded in rows of dresser drawers along with his silk socks. A large vanity dressing mirror was hung on one wall, and a settee was in the room. Meade besieged himself with nice things, from cars to jewelry, to the most exquisite vacations—everything was top dollar. He was living like the Clintons off his notorious client list and moved around his two-million-dollar Westchester county estate comfortably.

Today was a demanding day for him; first, it was a pretrial motion for one of his clients. After it was lunch with a prosecutor on another case at Gramercy Tavern on E20th Street in Downtown Manhattan to discuss a plea deal. Finally, he would spend the rest of the afternoon and late into the evening doing a mock trial for one of his star witnesses on an insider trading case.

Meade smiled in the long mirror. He was aging gracefully, looking younger every day. He was fifty-six years old with slicked-back hair, and he loved his golden spray tan. He was still a playboy at his age, having a buffet of young women in his bed, all hoping to be the next Mrs. Meade.

Arnold went through his walk-in closet and removed the perfect suit to wear today—a blue and white pinstripe Armani, with white-gold cufflinks, a solid blue tie, and his Ferragamo shoes. Dressed handsomely, he walked out of the master bedroom and into his gourmet kitchen. Meade opened his pantry and got the whole bean signature blend coffee he ordered monthly from Harrods in London because he had heard it's what the Queen of England drank. Arnold went to his built-in espresso machine ready to prepare a hot cup of coffee to go, but immediately he caught the surprise of his life. He had unwanted company this morning. He was startled by Mason and several goons lingering in his home.

"What the fuck!" he shouted. "Who let you in here?"

"Good morning, Mr. Meade," Mason said chillingly. "You do take a very long time to get dressed...just like a bitch!"

Instantaneously, Arnold Meade knew who sent them. He looked around and found himself surrounded; there was no escaping the inevitable. Suddenly, he felt claustrophobic as if the walls were closing in on him. He exclaimed, "Scott West sent you here to bully me...I've been around worse."

"Maybe. You do have quite the reputation."

"Get the fuck out of my house!" he shouted. Arnold had broken out in a cold sweat; his armpits were damp, the button on his shirt collar was strangling him, and beads of perspiration had trickled down the sides of his face. Still, he presented himself as in control when he wasn't.

"Look, we can do this the easy way, or the hard way, your choice," said Mason.

"I don't scare easily!"

"Is that so," Mason said coolly.

"It is!" he uttered with disdain.

Arnold Meade frowned heatedly at Mason and the men in his kitchen, keeping up the façade that he was unintimidated by their presence. He clutched the coffee canister tightly, wishing it were a pistol. Arnold had several registered guns in his home, but none at his immediate reach. He was in an unfortunate predicament, but it wasn't the first-time thugs and gangsters broke into his house and threatened his life.

Mason put a tablet into Arnold's hand. He was confused.

"Take a look," said Mason.

Arnold looked at the screen, and it was a live video playing on the iPad. Immediately he recognized the place. It was his daughter's home—her apartment in Manhattan.

"What's this?" Meade uttered with fret.

"You already know," Mason replied.

Meade's eyes stared at the live video streaming. The man was moving from the living room, down the hallway, and near the bedroom. The door was ajar, and the cameraman opened it slightly to capture the sleeping beauty. She was young, blonde, and beautiful—and she was alone and sound asleep, so far unaware that she was in danger.

"You better not touch her!" he growled at Mason. His nervousness quickly transitioned into full-blown panicky anger.

"We don't plan to if you decide to play ball wit' us," replied Mason.

He handed Meade a typed letter he quickly breezed through. "Are you fucking crazy?" he shouted.

"Sign it," Mason said seriously.

"Why would I commit suicide?"

"Sign it!"

Arnold Meade was hesitant. The letter outlined years of suicidal thoughts and the pressure he's felt throughout the years to keep winning high profile cases for criminals.

"I can't sign this!" he shouted.

"Someone's going to die today, Meade," Mason returned. "You decide on whether we commit a double homicide."

Meade was flabbergasted. He wished that he could go back a year so he could tell Bugsy West to go fuck himself. Arnold should have never gone against the grain. Scott West was a formidable opponent, but Arnold had put his chips on himself to win. That's what he always did. He won; he survived. Arnold was a survivor. But now he was put between a rock and a hard place.

"We don't got all day, muthafucka!" Mason griped.

"Look, we can work something out, can't we." Arnold wasn't done lawyering. "Get Scott on the phone and let me make this right. He doesn't want to kill me…I'm an asset to his empire. I will work any of his organization's cases pro bono. Call him, please, tell him what I said."

"Sign muthafucka!" Mason roughly grabbed Meade by his collar and tossed him up against the wall, his head hit the taupe colored interior with a thud. "Your times up!"

The pen was placed into Meade's hand. They forced him to take a seat at the table. The letter was in front of him, men with guns were intimidating him. They came with a Machiavellian game plan and backed him into a corner. The tears trickled from his eyes; he was literally about to sign his life away. But he didn't have a choice, his daughter was everything to him—she meant the world to Meade, and she didn't deserve to pay for his choices. His decision flashed before his eyes. Where was Bugsy right now while a gun was thrust in his face.

With a gun to his head, he signed the letter, his signature scribbled in black ink at the bottom. It was the last worst day of his life. Mason placed a silver Walther PPK near him, and Arnold realized that it was one of the many pistols he owned. *Of course, it is,* he thought. *These men are professionals.* Mason said, "Now pick up the gun and blow your brains out."

"What?" Meade was mortified. "You want me to kill myself?"

"It's a suicide letter, right? So, commit your suicide." Mason explained.

Meade was in sheer panic. The tears flooded his eyes, almost clouding his vision. He sat at the kitchen table dressed in his pristine suit and shoes, trembling with fear. He began to heavily sob, deep convulsions as his stomach contracted from the pain.

"Do it!" Mason shouted.

Still, Meade hesitated. This had to be a nightmare. He wanted to wake up from it, sweating and jumpy—but it wasn't. It was the real thing, and they weren't going away, not until he blew his brains out. The video of his sleeping daughter was still streaming, and to add insult to injury, a masked man was standing over his daughter dressed in black. He slowly pointed the barrel of what looked like a canon to her head.

"Don't make me ask you again!" growled Mason.

They stood around him, waiting for the bang—waiting for the deed to be done, to see his brains spray out and his body to slump forward.

Arnold Meade continued to weep. "You better keep your promise and not hurt her...." He picked up the gun with his trembling hand and grudgingly put the barrel of it to his temple. Meade placed his shaky finger on the trigger, and with tears engulfing his face, he hollered— "You motherfuckers!" —and squeezed.

Meade's head jerked once and then lolled headfirst on the table. The pistol dropped from his lifeless hand. There was a wager on whether Meade would do it, and a small percentage of Scott's men had made considerable money off the bet.

Fortunately for Catherine Meade, Scott West was a businessman. He knew that if anything happened to this prominent socialite, he would be at the top list of suspects. Mason called off the wolves at the daughter's apartment, and they left without harming a hair on the woman's head. Mason and his henchmen left the scene. They left Arnold Meade to rot in his four-thousand-dollar suit and inside his two-million-dollar home.

Chapter 31

They all got the same frantic phone call from Avery—something awful had happened. Lucky, Bugsy, Meyer, and Maxine all hastily arrived at the lavish penthouse and were immediately met with absolute chaos. Bugsy and Meyer had their guns drawn when they converged on the scene. Avery was lying against the wall with a bullet in him. He had been shot in the arm, his blood leaking, but he was still alive. Avery had also sustained head trauma, his skull had been cracked open with a large gash, a sight that could turn the most hardened person's stomach.

Nearby were two dead Mexican's. One unknown assailant had been shot in the head at point-blank range by Avery—his 9mm handgun resting in his dead hand. The other was filled full of holes that his body looked like Swiss cheese. The haunting sound of a baby screaming uncontrollably in the nursery, coupled with the nanny hollering with grief, had sent an eerie chill down everyone's spine. Maxine and Lucky shared the same terror—was their baby okay? They ran into the nursery, where the horror continued. In the room, everyone received the shock of their lives. The ghastly sight of something dreadful and so heinous had transpired—there was a dead baby in the crib. Its lifeless body lay in a pool of blood, the white sheet-soaked crimson. Gloria was in shock, crying hysterically, her face anguished as endless tears streamed down her cheeks. She clutched a baby in her arms.

Lucky and Maxine's eyes grew wide with fear and panic. And subsequently came the ear-shattering scream from a mother shocked into insanity as she realized her worse nightmare. Maxine screamed, "Nooooooooo!!! Dillinger, nooooooo! Please, God, nooooo! Bring him back to me!"

The plea was shrill, guttural—a high-pitched throaty noise, a scream that resonated with everyone within the sound of her voice. A mother's supplication for the impossible was heart-wrenching. Her son's throat had been sliced, a long cut ran across the front of his small neck, practically from ear to ear. It was so deep that bone was visible.

Lucchese was being gripped tightly by Gloria. Lucky, realizing her child was still alive, snatched her daughter from the nanny's arms and cradled Lulu so tightly she could have smothered her. Lucky cried too. Bugsy and Meyer were shellshocked. The sight of Dillinger dead in his crib made Bugsy so weak and emotional that his pistol fell from his hand as he stood there frozen. Not his son! Not his baby boy. It was unreal. It had to be a nightmare.

Dillinger was in his usual sleeping position, on his back—legs and arms spread wide. His round face, chubby cheeks, and pink lips were lifeless. His little cherub was gone. Meyer stood aghast, too. His fingers tightened around the handle of the gun as he gaped at a dead baby in its crib, and a mother swooning with absolute grief.

"Who kills an infant," Meyer growled. He, too, couldn't stop the tears from flowing, seeing his nephew had been brutally murdered.

Bugsy snapped back to reality and picked up his gun from the floor. He would kill someone. The only name he could think of was Scott.

"I'm gonna kill him!" Bugsy shouted. "He's a fucking dead man!"

Before Bugsy could storm out the room and go ballistic on everyone, Meyer was there to stop him. He blocked Bugsy's exit and pushed him back. Bugsy glared at his brother and looked like he was ready to shoot Meyer for getting in his way. He growled at his twin, "Get the fuck out my way!"

"Chill out Bugsy, I know you ready to kill Pops, but you sure it was him?" Meyer shouted, becoming the voice of reason. "It could have been anyone. We got two fuckin' dead Mexican's in the other room. Think nigga!"

Meyer stopped his brother, not because he didn't want his brother to avenge Dillinger, but Meyer thought this was drug-related.

"I told you he would do this! I fuckin' warned you!" Maxine screamed out, "Kill him, Bugsy! Kill him! I want that sonofabitch dead!" Maxine was overcome with guilt. One of the few times she left her son alone with the nanny, and this happened.

Emotions were spilling out, and tempers were exploding like bombs. Gloria, who was left alive, was ranting something in Spanish. She continued to shout and remained hysterical until Meyer finally asked, "What the fuck are you sayin' bitch?"

It looked like she was hyperventilating, but they didn't care about her condition. What everyone wanted to know was, who killed Dillinger? The nanny exclaimed, "The Mexican...he says, 'Lou, a Negra, will never be an heir to the Juarez cartel. This is your Madres fault!'"

Bugsy's ears perked up, and he wanted the nanny to repeat what she'd said, and she did. His eyes accusingly dashed across the room to Lucky. Why would the Juarez cartel think that Dillinger was Lucky's baby? And why would they believe Lucchese was a boy unless Lucky told them she was. Bugsy became confused. Could his sister do him dirty like that? Could she have set up his only child to be a decoy? He remembered that it was Lucky's idea that they move in together. So many clues were flying through his head about his sister. He seethed, but he wasn't sure yet. He wasn't sure about Lucky's deceit. But the dead Mexican's...the mention of the Juarez cartel, and finally Angel's treat to his sister. That was Bugsy's proof that Lucky had set him up—that she indirectly arranged for his son to be brutally murdered. He glared at Lucky and shouted, "You did this shit! You set up my son!"

Lucky looked at her brother, bewildered. She stood there holding her baby in her arms, Lucchese now used as a shield if Bugsy had thought about squeezing off a couple rounds into her. She hoped that Meyer would protect her from Bugsy's wrath.

"This is all your fuckin' fault, you conniving little bitch!" Bugsy shouted heatedly.

"It wasn't me! I would never hurt Dillinger!" Lucky screamed, defending her life. "I never told Angel that Lulu was a boy...that's a lie. Angel is trying to set me up, to pit us against each other...Bugsy, please, on my life...I'm innocent."

Everyone's nerves were frayed. It felt like hell on earth, and Bugsy and Maxine were overcome with grief. And now somebody had to pay for his son's death—anybody! He couldn't kill Lucky, not his sister, and the Mexican men were already dead. So Bugsy took his aggression out on the next best thing. He gripped the gun firmly and went to the sobbing and frantic nanny, put the guns' barrel to her head, and squeezed. *Boom!* Her blood splattered, and she crumbled to the floor—a bullet in her temple. Bugsy frostily glared down at her body and said, "You had time to listen to their threats, and you let them kill my son! You let them kill my fuckin' son!"

Tears streamed down his face. Bugsy tucked his smoking gun in his waistband and angrily pivoted. He stormed out of the penthouse in a blind fury.

Avery made his way into the nursery, looked at the carnage, and then at Meyer. He asked him, "You want me to go after him?"

"Nah, let him be. He needs to be alone right now." Meyer observed Avery, who looked fucked up. He was clutching his arm to help slow down the blood but had done nothing to address the nasty wound to his head. The sight of him made Meyer's stomach queasy. He wished the nigga would get some help. "Don't you need to get to a hospital?" Meyer said.

"This is more important," Avery replied.

"Ain't nothing else you can do here. I just wish you'd kept those fuckin' wetbacks alive so we could have killed them!"

"There wasn't anytime to subdue them, I had to react violently, or I would be dead too."

Meyer understood war. He eyed Avery suspiciously and asked, "What were you doin' here anyway?"

"Bugsy asked me to take Maxine's Benz to the shop. When I got here, she wasn't. I walked in on the melee and you already know the rest."

Meyer whistled. "We lucky you got here when you did."

Avery nodded and then took one last look at the ugly scene before leaving to get medical attention.

With the cops on their way to the horrific scene, Meyer looked and noticed that Maxine had crawled into the crib with Dillinger, and she sobbed heavily. Lucky was balled up in the corner with Lulu in her arms, rocking her infant daughter back and forth. The totality had Meyer at a loss for words, and he sighed in sadness.

Chapter 32

The bullet to his left arm was only a flesh wound, but Avery knew this when he got to the hospital. His arm had been placed into a sling, his head was stitched up, and he was treated and released the same day—patched up and ready to go. He walked through the hospital lobby and exited to the outside. It was a long night, and the tragedy was something he wouldn't forget. The death of Bugsy's infant son was traumatizing, and he knew that Bugsy would not stop until those responsible were tortured and murdered. That's why Avery knew he had to be extra careful. He lingered outside the hospital for a moment and lit a cigarette. He was waiting for his cab to arrive. Avery stood alone outside the Manhattan hospital and was somewhat nervous, but he had been in the game for a long time, and he knew how to move. His head was always on a swivel as he smoked his Newport and waited for his pickup.

Finally, the cab came to a stop near the curb a few feet from him. Avery flicked his cigarette away and climbed into the backseat.

"Where to?" the aging driver asked.

"Brooklyn," said Avery. "I'm going down by the Navy Yard."

The driver nodded and drove off. Avery sat back, sighed, and regularly surveyed his surroundings. He looked for any anomalies, or any familiar faces following him, but there weren't any. The streets were normal, the folks around weren't paying him any attention, and that was good. So after several minutes of paranoia, he relaxed a little and closed his eyes. The cab drove east toward the FDR Drive and then merged onto the Brooklyn Bridge. Brooklyn was familiar territory to him. It was his home, where he was born and raised but now lived on Long Island. Occasionally he missed it, but he was climbing the ladder of success and making moves in the underworld, so his domicile needed to be more secure.

An hour later, the cab came to a stop in front of a three-story bricked building on Cumberland Street. Avery paid the driver and climbed out of the cab. Once again, he observed his surroundings. The block was quiet at this late hour. Avery walked toward the entrance, and above his head to his right was a surveillance camera peering down at him. He looked up at it and nodded, they were watching him from within. Avery proceeded inside and was met with several armed thugs. His arrival was expected, and he could head up to the second floor, the stairs on his right. Walking into the vast and sprawling loft with the concrete floor and concrete pillars, big windows, and exposed brick ceiling, he looked at Scott standing near the window, and his queen stood beside him. They both turned simultaneously to look at Avery and awaited information from him. Behind him, he noticed Mason had entered the room too.

"So, what do you have for us?" Layla asked, not beating around the bush. Avery wasn't there for a social visit.

"It went down really ugly...too ugly, and Dillinger's dead," he said.

"Do tell," Scott said, not sounding broken up about the news of his dead grandson.

They wanted the harsh details. Avery was a double agent that Scott and Layla had planted to infiltrate their children. And so far, he was on point with information after information. There was a scare for him at one point, when Bugsy and Meyer suspected him of being the snitch, but what saved him from suspicion was that they believed Avery had no clue about their Yonkers location. But it was easy for Avery to find the second stash house when Bugsy thought he was keeping him out of their business. He had followed Chopper to the location and relayed the news back to Scott and Layla—three days later, they implemented St. Valentine's Day Massacre, Rah from Brooklyn's assassination, and the Yonkers warehouse murders.

The four, Scott, Layla, Mason, and Avery, were the only ones privy to this master plan of revenge and deception that Scott had conjured up. Mason and Avery had been around from almost day one. Gotti, Bonnie, and Clyde were like family, and when they'd heard what Maxine had done to them, both wanted to put a bullet in the bitch themselves. But Scott and Layla were unwearied. Avery didn't see how they were so patient, knowing that Maxine was the one behind the death of their youngest children. But what their older children did to Layla and Scott was unforgivable, he felt. Scott and Layla had spoiled those ingrates, and this was how they were repaid. It was clear why the two wanted their children destroyed. And when Mason discovered how Bugsy blocked him from speaking to his boss while Scott was incarcerated, he wanted to kill Bugsy, but he knew that wasn't his place unless Scott gave him the order.

Together, Scott and Layla were diabolical. Their plan was executing slowly, but not perfectly. First, they had Packer murdered and placed in Lucky's G-wagon. Layla wanted her daughter to feel exposed. They could have murdered Maxine long ago, but why rush the inevitable, when it would be so much fun taunting her. They wanted her to bury a child like they had buried three and then allow the pain to linger for a while.

"He killed the nanny," Avery said.

"It was expected," Scott said nonchalantly.

Gloria was in on the ruse, but the poor woman didn't expect them to kill the baby. Scott had paid the nanny to say that one Mexican cartel member had said to her, "Lou, a Negra will never be an heir to the Juarez cartel. This is your Madres fault."

Had it not been for the nanny saying those words to the grieving Bugsy, then their plan wouldn't have succeeded. They didn't expect the nanny to live long enough to spend her payoff. Both thought it would have been Meyer who would have killed Gloria, but it didn't matter. It needed to be done. No loose ends.

"Does he suspect you? You, after all, did come out alive with a flesh wound?" Scott asked him.

"I don't think so. Bugsy was too distraught over his son's death to think straight...but Meyer might be the problem," Avery said.

Layla finally spoke. "And Lucky? Is she dead?"

Avery shook his head.

Scott looked away, pondering other things that had unfolded. He and Layla were somewhat disappointed that the plan didn't evolve precisely how they thought. The couple convinced themselves that when their children walked into the room and saw Dillinger with his small throat cut open and dead in his crib, it would link back to Lucky and her hardheartedness. Angel told her to not have that baby, and she didn't listen—now look at the tragedy that unfolded behind her stupidity. And to push Bugsy to kill his sister, the icing on the cake should have.

Layla had discovered through Nurse Pattie that Lucky told Angel that the child wasn't his and that her baby was a boy named Lou, for short, not Lulu. Layla realized just how foul and trifling

Lucky was to not only her own mother but to her own brother and his innocent child. Layla knew that the only reason Lucky moved in with Bugsy and his son was if something like this jumped off. Bugsy's son, Dillinger, was nothing more to Lucky than a sacrificial lamb. Layla knew her daughter well, and it wasn't an oversight—it was calculated. Scott and Layla felt that with Bugsy not thinking, he would deduce how Lucky had played him. And in the aftermath, Bugsy would take his anger out on Lucky and finally do the unthinkable, kill his own sister and most likely force Meyer to kill his own twin in the violent melee. It was planned to kill three birds with one stone—and once Angel found out from Layla that Lucchese was his, he would honor his cartel's code and murder his daughter. But plans were just plans. Bugsy still had mercy for his sister after knowing the truth. So they had to keep pushing the envelope and devise another strategy.

Chapter 33

Dillinger John West was dressed handsomely in his pristine outfit—an all-white three-piece suit and waistcoat. His tiny hands wore white gloves as they crossed in front of him like a gentleman. He looked heavenly, like an angel, a cherub as he lay in the silk-lined, 18-gauge steel white casket, a heartbreaking moment for everyone. The news of Dillinger's murder created absolute outrage in the city, and across the country despite who his grandparents were. Everyone believed that his death was uncalled for, and hundreds of people wanted justice for Dillinger. Fingers pointed to the cartel when a news reporter connected the gangland tattoos on the deceased triggermen to the underground Mexican sicarios. The spectacle created unwanted attention for the narcos as the atrocious murder of an infant killed in his crib was about to become the catalyst of stricter anti-drug laws, harsher justice against the cartels and gangs, and the renewed call to build the border wall. A wave of protests and marches across the country had begun, and the feds had added more investigators to take down the infamous West clan. The slaughter at the Manhattan penthouse, leaving four dead, including a baby, had been headline news for days now, and his funeral had become a media circus with a zoo of reporters.

The Manhattan cemetery was flooded with people—more than anyone could count—dozens and dozens of folks gathered around the burial ground for Dillinger John West. The media was parked outside the cemetery with their cameras rolling on every movement and their mics ready to be thrust into people's faces with a flood of questions—and piggybacking with the media were a few well-dressed federal agents scattered throughout the cemetery, snapping their own pictures of certain persons of interest.

Dillinger's casket was inundated with flowers, teddy bears, and a few rosaries before finally being closed. Maxine stood near the casket dressed in all white with dark shades covering her tear-stained eyes. She was bordering nearly at a mental breakdown and slowly becoming unhinged. The past few days had been hell for her. The FBI interrogated her for hours. She was clueless, or feigned cluelessness, and everywhere she turned, people stampeded her with their condolences. She wanted to be left alone. She wanted to cry over her son in private, but in her world, solitude had been omitted. Maxine was flanked by Bugsy, who too couldn't hold back his emotions as tears streamed down his face. Surrounded by family and friends—and a few rivals, they watched their baby boy lowered into the ground as the pastor gave the eulogy.

Meyer felt his knees almost buckling as his little man was lowered into the ground. He just couldn't believe this was a reality. Lucky comforted him by rubbing his back and squeezing his hand when he had allowed his emotions to get the best of him. His sister was unprecedently composed.

"In the sweat of thy face shalt thou eat bread, till thou return unto the ground; for out of it wast thou taken for dust thou art, and unto dust shalt thou return," the pastor eulogized.

Everyone in attendance watched the casket sink lower and lower into the ground, including Scott and Layla. Bugsy invited Layla, and she brought Scott. From the church to the burial ground, it had been overflowing with white flowers—a blizzard of respect and condolences. Everyone was asked to specifically wear white in honor of Dillinger, but Layla showed opposition by coming to her grandson's funeral in a red dress like it was a celebration. The garish color didn't go unnoticed by all attendees, but the majority were too afraid to challenge her outfit choice. And Bugsy was too distraught to even care. He did his best to console Maxine, hugging her and holding her close, and while that was going on, Scott's stomach did backflips as he watched how affectionate the two were. He frowned behind his shades, knowing Maxine was living on borrowed time. She, too, would meet her fate, and it would not be pretty.

After the burial, everyone went their separate ways. Maxine hurriedly walked away from the area and climbed into the backseat of the limousine. She didn't want to be bothered by anyone. Maxine wanted to leave the cemetery and go home and grieve, thoughts of suicide infiltrating her fragile mind. Before she could close the limo door, a hand prevented the door from shutting, and it swung back open. Looming into Maxine's view was Layla. The two women locked eyes for a moment. Maxine wasn't in the mood for her pettiness—now wasn't the time, and if Layla was stupid enough to start something, then Maxine was ready to beat her down again.

Layla removed her shades and said, "My condolences for your loss. I know what it feels like to lose a child, I lost three, and still no justice for my children. But if you need anything...."

"I don't," Maxine quickly uttered, curtailing Layla's speech.

Layla bent down and leaned further into Maxine's personal space. Their faces only inches apart and countered with, "Take solace in knowing there's a special place in hell for kid killers."

Layla stepped away from the limousine, allowing Maxine to finally close the door and shut her out. Layla pivoted on her Red Bottoms and marched toward Scott. The feeling inside of her was bittersweet, knowing Maxine was suffering. The anguish was written on her face.

Layla and Scott walked arm-in-arm to the Bentley parked in the distance. Scott knew pictures were being taken of him and Layla. The FBI continuously clicked away, showing no subtleness. But Scott remained casual and relaxed and escorted his wife to the vehicle, and they quietly exited from the cemetery.

"What now?" Layla asked.

"Now…we lay the hammer down, and then we go on vacation. I need some time off anyway," Scott said.

Layla smiled. "Sounds like a plan."

Chapter 34

Lucky sat soaking in the warm bubble bath, enjoying an expensive bottle of wine. She finally unwound and freed her mind from any stress. Now that Dillinger was laid to rest, she felt Angel's reign on top would be over soon, and she wouldn't have to pay him for his men's murder. She wondered what made Angel jump the gun. He gave her an extension of time to gather the money and hop on his private jet with her son to prove her maternity. Whatever the reason, she didn't care. His actions made her brothers and every triggerman under their umbrella want to see Angel dead. They would war, and she was lucky that it wasn't in her name. Bugsy was calling the shots, so if anything happened to him, or Meyer, she could come out smelling like roses. Lucky would be a fool to think it would be easy to retaliate against a titan like Angel and expect to win. But the testosterone in her brothers told them otherwise.

On the phone, Lucky conversed with Angel, and he seemed normal—no mention yet of Dillinger. It was odd that he didn't reveal he had murdered her "son." Meyer advised her not to bring up that he was behind the murder unless he does, and she complied.

Finally, Angel said, "I heard about the tragedy on the news. Your family has a lot of enemies, yes?"

She knew Angel wouldn't wait too long to gloat. "You mean my *son*, right?"

"Your son," Angel repeated. "That dead baby was yours?"

Once again, Lucky was lucky that the national news outlets didn't post Dillinger's name or his parents' names to respect the privacy of a minor. They only reported that *'Infant West'* was the grandchild to *'Scott and Layla West,'* therefore, Lucky was able to confirm to Angel that he had indeed murdered her child. Lucky feigned sadness, making her voice choke up. "My baby…is gone…."

"It is your fault that you did not protect him, is it not?"

"My fault?" Lucky sniffled and pretended to weep.

"If we're meant to be one thing, it is protectors of those we bring into this world…but life goes on as does business. I'm a very forgiving man, but what happened in the Bronx with my men, will not be excused because of your loss. When can I expect my money?" he asked.

"At a time like this, you want to discuss money. I'm grieving, Angel."

"What about my men's families? Are they not grieving? Is your loss greater than those around you?"

"Send your men," she said. "The money's ready. My child was just laid to rest, so I'm not coming to you."

"Good. Besides that, how you been?"

Lucky felt he had some nerve. The boldness of him to ask how she was when he thought he had murdered Lou. She snapped and exclaimed, "How the fuck you think I'm doing!"

"You sound unstable," he replied.

"Unstable…are you serious?"

217

Angel remained nonchalant, and Lucky felt he was toying with her. He would never admit to the murder, especially when he had this much fun torturing her. So Lucky continued with her sarcasm, knowing that men like Angel always felt they were invincible. But her brothers would make him pay. Bugsy was determined to go through great lengths to bring about justice for his little boy.

"Okay, I will say goodbye for now. And Lucky…"

"Yes, Angel."

"Be careful."

The box truck crossed over the G.W. Bridge and fused with the Bronx traffic. The three men in the cabin sat idling in heavy traffic for over an hour until they finally arrived at their destination—a new location in Inwood, Manhattan. It was a bricked clothing factory on Broadway, a front for drug distribution.

The truck pulled into the warehouse and awaiting the men were Bugsy, Meyer, Chopper, Avery, and several other triggermen. The vehicle came to a stop inside, and the doors closed. The three Hispanic men climbed out of the cabin to get things started. They were on time to receive the large shipment of cash due to their cartel. They came armed but figured what happened at the other Bronx location a few weeks back wouldn't happen again.

The driver was leery that Bugsy had so many armed men inside the warehouse. "Y'all expecting trouble, amigos?"

Bugsy replied, "Better safe than dead."

"We load up the cash, and we go," the driver said.

"That's fine by me," Bugsy said.

The driver nodded to his acquaintances. The men opened the rear doors of the vehicle and were prepared to load. The driver was armed with a pistol, and he looked uneasy.

"Why you so nervous, nigga?" Meyer asked him. "You got something to hide?"

He and Meyer locked eyes, the man didn't respond. The gun in his hand was a sure sign of distrust between him and them. His head swiveled, and he counted nineteen men inside the room. Nineteen—it was an uncomfortable number against three. The Hispanics looked around at their surroundings and felt things were tense. They didn't feel welcomed.

Bugsy felt only contempt for anything attached to Angel. These men were at the bottom of the food chain, but he needed to start somewhere. Bugsy stared at the driver and asked, "You have kids?"

The driver seemed confused by the question. He answered, "We don't discuss personal business. You know that."

"We don't, huh," Bugsy uttered. "You know I had a son, right?"

The men didn't care about his family, and they didn't care for the chitchat. They were there on behalf of the cartel to collect the money and be on their way. They wanted no drama, but it was coming to them whether they were ready for it or not. And then it happened, Meyer couldn't contain his composure anymore, and he fired his gun quickly—*Bak!* He shot the second man in the face. The other two men were startled by the outburst of violence. The driver attempted to lift his gun and react, but a cord was wrapped around his throat and squeezed. The last man in the rear was immediately jumped and pistol-whipped. They were swiftly overpowered.

The driver glared up at Bugsy, trying in vain to loosen the cord around his neck. He squeezed out, "You…are making…a mistake!"

Bugsy frowned heavily at the man on his knees with the cord around his neck and replied, "Your fuckin' boss made a mistake!"

The two men were kidnapped and taken to a different location. The dead man's body would be disposed of, he couldn't be found.

Chapter 35

It had been days of severe torture, but the two Hispanic males were resilient and loyal to the cartel. Meyer did everything in his power to make them give up key locations of not only stash houses belonging to the cartel, but residential places where Angel lived. They remained silent in fear for their families. Meyer and his goons brutally beat the men—repeated pistol whippings, cutting off fingers and toes, working his way through their hands and feet. Soon, the two men looked hideous—their faces looked like chopped meat. Their breathing became sparse, and they were barely alive. But still, the men refused to give up their boss because it meant that their families would die.

Meyer and Chopper grew frustrated. They both tried everything to extract information from them. Meyer never had seen men so stubborn and so resilient. He had to respect their gangsta and their commitment to the cartel. Bugsy respected nothing about them. The only thing he wanted was information.

"These muthafuckas are stubborn, Bugsy…look at them, ain't nothin' left to torture or take apart, and they still ain't saying shit," Meyer said.

Bugsy fumed. He would not give up, this was his only option. He had to get something from them. These men were standing between his revenge with Angel. And then it dawned on Bugsy, what did they love the most—their families.

"I have an idea. Keep them alive until Meyer returns," he said to Chopper.

Chopper nodded.

Bugsy got their information, their addresses to their homes from their licenses. If they feared the cartel that much, then they would fear him a lot more. Bugsy was a furious man, and nothing would stop him from ensuring justice for his son. He instructed Meyer to take Avery and a few henchmen with him and fly down to Florida, kidnap their families and drive them back to their location.

Maxine couldn't eat, sleep, have sex, bathe, or even think straight. She couldn't get over the death of her baby boy. Maxine walked around in a trance-like state, beside herself with agonizing grief. Maxine had concluded that they were all poison, every one of them. From day one, they did nothing but ruin her life and cause her despair. Layla took away over twenty years of her life, and Scott never loved her, she believed. And Lucky was the catalyst that got Dillinger murdered in his crib. Maxine felt betrayed by everyone, including Bugsy. She wanted him to kill his father—he did not. Maxine begged him to murder his sister—he refused. The West's took everything from her, and now she was losing her sanity.

Bugsy noticed that she was unstable. He locked up all the firepower he had in the house and cleared the medicine cabinets of all painkillers and hoped that would be enough. He worried that Maxine would take her own life, so he called the house hourly.

Everywhere in the penthouse was a reminder of Dillinger's short life. Bugsy didn't want to live there anymore, the haunting of his son was too much for him to bear. But Maxine refused to leave. She believed that she could still feel her son's presence in the penthouse, crying out to her in pain. Maxine wasn't there to protect him. She prayed God would have mercy on her soul.

Maxine wasn't lucid when she stumbled through the long hallway dressed in a dingy T-shirt and sweats. She wobbled, hugging the wall for support under the cloak of darkness, heading toward Lucky's room. Lately, she had been drinking Hennessey straight from the bottle to dull her pain, but nothing helped. It wouldn't go away. The stain of her son's death followed her like a shadow.

Maxine found the bedroom door ajar. For several minutes, she stood over the sleeping bitch who caused all her misery. Maxine raised the serrated knife over her head with her eyes glued on Lucky. Madness overcame her, and she plunged it down into Lucky's sleeping frame, with full force. Unfortunately for Maxine, her attack didn't hit center mass. The knife tore through Lucky's upper arm, startling the young woman. Lucky's eyes flew open in panic, and quickly she fought for her life.

"You fuckin' bitch! Aaaaaaaahh…get her off me. Get the fuck off me!" Lucky screamed.

Blood and panic saturated the room, as Lucky wrestled with the crazed Maxine, she felt the knife stab her again. She continued to fight for her life. The screaming woke up, Bugsy, who charged into the room and observed the chaos happening. Instantaneously, Bugsy gripped Maxine's forearm and desperately tried to prevent the knife from thrusting downwards into his sister again. Still, Maxine violently jerked from his grasp, and in doing so, she cut Bugsy's hand. Blood was everywhere.

"She killed our baby! She killed our son!" Maxine shouted intensely. It was as if she was possessed. Her eyes were so black as if light or life was ultimately absent from her soul. She was a black hole of rage.

She fought Bugsy with a vigor he didn't know she possessed. He didn't want to hurt her, but he also couldn't allow her to hurt them any more than she had. There was a power struggle; it was a bull of a fight, but eventually, he triumphed, and Maxine was thrown to the floor and restrained. The results were a lot of heavy breathing and a few minor injuries. Lucky suffered from a couple stab wounds, but none were life-threatening. She escaped death by a miracle.

"You crazy fuckin' bitch!" Lucky shouted.

Maxine screamed in anguish—the core of her pain echoing throughout the room.

Bugsy stood in awe. Everything about Maxine was in disarray, from her hair to her well-being, she was off her rockers. He could only stand there and feel sadness and sympathy for her. Everything she's been through; it was all leading to this moment. The signs were there, he simply ignored them.

Once again, their home had become a magnet for law enforcement and paramedics. Lucky was being treated for her injuries on the gurney while Maxine was being carted off to jail. Their home had become a cesspool of one tragedy after another. While Lucky was being carried to the hospital, Maxine was in the back of an unmarked squad car and she still incoherently ranted about murder and her dead son. She had lost all her mental faculties, and eventually, she would be placed on a 72-hour hold. Bugsy would be left to pick up the pieces. He already had enough on his plate to deal with. Now he had an escalating family affair and a fragile, emotionally unsound baby mama.

Chapter 36

Two days later, Meyer forced a mother and young boy into the undisclosed room and pushed them down to the ground in front of the tortured man. The man took one look at his family, and he immediately felt absolute fear. He cried out to them in Spanish. His wife was on her knees crying, her face awash with tears—seeing the horrifying condition of her husband. It was an ominous reunion. Meyer towered over the wife and put a 9mm to the back of her head, and he glared at the man. "Now, where did we leave off...you and I?" Meyer growled at him.

"Please, noooo! Noooo! Let them go, please! Kill me and let them go!" he screamed in horror.

"It's in your power to let them go, talk to me...tell me what I need to know about your boss, Angel," Bugsy said.

Days of torture, and it took only two minutes for the man to sing like a bird after seeing his family in imminent danger, and he told Bugsy everything he needed to know about Angel.

"Thank you," Bugsy said.

Bugsy index finger pressed against the trigger of the 9mm, and the wife's head exploded, her body dropped. The screaming that came from the male was haunting after witnessing his wife's execution. He then killed the boy, a bullet to the back of his head, and his body fell next to his mother's. Now the man had no reason to live, he wanted to join his family on the other side—Bugsy gave him his wish. Bugsy executed the last man, putting a bullet in his forehead.

"Get rid of the bodies. I don't want them found," Bugsy instructed.

Chopper and Avery nodded. Bugsy left the room, still unsatisfied. He climbed into his Escalade with Meyer and left the undisclosed location while his men were left behind to make them disappear for good.

"They never checked in," Angel said to her.

Lucky feigned shock. "What...how's that? The exchange was made over a week ago, and they left accordingly, Angel. I have no idea what happened to them, I swear."

"I find it hard to believe that lightning may have struck twice. It's becoming a thing with you...problems," Angel said.

"I have no problems with you, Angel. Your men came and left with twenty million of my cold hard cash. Things went smoothly. Where they went after they left us, I have no idea."

Angel hung up. It was abrupt. Lying to him was tough, but she did it. Lucky just needed to bide her time before her brothers found and murdered him—if that was possible.

Bugsy was there with a massive bouquet of roses and a reassuring smile to pick Maxine up from Bellevue. The doctor said her actions came from exhaustion. He assessed that after the sudden death of her son, she hardly had any sleep. That, coupled with her alcohol consumption, made her unstable.

Maxine was silent as Bugsy discharged her. Her eyes told him that things would never be the same between them. He wanted to give her some good news.

"Lucky's moved out," he said. "She won't be bothering us anymore. We can fix this, work on us."

Maxine didn't utter one word. There wasn't a way she could get past these events. She knew that had she not been under the influence of alcohol, Lucky would be a dead bitch. He continued, "I think we should move too so—"

"No!" she snapped. "I'm not leaving, but you should."

Bugsy smirked. "What do you mean by that?"

"I need my space to grieve my son, and I can't do that with you there. That isn't your apartment anyway, it's Scott's. You can move back into your apartment, and I want you to do that asap."

Maxine was lying on the couch, eyeing the foyer as Bugsy rolled each one of his suitcases by the door. She was watching him like a hawk. He couldn't leave fast enough. Maxine could tell that Bugsy thought this would be temporary, he was always looking on the bright side of things. But their relationship was as dead as Dillinger, and nothing could revive it.

"That's all you're taking?" she asked.

He looked down at the suitcases as if he didn't know what she meant. "It's all I can handle by myself."

"Why didn't you call movers or have Chopper help you? We don't need this to drag out, Bugsy. You have a lot of clothing, shoes, weaponry here—all things I don't want to look at."

He wasn't letting her go that easy. Bugsy would stall if it got Maxine to realize she still loved him.

The banging on the front door didn't even startle her. If shooters came—then they came. She would just get to be with her son again that much sooner. However, Bugsy wasn't as lax. He had his hand on his pistol, and he cautiously approached.

"Who is it!" he yelled.

"Your mother."

Bugsy turned to look at Maxine, who rolled her eyes. This is precisely why she wanted him gone. The door was quickly unlocked, and a frantic Layla came barging in.

"Your father is missing," she hollered, her face flushed with tears.

Those words made Maxine sit straight up. Layla had her full attention.

"What does missing mean?" he wanted to know.

"Are you mentally challenged!" she shot back. "It means Scott's disappeared into thin air like a magic act."

Bugsy smirked. He exhaled and asked, "Are you sure. When was the last time you saw Pops? Did y'all have an argument?"

"Stop speaking to me like I'm a fuckin' moron. Your father's been gone since yesterday morning. He went to the gym and never came home. None of his men have heard from him, I spoke with Mason, and he's out there looking, but so far he's just gone."

"What about the feds? Local precincts...hospitals?"

"Done, done, and muthafuckin' done!" Layla was frantic. "I swear if any of y'all are behind this shit...," she let her voice trail off.

"I promise you we ain't had nothing to do with Pops missing. In fact, I'm going to get our men on it right away."

Layla never acknowledged Maxine, nor did she say anything about the pile of suitcases by the front door. Bugsy got on the phone to let his siblings know about their father. He also called Chopper and Avery to round up a search party. Maxine finally saw a silver lining. She thought that Murder Incorporated had stolen her money. It had been so long without results. She knew that they could search all they wanted—Scott West wasn't coming back from the dead. Next up was Layla.

Chapter 37

O pie became the man by her side, day and night she was making moves behind the scenes looking for a new connect, scouting out new territory to seize just as she had done with Delaware. Lucky had become something of a double agent. She had to be there for her brothers and the ongoing war with the Juarez cartel. And then subtly line up all her ducks in a row. She traveled everywhere with Opie—the tristate area, Connecticut, Albany, and the south, scouting out locations and making inroads. Her hustle left little time for her to be with Lulu—and the nannies continued to be surrogate mothers.

It was late in the night when Lucky arrived home from handling her side hustle. Her brothers thought she was spending her days and nights with a nigga, and she allowed that lie to linger. Having an imaginary boyfriend was the perfect cover for all her absences. Her Benz came to a complete stop into her parking space, tired, she stumbled toward the elevator and made her way home only to find she had company. Meyer was seated in the living room, cradling Lulu in his arms and looked every bit like the loving and caring uncle he was. His look from Lulu to Lucky transitioned.

"Another fuckin' late night wit' you and that nigga," he said.

"Meyer don't start with me. I'm not in the mood," she said. "How the fuck did you get into my house anyway?"

He ignored her question and replied with, "You out there frolicking wit' this muthafucka and you ain't takin' care of your daughter. You an unfit mother, Lucky." His words were blunt and cutting, but he didn't care.

"Don't you dare judge me, Meyer...who the fuck is you anyway?!"

"I'm the one here making sure Lulu is okay," he shouted.

His loud outburst scared Lulu, and she cried in his arms. She cried because Meyer was so agitated.

"See what you made me do!" he barked at Lucky. He stood up and handed Lulu to the latest night nanny, Selma, that at once tried to console the crying infant. She exited the room with the baby to leave the siblings to talk in private.

"Just get the fuck out my house, Meyer," Lucky cursed.

"You need to get your fuckin' shit together."

"My shit is together!" she retorted.

"Not wit' Lulu, it isn't! I already lost a nephew; I'm not tryin' to lose my niece too."

"She's not your business!"

"She is my business, Lucky. She's family, and that baby is the only innocent thing in this fucked up family! And I swear, if you..."

"If I what?" Lucky rebuked, stepping closer to her brother and nearly getting in his face. "If you want to care about a fuckin' baby that bad, then go have your own with that bitch Zoe. Or did you chase her off, too!"

Meyer frowned. She had no right to bring her up. He clenched his fists, and he could punch his sister's lights out, but he didn't react. Instead, he continued to berate her. Lucky didn't want to hear the truth from him; it was the reason she was so defensive. Truth be told, Lucky was too young and unfocused to be a mother. Her attention was elsewhere. She loved Lulu, but she wasn't the affectionate type. She wasn't mother material.

"Don't fuck wit' me Lucky," he warned her.

Lucky matched his intense scowl, and angrily replied, "You don't fuck with me!"

Lucky walked into her kitchen to cut her a piece of Junior's cheesecake she had bought yesterday with Meyer right on her heels. He wasn't done arguing until he saw her pull out his favorite dessert.

"Yo, let me get a slice."

His sister rolled her eyes as she grabbed two plates, forks, and a cutting knife. She sliced a large piece for him and a smaller one for herself.

"Y'all find Scott yet?"

Meyer shook his head while stuffing a large spoonful of cheesecake into his mouth. "Nah, Pops just vanished into thin air."

"He'll turn up soon," Lucky tried to convince herself that he wasn't dead. Her brother did the same.

"Exactly. Pops just needed some time away from Ma. You know she can drive anyone away."

They chuckled, and then there was an awkward silence. Lucky said, "He's dead, isn't he?"

Meyer exhaled. "It's looking that way."

Maxine dropped off the final one-million-dollar balance to Marisol, so Murder Inc. could finish the hit on Layla. But she had added more names to the list.

"Speak with Juan-Pablo and tell him the Garcia cartel wants Bugsy, Meyer, Lucky, and her daughter, Lulu eliminated."

"Their children? Bugsy, Meyer, and Lucky? Why?"

"I don't know why. Just have Juan-Pablo get it done!"

"And the baby too? Are you sure they want the baby dead?" Marisol asked.

"That's what I said, right?"

"I can tell you now that Juan won't kill a baby! There is a code."

"For a million dollars, he won't?"

Marisol snapped, "I said no!"

Maxine felt she could live with that. With everyone dead, what kind of life would Lulu have anyway? "A'ight, I'll let them know, but they won't be happy."

"Too bad," Marisol stated. "And the same arrangements. Drop one-point-five million and balance upon completion of the first hit."

"One-point-five million?"

"You want three hits...do the math, that's three million for Bugsy, Meyer, and Lucky, Juan takes half upfront. Once he murders the first sibling, you'll pay the balance. You know how this goes why am I explaining again?"

Maxine didn't like how Marisol was speaking to her. She was talking greasy. Marisol was a different person than the last time they had met. She decided to not take it personally. Maybe Marisol was going through something. She said, "Tell him to hurry the fuck up with Layla! Ain't nobody got time to be waiting on murder."

The men were fatigued, each man balancing off less than four hours of sleep per night. This routine had been going on for weeks. The West organization had been at war with the Juarez cartel, scouring the crevices of the tristate looking for its founding member. Scott was presumed dead, but his family still wanted his body back so they could give him a proper funeral.

Layla was beside herself crying most days and each night for her other half. She wanted her husband back and never bit her tongue in accusing her children of being behind his abduction. Meyer tried to console his mother, feeling saddened that she was in so much pain. He had never seen his mother so vulnerable, but he understood. Death had gotten too close and too personal with them, and Meyer would be lying if he said that he didn't want a time out. He wanted just enough time to process that his siblings were dead, Penelope with his unborn child, Dillinger, and now the family's patriarch. Scott was gone, and it seemed they would never know how he met his demise.

Meyer answered his cellphone and got the shock of his life. "We need to talk."

Chapter 38

I wanna see you," Bugsy asked an uninterested Maxine. "We can't let it just end like this. Not without having some sort of closure, baby. What did I do? Why have you pushed me away?"

Max twirled her eyes around in her head, annoyed at his begging and pleading. She was long over Bugsy and had been fantasizing about what her life will look like once she's successfully had the whole West bloodline wiped out. Only Lulu would be left, and Maxine could take care of murdering Lulu on her own—payback for her son. And with the huge insurance policies she had taken out on Scott and Bugsy, which had the double indemnity clause that paid out double if one were murdered or died in an accident, she would have twenty-million-dollars payable to her. Maxine would also have access to the safe's in her apartment and Bugsy's that held money and jewelry. She would sell all their paintings and furniture and would never have to work again. Sadly she wouldn't be able to inherit any of their legal holdings because they weren't married or takeover his illegal operations, but Maxine would be financially set up for the remainder of her life.

When Maxine didn't answer, Bugsy continued to beg. He asked, "Where are you?"

She looked down at the finishing touches on her manicure and sighed. "I'm out. Why?"

"Because I'm at the penthouse, and I wanted you to come home."

Maxine sucked her teeth. Something Bugsy hadn't ever heard her do. She was showing a side of her that had laid dormant while they were together. "I'll be home soon. And Bugsy—"

"Yes?"

"Don't ever enter my apartment again without permission. You don't live there, don't make me say it a third time."

Maxine waltzed inside her apartment with a chip on her shoulder. Her lips were twisted, and she frowned heavily. The doorman escorted her upstairs because Max had bags upon bags of expensive clothing. Today she had treated herself to a shopping spree compliments of her ex.

"Thank you, Randall," she said and handed him a crisp one-hundred-dollar bill. He smiled graciously.

"No, thank you, Ms. Henderson."

Maxine closed her front door, placed her handbag on the side table, and heard movement in the living room. Without removing her coat, she investigated. "Bugsy," she called out.

"I'm in here."

When she walked into the living room and saw his face, and several other familiar faces all under the same roof, Maxine was stunned.

She stood there frozen in shock—her heart dropped into her stomach, seeing Layla, Lucky, Bugsy, Meyer, Chopper, Avery and Mason standing next to each other. *What are they doing here?* She asked herself. She had a hint, but it was terrifying to know she was probably right.

"Hey, bitch!" Layla barked at her.

"Your fuckin' luck ran out, didn't it?" Lucky followed up behind her mother.

Maxine felt her heart beating like African drums in her chest. She turned toward Bugsy for help. She asked him, "What's going on? What is this?" At first, he couldn't look at her, and then when he did, only disgust, anger, and feelings of betrayal showed on his face.

"You've been living on borrowed time, bitch," Layla growled at her ex-friend. "Now, it's time to collect!"

Maxine tried to call their bluff. She needed to show strength if she was to get out of this situation alive. "Look, either someone tell me what the fuck is going on or get the fuck out of my house."

Just then, she heard, "Your house, huh?"

Maxine spun around to see Scott walking in the room, his hands stuff snugly into his suit pants pockets. He looked incredible for someone who had come back from the dead. And trailing behind him was each member of Murder Incorporated—Juan-Pablo, Diego, Luis, and Miguel, including Marisol. Maxine closed her eyes and willed them back open. Damn, she had fucked up.

Murder Inc. had tailed Scott for weeks, always missing an opportunity to snatch him up because either Scott's men were on point or the feds were doing their own surveillance of the man. This hit was complicated, so the men thought about hitting Layla first. That was vetoed because they knew that if they got at his wife, it would put the kingpin on notice, and they would never fulfill both contracts. Each day they sat in the car doing their rounds; they would politick. And the one question they kept coming back to was why did the Garcia

cartel outsource this hit? It didn't make sense, and since they didn't want to be on the cartel's radar, they followed Maxine.

It didn't take long for Juan-Pablo, who knew the twins to realize that Maxine was now with Scott's son, Bugsy, and that baby was the son's and not the fathers. Juan-Pablo approached Scott on a street corner to show the kingpin he wasn't a threat and was shocked and equally flattered that Scott knew exactly who he was.

"Juan," Scott said and extended his hand for a shake.

Juan-Pablo nodded. "How you know my name?"

Scott looked him dead in his eyes and said, "I know everything. I run New York."

The two men sat like old business associates in Cubana, a cigar bar in Soho, and Juan filled Scott in on Maxine's plan.

"She said that the Garcia cartel had sanctioned the hit on you and your ex-wife—"

"My wife," Scott corrected.

"Your wife. She gave us a million upfront and will pay the balance upon completion. I can give that back to you as a sign of respect."

Scott inhaled his cigar smoke slowly and then exhaled. "That won't be necessary. You keep it. And do me a favor."

"What's that?"

"Collect the balance from her. I got a plan."

As Maxine stared into the faces of the men who had betrayed her, she wanted to scratch their fucking eyes out. She needed an ally, and it had to be Bugsy. He had once told her he would die for her; she hoped he was ready to honor his words.

"Whatever's happening, Bugsy, I'm being set up!" she cried out. "You know they've never wanted us together. First, they take our son, and now they want to come between us."

"I read the letter," Bugsy said.

"What letter?" She didn't know about any letter.

Calmly, Bugsy walked toward the woman who was someone he had deeply loved and now felt only contempt. He handed Maxine a letter that had passed through each siblings' hands, a letter that had a thousand tears dripped on it, a letter that would fuck up her whole world. They all read Tarsha's final words written to Scott. It was the truth. Tarsha knew details and dates all given to her by Wacka. Tarsha explained the missing engagement ring, the blackmail, and how Layla had unknowingly financed the murder of her children.

Maxine's body shook involuntarily. Wacka had belched up her past. This was chickens coming home to roost. The flood gates had opened, and the truth finally came pouring out. Maxine stood there, surrounded by animosity, swallowed up with despair. How was she going to talk her way out of this one?

"I'm being set up. I told you about them, Bugsy, didn't I? Remember, I told you that Wacka and Tarsha were trying to set me up! I'm innocent. Please believe me. Whatever they said about me is a lie!"

"You were always a fuckin' coward!" Layla spat, unable to tolerate the lies. "A needy, weak bitch who instead of going after the person who put your dumb ass behind bars you went after three defenseless children…what kind of shit is that? There's something mentally wrong with you! You're sick in the head."

"Coward, …weak?" Maxine snorted. "I beat your ass once, and I'll do it again! Ask Lucky how weak this bitch is!"

Lucky shifted on her feet, uncomfortable with the subject.

Layla laughed out loud. "You think 'cause you learned a few karate moves in prison that makes you strong? A warrior? I beat you with my mind,"— Layla's index finger tapped her temple. "No triggermen, no corner boys—just you and me. The moment I got you to take the fall for Sandy's murder, I won. War is a series of battles. A dance won through strategy, not brute force. You spent two decades working on your triceps and biceps, doing pushups and pullups for revenge when you should've been reading—mental cardio bitch! Studied how to not find your ass in this situation!"

Maxine's nostrils flared. How was this fair? All these adults against only her.

It was Marisol's turn for retribution. She never liked Maxine from day one. Marisol pressed play on her iPhone, and Maxine's voice boomed into the now silent room, and she was heard negotiating the murders of not only Meyer and Lucky but Bugsy and Lucchese too. This was bad. This was beyond what Bugsy could have ever fathomed she was capable of.

Maxine stared at Bugsy and physically saw his heartbreak. Bugsy didn't think he could feel more pain than when he laid his son to rest, but Maxine had surpassed that agony. He felt like such a fool.

Maxine wasn't done trying to manipulate. She uttered, "I love you…."

Bugsy barreled toward her and slapped her so hard that Maxine forcefully spun around and hit the floor. The tears trickled from her eyes, and everyone in that room loved every moment of it. Maxine didn't pick herself up; instead, she looked up at Bugsy towering over her with a menacing gaze. There would be no more begging or pleading from her, knowing this would be the end of her road. They all were yearning for her demise, and Maxine couldn't talk her way out of this predicament.

Suddenly, Bugsy attacked her again—no more slaps, but his fists hammered down on Maxine repeatedly, knuckles crashing against her jaw and her temple as she cried out, quickly she became disoriented. Bugsy rained down hell and fury on Maxine, like she was a male stranger to him. To everyone's amazement, Max scrambled up off the floor and swung too; she would not die without a fight. Max swung wildly, trying to back Bugsy up off her. One punch landed on his chin, which only infuriated her former lover beyond reason. His once sanguine and confident outlook on their relationship had been reduced to violence and murder. He wanted to end her.

The family watched, no one interfered, and for a moment it was Bugsy's show, and he didn't disappoint. He looked like Ali going for the knockout. Punch after punch, after punch landed on the pitiful looking female and Maxine's blood spewed out—her face cracked and made an awful sound. Bugsy nearly beat her to death but stopped to breathe. His knuckles were red, bruised, and swollen. Maxine fell to her knees, her footing slipped in a puddle of her blood. She could no longer fight back, and strangely, she accepted her fate. Maxine could barely see. She could barely move, her body depleted. Her breathing was sparse; it was the end of the road for her.

Now, the entire family stood around her, glaring at the beaten sociopath.

"Get it over with," she said defiantly.

Scott spoke, "In due time, Maxine. There will be no quick death for you. I've hired the best, and when I say he's the best torturer in North America, I tell you no lie. You will die a few times tonight, be brought back to life, only to die again! Mark my words, you will die thrice for each child of mine you had buried."

Scott had hired Alan Crippen. He was the best of the best of them and was waiting for his next lab rat. Alan was waiting at a clinic he owned in Sag Harbor, New York, not far from the Hamptons. There, he had a full medical lab where he could live out all his sick, twisted fantasies. He specialized in bringing his victims to the brink of death and then reviving them so he could torture them more. The record number of reviving one person up to date was thirteen times. He literally had one victim who he had killed over a dozen times before the man finally succumbed to his injuries, and on the last attempt, he could not be revived. Scott had arranged an insidious way of causing her death, but he felt she deserved nothing less than depravity.

Bugsy crotched beside Maxine, ready to cover her mouth and wrists with duct tape so she could be quietly transported, but before he did so, she had one final thing to say to him. "At least I'll get to see *my* son again…so fuck you!"

He covered her mouth with the tape, silencing her sarcasm. He then replied, "Where you're going, *my* son won't be there." Bugsy wasn't finished with the assault. His fists again smashed into Maxine's head, upper body, back, and stomach until he had knocked her unconscious. Meyer and Scott had to drag the emotionally unstable Bugsy off her. No one in that room wanted Maxine to die that easily.

Chapter 39

With Maxine's body limp, it would be Layla and Lucky with the ultimate task of transporting Maxine to her doomsday. Scott said, "Mason carry this trash down to Lucky's G-wagon."

Mason scooped up Maxine's lifeless body like a husband carries a wife, while Layla grabbed their victim's purse. Layla wanted to keep Maxine's handbag as a reminder of her demise. She would have it framed in plexiglass and placed in her closet, so each day she got dressed, she would think about the day she snuffed this bitch's lights out.

Scott continued, "Throw this bitch in Lucky's trunk—"

"My trunks full," Lucky said.

Scott was about to offer his SUV for transport when Bugsy chimed in, "Mason throw her in the backseat…and Lucky, make sure you put the child safety on so she can't escape. Call us when y'all get to Sag Harbor. We'll be right behind y'all."

Mason carried Maxine's battered body to the private elevator and pressed the parking garage where Lucky's G-wagon was waiting. Once in the lot, Lucky had a change of plans. She looked at the bloody, almost dead corpse and frowned. Bugsy had put a hurting on Maxine, and there wasn't any way she would let her bleed all over her vehicle.

"Mason, we gonna take Maxine's car."

"My car!" Layla corrected. "My husband's money bought this Benz and what's his is mine."

They were in the middle of murder and mayhem, and Layla couldn't resist marking her territory. She would war with Maxine over Scott until her nemesis took her last breath. Lucky's eyes rolled in her head, but she said nothing. She checked Maxine's coat pocket and purse for her keys, but they weren't there. Aggressively, she checked her jeans and found them.

Lucky hurried off to retrieve Maxine's vehicle while the other's stood impatiently and cautiously to the side—just a few feet out of the view of the building's surveillance cameras. Layla stared at the unresponsive Maxine in Mason's arms with disgust. She glared at the kid killer and wanted to rip her apart with her bare hands.

"It's in your best interest to not wake back up, bitch," Layla whispered in Maxine's ear. "If you thought what my son did to you was unbearable, just wait until you feel what my husband and I've planned…."

Mason listened to Layla mercilessly berate Maxine and hoped that the impending torture could give the two people who were his bosses and whom he considered friends, closure.

Lucky backed the Benz sedan up just a couple feet from Mason and Layla. She hopped out and popped the trunk. Everyone exhaled as they stared down at Dillinger's carriage, a new walker, and other items her dead son would never get to use.

"Fuck!" Layla cursed. Why hadn't they prepared for the transport more efficiently?

"What y'all wanna do?" Mason asked. His arms were tiring of holding Maxine, her body feeling like dead weight.

"Put her in the backseat," Lucky instructed, taking control. She ran and checked, and the child safety lock was already on. "She can't get out."

"Let that bitch try," Layla said and pulled out her pistol. "And I'll blow her fuckin' head off!"

Chapter 40

Murder Inc. felt like they had made the right move coming to Scott about Maxine's diabolical plan. This was their avenue into the Garcia cartel, and they didn't even have to get their hands dirty. And for Scott to allow them to keep the two-million-dollars that Maxine had given them was mind-blowing. They loved working with men of this caliber.

Mason had rejoined the party. All the men and Marisol stood around the living room, smiles all around. As if the fact that Maxine was being driven to be tortured and ultimately murdered didn't happen. As if Scott West hadn't just come back from the dead. As if a confession letter wasn't just read. As if a murder-for-hire tape wasn't just played.

Scott poured his guests a three-finger glass of Macallan 25, and everyone clinked glasses in a celebratory manner. The Cuban cigars came next. The living room quickly filled with laughter and thick smoke rings.

"I owe a lot to this man," Scott said and nodded toward Juan-Pablo, who beamed. "He had a difficult choice to make, and he made it."

Juan looked at Marisol, and she was grinning from ear to ear. He was her man, and he had taken them to the next level with his wit and quick thinking. No one could outsmart him. Not in her book.

Scott continued, "He did what was best for him, his crew, and his family." Scott nodded toward Diego, Miguel, Luis, and Marisol—all felt like they were being inducted into the Hall of Fame. "And this is how I do what's best for me, my crew, and my family."

Mason, Bugsy, Meyer, Avery, and Chopper all pulled out wires, wrapped them tightly around their unsuspecting guests of honor necks, and strangled the lives out of them as Scott watched. Each strangulation took over four minutes, some longer, as each person struggled. Truthfully, these weren't easy kills. Everyone fought hard for their lives, including Marisol, scratching, and clawing at the hands of their assailant.

When the last body dropped to the floor, Scott said, "Get them the fuck outta my fuckin' house!"

Scott didn't believe in absolution. The fact that Juan-Pablo would even take the contract on his life was a violation to him. And if Scott didn't put him down now, he would have to later. A man like Juan-Pablo and his Murder Inc. crew could never be trusted, and it would only take a matter of time before they revisited the subject of murdering Scott West.

Scott continued issuing orders, "Mason, I want you to take Zaire and Kane with you to Bonita's and find my muthafuckin' bread. Kill Marisol's mother and whoever you deem as a threat. Hit the rest of Murder Incorporated's families and leave no witnesses. Before the sun rises, I want all ties to Murder Inc. to be permanently dismantled."

The large suitcases were brought out, and a body was placed in each. That apartment had enough heat, so disposing of the bodies with the utmost discretion was imperative. Everyone loaded into the private elevator with their respective suitcases and headed to the parking garage. When the doors opened, Bugsy noticed the anomaly. He saw Lucky's G-wagon, looked around, and noticed that Maxine's AMG Benz was gone.

"Fuck!" he called out, and everyone froze.

"What's up, bruh? What's going on?" Meyer wanted to know, as did everyone in the garage. The men placed their hands on their pistols, thinking that a threat was coming around the corner. But Bugsy was on his cell, dialing his sister.

"Lucky, watch Maxine. The child lock in her car—"

"I know," Lucky yelled. "The bitch made us crash the car on the Brooklyn Bridge. She's gone, Bugsy."

"What do you mean, gone?"

"Your lunatic baby mama was so shook about being tortured that she jumped off the bridge. She's dead!" Lucky was angered and disappointed that they wouldn't get to see her suffer. "The coast guard and helicopters are all out here. The bridge has been shut down…it's fucking chaos."

"You sure she's dead?"

"No one can survive that fall, and if they did, they couldn't survive long in that frigid water. This will be a body recovery, not a search and rescue."

"What's that?" Bugsy heard an unrecognizable sound, a screeching wail that had echoed through the phone.

Lucky whispered, "That's Layla. When she saw Maxine climb over the railing of the bridge and then jump, she lost it. She was looking forward to her suffering, so nothing I say can console her."

Bugsy hung up and felt ambivalent. Maxine had hurt him deeply, but he would be lying if he said that he wasn't mad she died her way and had avoided days of torture. He announced to the garage full of killers Maxine's fate, and everyone went ballistic.

"That's one lucky dead bitch!" Meyer said.

"She didn't deserve a quick death," Mason added, feeling that her neck broke as soon as she hit the water from that height.

"That shit ain't right…not after what she did to Gotti, Bonnie, and Clyde. Where's the justice?" Chopper chimed in.

Finally, Bugsy said, "Dead is dead."

Their whole plan was coming together. They'd purposely held off on exposing Maxine until they murdered her baby. It was a coldhearted act, and they wanted Maxine to suffer as they'd suffered. Layla refused to have any grandson of hers tainted with the same blood as Maxine's. And now that Maxine and Dillinger were out the way, it was only a matter of time before Bugsy and Lucky followed the same fate. They felt they were at the point of no return. Once they ordered the death of a baby, there was no turning back.

"I heard you took Maxine's suicide hard," Scott said. He had just come home after a long night of body disposals. "What's wrong? Talk to me."

Layla was lying on the couch with a cold rag over her forehead. Her eyes were puffy, her face streaked with tears, and she felt nauseated. Layla had cried until no more tears were produced. When Maxine sprang up from the backseat and kicked Lucky on the side of her head, things went in slow motion. The car veered across a lane and was hit from behind by another vehicle. The Benz smashed against the bridge's metal beams until it came to a forced stop. Both airbags dislodged temporarily dazing Lucky and Layla as Maxine scrambled to get out of the backseat.

With what little life Maxine had inside her, she used to slowly zombie walk the bridge. She tried to scream out, to ask for help, but she didn't have the energy to formulate any words. Horns honked and angry New Yorkers who drove by cursed the insane woman who seemed to flee from the scene of an accident. When Layla and Lucky finally exited the totaled vehicle, Maxine was nearly across the bridge. The mother and daughter took off running.

The male driver who had rammed into their trunk was confused. Why had the occupants of the car taken off? The uninsured driver started his vehicle and fled too. He passed Layla and Lucky and made a speedy getaway.

"Maxine," Layla called, and she turned to face her abductors. "Stop running...we won't hurt you."

Maxine could see Layla reaching for her gun, and she had a decision to make. With the last ounce of momentum she had, Maxine scurried to the railing, climbed over, closed her eyes, and jumped.

Dillinger, mama's coming, she thought as her body floated through the air before crash landing into the icy East River water below.

Layla had watched in horror. As Maxine's body sank out of view, so did her heart. This wasn't supposed to happen.

"All our planning, all that fuckin' waiting, and for what? For her to go out on her terms. I promised that bitch that she would suffer."

Scott could see the turmoil on his wife's face. Layla didn't look angry; she looked defeated. Maxine was her rival for decades, so Layla wanted a spectacle when she took her revenge. He sat down next to her and took her hand into his. Scott said, "Layla, you know how the game goes, it's unpredictability. That's what you love about the hustle—there's always a challenge. Let's not dwell on how Maxine met her demise, let's celebrate that she's dead."

"But our babies, Scott...."

"Our children have been vindicated. They're in heaven knowing that their parents were the catalysts who ultimately brought about Maxine's end. She's gone...never coming back. Let's move forward because we still got more shit to do."

Chapter 41

Bugsy took a large swig from the Jack Daniels; the brown liquor went down his throat quickly—a quarter of the bottle left to finish. He sat in the driver's seat of his Bentley, parked near Central Park. He wanted to be alone. He wanted to get drunk and forget about his problems, but it was difficult. Maxine's body was floating somewhere or crashing up against large rocks or might never be found. Bugsy was hard on himself. How could he have not seen who she was? She had convinced him she was the opposite of his mother when they were cut from the same cloth of treachery. It was his world, and there was no escape from it. Bugsy wanted to become unhinged. He didn't want to care anymore—maybe drink himself to death—or perhaps a rival would blow his head off. He cursed himself. He seethed, he wept, he mourned. He was angry and alone. And then he thought about her—the one woman he loved. The one woman he knew would never betray him. The one woman who had always been there for him and who he wanted children with. She didn't come with a checkered past or baggage, and she didn't have previous relationships with anyone in his family. She was honest with him, pure. It was his lifestyle and his deadly organization that drove her away. But now he wanted her back. Bugsy strongly felt he needed Alicia in his life—now more than ever.

The next day, he reached out to an associate named MacArthur. He wanted Mac to track down his old flame.

"I'll see what I can do," said MacArthur.

"I just want to know where she is and if she's okay."

Mac took less than a week to track down Alicia. He came to Bugsy with the news. "She's staying in Connecticut…rents a cozy three-bedroom home right outside of Stamford. She's still in the medical profession, works the graveyard shift at Stamford hospital."

It had been over a year since he last saw her, and he greatly missed her. She was his everything. She was the woman he wanted to marry. He had become so broken up about her he ran into the arms of Maxine.

Bugsy arrived at her two-story home in the quiet and suburban part of Stamford. It was the early evening when he parked in front of a navy-blue house with a long white front porch and white shutters. There was a narrow driveway leading to a one-car garage. The place was neat, with manicured grass, lovely flowers lining the walkway to the front porch, and trimmed shrubbery. It was cozy and quiet, and the neighborhood where people kept to themselves and greeted you with 'good morning' and 'good evening.' It was the perfect place for Alicia.

Bugsy climbed out of his car, looking handsome like always, carrying a large bouquet of flowers. He came unannounced, invading her privacy, and hoped that he wasn't too forward. He approached her front door and knocked. He waited, a moment went by, and there was no answer. He banged repeatedly and still no response. He didn't travel to Connecticut to turn around and go back home so he would wait—Alicia was worth it. He walked back to his car and sat behind the wheel, and to pass the time, he assaulted the liquor bottle.

A few hours went by, and Bugsy felt his legs getting cramped. He was just about to get out and stretch his legs when a Lexus jeep pulled into the driveway and parked. Bugsy perked up. Music was blaring from the vehicle, and Bugsy could make out that it was Alicia sitting in the passenger's seat. It bothered him she was with a man. He fumed, immediately climbing out from his car and hastily approached the passenger's side. There was no second-guessing his actions. He tapped on the passenger window, startling the vehicle's occupants.

"Bugsy," she uttered with uncertainty.

She rolled down the window to get a better look at him. And there he stood, at her home, after all this time had passed. "What are you doing here?" she asked him.

"I need to talk to you. Get out the car," he said with authority in his tone.

Alicia didn't know where to begin with him. She felt ambivalent about his unexpected visit to her new home and her new life. Bugsy acted like she was alone as if there wasn't a male driver sitting right next to her.

The man frowned at Bugsy. He felt disrespected. "Is this dude serious?" the driver griped. He glared at Bugsy, but Bugsy wasn't budging. He desperately wanted to have a word with Alicia, in private, and he clarified that to her male friend. But the driver wasn't having it. He turned off his ignition and jumped out of his car and approached Bugsy. Alicia tried to stop him, but the fuse had been lit. The handle of Bugsy's gun smashed against the man's face, bloodying his nose, making it leak like a drippy faucet. He shrieked from the pain and cupped his injury with both hands. Bugsy struck him again and again, pistol-whipping the man until he succumbed to his knees. Tonight, Bugsy would show this man he should have stayed seated behind the wheel and not fuck with him. Alicia sprung from the passenger's side in panic and immediately came between them.

"Stop it!" she shouted. "Please! Stop." Her eyes cut angrily at Bugsy. She felt disgusted by his actions. "What is wrong with you?"

Suddenly, Bugsy looked remorseful. He didn't mean to lose control so quickly. "I'm sorry, baby…I just needed to talk to you. I needed to see you," he pleaded with her.

She looked down at her friend, and he was in bad shape, but he would live.

Bugsy put away the gun, and then he reached into his pocket and pulled out a wad of bills. He peeled off two-thousand-dollars in hundred-dollar bills and tossed it down at the man's knees. He then said, "If you need more, let Alicia know. I apologize. I lost control." He looked at Alicia, who still looked at him angrily and said, "I'm sorry. I didn't mean for this to happen."

"What do you want from me, Bugsy?"

"A moment of your time, please, Alicia," he replied anxiously.

Neighbors peeked out from their windows, and Alicia didn't want the cops coming to her front door. She loved her new home and wanted no drama at her place. But Alicia had never seen Bugsy looking so unbalanced. For as long as she knew him, he was always well put together. And in control, from his emotions to his physical being. Now, he was falling apart.

She turned and looked down at her friend. He picked himself up from his knees and held a handkerchief to his nose, trying to stop the bleeding. She sighed. Five minutes back into her life, and there was already violence.

"I'm sorry," Bugsy uttered to him and her once again.

The man was defeated. He knew when to call it quits—Bugsy was a gangsta, and it showed in his eyes. Quietly he picked up the cash from the ground, got in his Lexus, and left, knowing that with a man like Bugsy, you don't call the police.

Alicia glared at him. "What do you want?"

"Can we go somewhere?"

She felt reluctant to leave with him. Alicia noticed her neighbors were still gawking at her from their windows, the last thing she needed was a problem with her landlord. She left with Bugsy before her street turned into a reality show. She climbed into the passenger's seat of his vehicle, and they drove off.

"Where are you taking me?" she asked him.

"Somewhere quiet," he said.

She rode in silence. She was still upset with Bugsy, but something about him made her body tingle with excitement. She missed him, too. But could she deal with his dysfunctional family and his chaotic lifestyle again? It was a question that spun around in her mind repeatedly.

Their drive ended up at a hotel, and Alicia didn't look too pleased where Bugsy parked. She cut her eyes at him and said, "Seriously, …you bring me to a hotel?"

"I didn't hear you invite me inside your home," he said.

"But a hotel? You couldn't drive to a restaurant?"

He moaned. "If you feel uncomfortable…."

"I'm not!" She chuckled strangely and continued with, "I just witnessed you beat the shit out of my friend, and now I'm at a hotel with you. I must be losing it too."

She looked at him, and he was so handsome—still fine. But his eyes were sad. *Is it because he misses me?* She thought. She exhaled and said, "C'mon, let's talk."

Bugsy paid for the room for one night, and the two went to the fourth floor and entered a cozy, one-bedroom where it would be just them two. Bugsy sat on the bed while Alicia stood with her arms folded across her chest, placing a barrier between them. When he looked up at her with more sadness than she had ever seen in her life, she asked, "What's happened? What's going on? Talk to me."

Mournfully he announced, "They murdered my baby boy, and I don't know how to cope...what to do? I'm fucked up...and I need help."

The announcement leveled her. So much had happened since they parted ways. Bugsy was in tears. He was in an unfathomable pain and falling deeper into despair. Alicia had never seen him like this before. It was bad. But she was in shock he had a baby. Suddenly, she felt a tinge of jealousy from the news. However, she needed to table her feelings and focus on Bugsy's pain. The words 'baby' and 'murder' shouldn't be in the same sentence. But coming from his world, they were.

She sat down next to him and rubbed his back. Round, slow motions meant to soothe and console the grieving father. She would allow him to cry on her shoulder or in her arms—anything to ease his pain. Bugsy was a man's man, but he looked so distraught that it almost canceled out who he was and what he was about.

"I'm here, Bugsy," she said sincerely.

He huffed. He locked eyes with Alicia, and right there, he knew he could always trust her. She was as beautiful as ever—an angel on earth. Her angelic features brought about some comfort in Bugsy. There was no disputing it; she was the best thing that ever happened in his life.

"There's a lot to say, so I'm just gonna say it. I need you, Alicia. I want you back. My world has been hell without you," he confessed.

"What happened to your baby?"

"My little man, my son, his name was Dillinger John West, and he was murdered in his crib."

Alicia's mouth gaped open. "Oh, my God, no!"

"They slit his throat like he was an animal. It was all over the news. You didn't hear about it?"

She shook her head. How could she have missed this horrific news? Tears streamed down her high cheekbones, and Bugsy consoled her. Alicia took the story harder than he thought she would. Bugsy talked, and he spared no details. He looked at Alicia and told her everything—minus him murdering anyone.

"I'm sorry this happened to you, Bugsy. That is so tragic. But I'm here for you, baby...I'm here."

He nodded. Those words were reassuring to hear, needed to get his mind right. He had to become focused again, and he knew he needed Alicia for that. She gave good advice and, most important, he trusted her.

"Damn, I missed you," he whispered.

"I missed you too," she admitted.

Things transitioned from anguish to intimacy. They couldn't stop looking at each other. And then it happened, they shared a passionate kiss. It felt amazing for him to touch her lips again like fireworks were going off inside of him.

"I love you," Bugsy said breathlessly.

"I love you, too."

It didn't take long for her clothes to peel off, and his, and Alicia lay naked underneath him, parting her legs and allowing him inside of her. He penetrated her slowly, and they made love.

After an hour of passion, Bugsy fell asleep while Alicia was wide awake.

Morning came, and Bugsy woke up embracing Alicia in his arms. He looked at her and whispered, "I don't wanna lose you again. Can we start over?"

She sighed. "Maybe, Bugsy. But I need time and some space to think."

"I'll give you all the time and space you need."

Chapter 42

Angel lit his Cuban cigar and stood by the large window and smoked contentedly. He took comfort in his sprawling compound on South Beach, the contemporary structure was over 8,000 square feet with an Olympic size pool and a large guest house. The place had two kitchens, an exercise room, an elevator, and a tennis court. He watched the landscapers working on his lawn and admired how they always took outstanding care of his property. He liked his grass manicured, and the trees and hedges trimmed neatly. He took pride in his estates and his expensive vehicles. His South Beach residence was well appointed, with all the high-tech amenities one could ever dream of. His armed security team regularly patrolled the area with automatic weapons, and he had CCTV cameras pointed everywhere.

From the window, he observed his wife, Dahlia, and kids enjoying the infinity pool. His wife was a beautiful woman—a goddess in his eyes with long sensuous hair, a bright, broad smile, and fiery disposition. She gave him three children—two boys and a girl, and he gave her her heart's desires. Dahlia didn't lift a finger around the estates, Angel had hired a gaggle of servants to wait on his family around the clock.

Angel finished the cigar and went to join his family. His wife was sunbathing in one of the lounge chairs, her tanned skin glowed under the hot sun. She wore a skimpy two-piece bikini valued at $400. She was dripping in diamonds and pearls, her wedding ring and band weighing down her dainty finger.

"Who are these three little fish posing as my children…," he said to them in Spanish.

His children giggled, climbing out from the pool and continued to horse around, laughing and chasing each other.

"Listen," he announced. "It's time to go and get ready for dinner. We have a reservation for six."

The kids were excited. His wife gathered her little ones, and they all retreated into their home to shower and dress for the evening.

Angel looked handsome, and his wife looked stunning. His two sons and daughter were dressed like members of the royal family in their conservative outfits. The black Rolls Royce Phantom sat idling out front, and their chauffeur stood near the rear door, waiting for the family to climb into the vehicle. As they approached, Angel's eyes looked over at the landscapers, and he noticed they were taking longer than expected to finish. It appeared they were lingering. He stared at a few men, seeing that several landscapers were watching him. It was strange. Angel's gaze went from one of the men's faces traveling down to his hands, and he saw the weapon—an Uzi, it was cleverly concealed and removed from a black garbage bag. Immediately he alerted his men, shouting, "It's an attack!"

His words boomed out like an explosion, and right away, several landscapers went from working men to hitmen. Uzi's and automatic weapons were briskly brandished and aimed toward Angel and his family. They didn't hesitate to open fire.

Rat-ta-tat-tat-tat-tat-tat-tat!

Bak! Bak! Bak!

Angel drastically pulled his wife and kids down to the concrete as gunfire erupted. His armed goons immediately returned fire. Bullets saturated the front entrance to his home as an intense gunfight erupted. The glass to the Phantom shattered and shards of glass rained down on them. His chauffeur, unfortunately, was riddled with bullets, his body plummeted to the ground near his kids. They were horrified at the sight of him and the violence.

Rat-ta-tat-tat-tat-tat-tat-tat!

"Protect the boss!" Angel's lieutenant screamed.

From each side, men went down in the violent melee. Angel did his best to cover his family from the barrage of bullets. He shielded his kids with his own body as they hugged the ground. His wife used her body to shield them too. She looked over at her husband with a deep fear and panic written on her face.

"Kill them all!" Angel shouted.

Angel knew he couldn't be a sitting duck for too long. There were many men suddenly coming from out of nowhere. His soldiers were doing their best to wipe them all out, but his enemies were vast and skilled. Angel's cousin, Louis, took extreme action. He risked his own life by charging into battle with the Heckler & Koch MP5A2 and mowed down several men.

Louis geared up near the driver's side, letting off a volley of shots at their foes, and yelled, "Boss, get them in the car! Now!"

Angel picked himself up and hurriedly shoved his kids and his family into the backseat of the Phantom. His enforcer, Oscar, pulled out the chauffeur and thrust himself behind the wheel of the vehicle, and it sped off from the violent fight. The car fishtailed at first and fled at top speed as it continued to be riddled with bullets. Angel was grateful for Louis and Oscar. But he fumed. Where was Alejandro? He was his top enforcer, and he had allowed this to happen.

His two sons and daughter were crying hysterically. They had been cut by flying glass, and their elbows were bruised and scraped from the hard fall. His wife was in shock.

"Muthafuckin' putas!" Angel angrily shouted.

An attempt on his life was typical. He had narrowly escaped many hits against him. But none had ever come so close to a property he bought for his family. They had escaped unharmed, but the fact that their lives had been put in danger meant that whoever sanctioned the hit would suffer the consequences. He would kill them all.

His first thought was his longtime nemesis, The Garcia cartel. They hit him; he hit them back twice as hard. It was an ongoing feud between both cartels.

He took a couple hours to get his family on a private jet to fly them back to Mexico to their fortified estate where they'd be safe. He had officially declared war with the Garcia cartel when he'd murdered Hector Garcia, the nephew of the drug kingpin, Javier. Angel thought his rival wouldn't find out; apparently, he did. Now, may the best cartel win.

Chapter 43

The cellphone chimed in the bedroom, waking up Scott from his sleep. It was early morning, and Scott turned in his bed, reaching for his ringing phone on the nightstand. He noticed that Layla wasn't lying next to him and could hear the shower running. He answered the unknown number. Immediately he heard Javier say, "Did I wake you?"

Javier calling him at this time of the morning meant only one thing; that it was urgent. Javier had his undivided attention.

"No, what is it?" he asked.

"As you know, I'm at war with the Juarez cartel. Two of my compounds were hit late last night, a lot of casualties. I lost a lot of good men."

"What can I do to help?"

"I'm aware that your children are doing business with them. So as a courtesy to you, who I respect, I want you to know that your children could become collateral damage. And if so, if they are caught between any crossfire that there won't be an issue with you. Their ally is my enemy...but you, Scott, I still consider a friend."

Scott sat quietly for a moment, and then replied, "Fuck 'em! If they're stupid enough to side with our enemy, then they chose death."

"This is why I always liked you. You're grounded with loyalty."

"You and I have many years together, Javier, and I respect our friendship and our business arrangement."

"That is good to know," Javier replied. "I'll be in touch."

It was a brief conversation. Scott lingered on his bed, contemplating the fallout his children would have from their continued disloyalty.

Layla came out of the bathroom, toweling off. She looked at her husband and asked, "Who was on the phone?"

"Javier."

"What did he want?"

"My blessing," Scott replied.

"For what?"

Scott explained, "He knows that our children are working with the Juarez cartel, and they're at war."

"Oh."

"Not what we planned but a plan nonetheless."

Layla was concerned. "But what about Meyer?"

Avery advised them that their children went after Angel for Dillinger's murder—which was exactly how Scott and Layla wanted it to play out. However, Angel must have believed that the hit came from the Garcia cartel. What Scott didn't know and couldn't factor in as a variable was that his daughter had murdered the nephew of Javier Garcia in cold blood at the behest of Angel. The only people who knew that fact was Lucky and the Juarez cartel, so, therefore, Angel assumed the heat came from his archenemy.

Scott didn't like it. The plan was now capricious. With Angel focused on the Garcia cartel, Angel left himself wide open to be taken out by his children. And with Angel gone, then the feud between the Juarez and Garcia cartels quickly dissipates, and his children would be spared.

"There's a chance they could walk away victors in all this."

Layla thought for a second and gleaned where her husband's head was at. "You know, we can still handle Lucky and Bugsy ourselves."

Scott's head shook rapidly. They needed to refocused Angel's attention back to the real focal points—Bugsy and Lucky. Scott needed Angel to unwittingly do their dirty work. "Go stand and look out the window. Fifty-stories down is an unmarked van with federal agents just waiting for us to move recklessly. They've increased surveillance on us after Dillinger's murder. I've said this once, Layla, but it'll be death by a fed before I do life behind bars."

She understood and wanted to help. Her husband had spent too much of his days planning this out down to the last detail. She said, "Don't worry, I'll meet with Angel personally and drop a dime on them. He likes me. We'll talk."

Scott smiled. He loved it when they plotted together.

Layla sat in the backseat of the Bentley and stared out the side window. The luxury vehicle traveled through one of the most impoverished areas in Mexico. The town was south of Chihuahua. It was rough and battered with poverty. To Layla, the city seemed to be a bleak-looking place with dusty and partially paved roads and dirty looking people. The buildings and homes looked dilapidated, and many lacked basic amenities like toilets or clean water. Their roofs were made of thin layers of either metal, plastic, or even cardboard material. Layla had never seen poor like this, some kids without shoes, and everyone had a look of hopelessness.

But she wasn't a humanitarian nor was she there to give charity. She was only there to meet with Angel. So Layla sat back and traveled through the town, turning her head from the dreary folks and focusing ahead. The driver continued down a dirt road, and they soon arrived upon two towering iron gates, and behind them was a sprawling compound. The gates opened, and they proceeded toward a two-story well-fortified structure that didn't look welcoming to any visitors. Everywhere Layla looked, there were armed men, and some with dogs that looked like their teeth could cut through bones—also, lots of guns and armored vehicles. Everything about the place was a direct contrast to the poor and luckless town she just passed through.

The Bentley came to a complete stop in front of a long and wide porch with several concrete pillars. Several men with machine guns stood around and watched the vehicle intently. Layla sighed and uttered to herself, "Here we go."

She swung the door opened, and her stylish heels touched the ground, and she stood up, looking ahead. *Fuckin' Mexico*, she thought. She hated the place already. It wasn't her cup of tea. Soon, she was escorted into the building, guided through the long hallways, and invited into a room. Inside the room was Angel seated behind a desk, looking less than merciful. He was at war with another cartel, and they almost killed him and his family. Every move he made was calculated, and every person he met with skepticism. He looked at her and said, "Welcome to my lair."

"Said the snake to the frog."

Angel shrugged. "You came a long way. What is it that you want that you couldn't tell me over the phone?"

Layla couldn't wait to leave and get back on American soil. "I came to ask for a favor and forgiveness from you."

"A favor and forgiveness? Do I look like I'm in a favorable and forgiving mood? Men nearly wiped out my entire family."

"I heard, that was tragic," she said with empathy. "I'm sorry that had to happen to you."

"You didn't travel all this way to Mexico to show me sympathy, so what is your favor and forgiveness?"

"What can I do to stop the hit on my granddaughter?"

Angel was far from a simpleton, but he was genuinely puzzled. He replied, "Your granddaughter."

"Yes. You've already taken my grandson. I don't wanna lose anyone else. My son, Bugsy, it was his son you killed, and he wants his revenge."

Angel was taken aback by Layla's words. Though he was upset, he didn't show it. "I had nothing to do with a baby being murdered. You are mistaken," he said. "But Lucky, she did have a girl and not a boy?"

"Yes, of course. She's a beautiful baby girl, and her name is Lucchese Lily West. We call her Lulu for short. She's my first granddaughter, and we can't lose her, Angel."

Angel sat there brooding, and then Layla added the icing on the cake by saying, "Would you like to see pictures of her? Of your daughter?"

"Of course," he said.

She removed several pictures from an envelope she carried and placed them on his desk in front of him. It was as if he was inspecting every image for authenticity. He looked closely at Lucchese with her light skin and bone-straight black hair indicative of her mixed-race to Angel. The baby looked just like his daughter, Ariella when she was a toddler, proof to him he could be the father. He sat there, deducing everything that transpired. He realized the reason his men were being killed and that his own family was almost gunned down. *Lucky, that slick fuckin' bitch*, he thought to himself.

"I promise you that I had nothing to do with the hit on your grandson and that I have no plans on killing a child, especially my child," he said.

"But Lucky tells me otherwise. She feels threatened by you. She said that you've threatened to kill the West's third-generation because she ended her relationship with you."

Angel was amused that he was described as a spurned lover. "I assure you, your daughter has quite the imagination. I would never take a child from their mother. Do I look like an animal to you?"

"No, you don't." Layla smiled. "But it's Bugsy you need to convince. He believes otherwise."

"I will contact Bugsy personally and let him know that I had nothing to do with his son's murder. And will also offer my assistance to help find out who did. Layla, please, don't worry. Sí?"

"Yes."

She knew it was a lie, but she loved every word of it. She felt that Angel's attention had shifted back toward Lucky and, ultimately, Bugsy. Her trip to Mexico was concluded.

Chapter 44

Her legs were tangled around his, his arms were placed around her curvy frame. And her breasts and nipples were pressed against his bare chest as the two laid naked under the sheets. It was only hours ago that Bugsy had made intense love to Alicia. The way he was inside of her, it was tantalizing and the way he held her afterward as if he never wanted to let her go—it was love. Alicia opened her eyes to see Bugsy awake. He smiled at her while running his hands over her body. He ran his hands down her backside and whispered, "Good morning, baby."

"Good morning," she returned.

It was a beautiful sunny morning, and the two wanted nothing more but to linger in bed and remain close. Alicia welcomed Bugsy into her home and into her bedroom, and they made every minute count.

"I need to use the bathroom," Bugsy said.

"Go ahead. I'll be waiting right here." She smiled.

Bugsy seemed hesitant to remove himself from her warm grasp, but nature was calling. Butt naked, he climbed out of bed and went into her bathroom. Alicia had only thought about him lately. Being so close and intimate with Bugsy again made her realize how much she missed him. Alicia had dated two men after she broke up with him, they were kind, handsome, but they weren't Bugsy. It was a no-brainer when she went back to him.

For days they stayed cooped up in her home ordering take out and making sweet, passionate love. Alicia had vacation days, so she used them to be with Bugsy. The two lazily relaxed in her home, watching Netflix and chilled, renting movies, playing cards, and simply conversed. Bugsy felt like he was on vacation, and he acted as if he wasn't at war. He was back where he wanted to be, with Alicia, living a simpler life with her, though he knew it was only temporary.

Meanwhile, in NYC, Meyer had gotten back with Lollipop, and she had easily forgiven his long absence. And for a moment, it seemed like they were the proud parents of Lulu. Lucky was always away, off somewhere being sneaky. Meyer would occasionally go by Lucky's apartment and take Lulu from Maria for a few days. And it didn't take long for Bugsy and Alicia to become involved in his niece's life too. Lulu had become essential in Bugsy's healing over the murder of his son, and seeing how Alicia had fallen for the baby with the prettiest face ever, it put him in a friendlier mood. Everyone enjoyed having Lulu in their lives. She was always smiling and trying to speak already. She was alert for her age, and Meyer called her a baby genius when she did some of the smallest things. And soon, the uncles were fighting over who Lulu got to spend the night with. The twins, two hardcore gangstas, were becoming like two men and a baby, feeding bottles and changing diapers, and their better halves enjoyed seeing the bonding with their niece.

Layla sat sipping a margarita on the terrace high above the city, enjoying her privileged lifestyle. She felt that her meeting with Angel went well, and knowing that soon, the outcome of her meeting would unfold.

Her cellphone rang. It was Scott. "Make the calls," he instructed. Layla called each one of her children and invited them to travel with her and Scott on vacation to Australia. As expected, Bugsy and Lucky unequivocally told her no.

"I can't make it," Bugsy told his mother.

"I got shit to do," Lucky replied.

There was not a chance in hell they would fly across the world to spend quality time with their parents. After the deaths of Maxine and Murder Incorporated were carried out, the family splintered again. Everyone went their separate ways because murdering enemies couldn't be the glue to put the West family back together. Too much betrayal, too much death, and too many lies had been exchanged for anyone to let bygones be bygones.

Meyer contemplated the trip. He felt it was an excellent time to get away, perhaps bring Lollipop, but once he discovered that a flight from the states to Australia was nearly twenty-two hours long, he too declined the trip. Who could spend damn near an entire day trapped on an airplane was insanity? It wasn't for him.

Scott and Layla didn't want their Judas children on vacation with them and was relieved that they all declined. Both knew that any day the shit would hit the fan, and to avoid federal scrutiny, they would leave the country, and hopefully come home to the aftermath—ultimately with both their children finally dead.

Chapter 45

As the two black Range Rovers sped down the desert dirt road, a cloud of dust billowed behind them. Angel sat in the backseat of the first vehicle, and he was flanked by his armed goons. He sat in silence, contemplating the weight of this meeting. For miles and miles, there wasn't anything but wasteland—the roar of the two vehicles the only sound around for miles.

A mile ahead, the driver could see some activity. There were two vehicles at rest, waiting on their arrival. Seeing this, Angel perked up. His meeting with Javier Garcia was only moments away. He could already see that his rival had come with his own small army of men. Angel fixed his eyes ahead and prepared himself for a serious encounter with a man just as powerful and wealthy as himself.

The Range's came to a stop a few yards away from Javier's two Hummers. Doors opened, and several men climbed out of the vehicles, their automatic weapons trained on their rivals. This was a cordial meeting between the two drug lords. It was one that Angel had called to establish a truce between both factions. They agreed to meet at a neutral location, and they both came with some serious firepower.

Javier and Angel walked ahead of their men to converse in private. They didn't greet each other with handshakes because it wasn't that type of party. Angel squared off with Javier, and said, "I had your nephew killed, but it was done so under false intel." That was only half the truth, the half that mattered.

Javier frowned heavily. "And why shouldn't I have my men blow your head off right now?"

"Please, Javier, no threats."

"Under false intel or not, my nephew's death needs to be avenged," Javier said.

"I can help with that. I may have information that you'd like to hear."

"There's no such thing as help from you, Angel," Javier griped.

Angel knew he had to be the voice of reasoning. He understood that the two Mexican cartels would always be at war, fighting over borders, drugs, and territory. However, he needed to focus his resources against one empire, the West Empire.

"The West organization are our threats," said Angel.

"I have no quarrels with Scott West."

"Neither do I," Angel explained, "But his children are not just my enemies. They're yours too."

"Stop with the games," Javier roared. "We both know that they are under your umbrella, so how is that an issue for me!"

"Because it was Lucky West who pulled the trigger," Angel explained. "And I sanctioned the hit, but as I said, it was under false intel from the West children."

Javier's interest was piqued. But he was too enraged to come to any agreement between them. Until he got justice for his nephew, there was no reasoning—no bipartisanship between them.

Javier said, "We war until both of us are dead, and when we're gone, our children will take over and continue this conflict."

Angel knew there would never be a lasting reconciliation between them, but he couldn't have his men fighting two wars at once. He locked eyes with Javier determined to accomplish something before they both went their separate ways. He said, "What can I do right now to pause this discord between us?"

Javier smirked. "Well, that's simple; I would need to kill a member of *your* family."

He was serious. Angel dwelled on the thought for a moment, he uttered the word, "Done!" and then he looked back at two of the goons with him. Alejandro was his brother, and Louis was his cousin. Angel yelled, "Bring Alejandro to me now!"

His men snatched up the least favorite, the weakest link, and quickly seized Alejandro, dragging him forward as he resisted. He cursed. He fought but to no avail.

"Angel, what the fuck is this? What are you doing? Are you crazy?!" Alejandro screamed out.

"This is my brother," Angel explained. "Ranked equally, if not higher than that of a nephew. Do with him what you must. You have my blessing."

"I accept this exchange," Javier retorted.

"Angel, please…what have I done to you?" Alejandro begged for an explanation.

"I never liked you, Alejandro," Angel replied coldly. "He's all yours, Javier."

Javier nodded. Angel was a heartless and cold-hearted sonofabitch. Alejandro was his half-brother, and he blamed him for many things but most recently for being sloppy at his South Beach home, allowing several men to infiltrate his property and put his family in harm's way.

Javier's men roughly grabbed Alejandro, and they dragged him back to one of the Hummers as he screamed, "Nooo! Don't do this!" while Angel and the others looked on detached.

"For now, you have your truce…for now," Javier said.

"I'm glad we were able to come to an understanding," Angel said.

He turned and marched back to the vehicles, not even once looking back at his captured brother. He had to sacrifice family for the greater good of the cartel.

Chapter 46

Layla lounged around topless on the sunny deck and enjoyed the sundrenched and beautiful warm Australian weather. It was the holiday of a lifetime—luxury and paradise, as the couple was living *La Vida Loca*. They rented a wonderful beach house that sat parallel to the idyllic beach and pristine coastline of Bryon Bay.

Scott and Layla were unwinding, drinking margaritas, and having great sex. They'd leased the beach house for six months, feeling it was a long enough time to stay away and let everyone kill each other. They would simply sit back and enjoy the sunsets, have romantic dinners, lingering great sex, swim the ocean, tour Australia, and have significant time away from the chaos in New York.

Layla took pleasure in the exceptional view of the ocean as her nipples glowed under the sunlight. She took a sip from her margarita and smiled at Scott. He was shirtless, wearing a pair of long swimming trunks, his masculine physique still toned and sexy as ever. They had planned on renewing their wedding vows while on the continent, and this would be their perfect honeymoon. They had privacy and peace, and they were appreciating their lives and appreciating each other. The time when they were a family of eight was so long ago. Now, both had convinced themselves that any outsiders, including their children, were enemies.

Bugsy stood over the Mexican man down on his knees and placed the barrel of the 9mm to the back of his head. He didn't hesitate to pull the trigger, his body propelled forward, crashing face down, his blood spilling. Bugsy still fumed. He looked around him, and along with the man he killed, there were a half dozen dead men spread out in the compound owned and operated by the Juarez cartel. They killed everyone in sight, a high enough body count to make the Juarez cartel cringe, but their main target wasn't there.

Bugsy was on a bloody crusade against Angel Morales, and he had his army to back him up—men dedicated and crazy enough to follow him into hell and try to overthrow the devil himself. It seemed like he and his twin brother had switched identities, where Bugsy had become the hotheaded killer. He aimed the gun at the corpse and fired—*click-click-click*—he emptied his clip.

"We need to go," said Chopper.

Bugsy stood in silence, glaring down at the man he just killed. He was somewhere else for a moment, in a trance. His hand clenched the smoking gun tighter.

"Bugsy, we can't stay here all day. We did what we needed to do, let's go," Chopper repeated more urgently.

Chopper, Avery, and Bugsy exited the crime scene. The men climbed into the Suburban, and the vehicle sped away from the compound. The guns they just used to kill several men were tossed into a black trash bag to be disposed of.

"I'm lying to her," Bugsy finally spoke out the blue, bringing his attention to Chopper.

"What you mean?" Chopper asked. "Lying to who?"

"My woman, Alicia, I lied to her and said I wasn't with this gangsta shit anymore. I lied to get her back, and I'm lying to keep her around because I can't lose her again. But now I'm in this shit knee-deep, and it's sucking me in faster than before," he said, looking ahead and not once looking Chopper's way.

"You do what you gotta do because they violated you when they murdered your son, he was a civilian. But when the day comes and you need to chill, or you still need to kill, whatever it is you choose, I'm always gonna have your back. So I'm wit' you, either way, Bugsy...remember that," Avery added his two cents.

"Me too," Chopper made known.

Four black Lincoln Navigators came to a stop in front of a brownstone, making the block look like the President of the United States had arrived in Harlem. But behind the tinted windows and the fleet of vehicles was the heavily guarded, Bugsy. He sat in the backseat in one of his newly acquired armored vehicles and gazed at the brownstone to his right. He was worried. He hadn't seen or heard from Chopper in almost a week, and that was an anomaly. Chopper always checked in, and he was always around, and for his righthand man to suddenly disappear, go missing without a trace, he knew something was wrong.

Bugsy climbed out of the backseat and followed by several henchmen approached the lavish-looking brownstone. He entered the residence. Chopper lived a private life and a cautious one. The enemies they'd made over the years, they had to move stealthily, always stay armed, head on a constant swivel, and remain paranoid. Bugsy could count on one hand how many folks knew where Chopper rested his head.

Bugsy entered the home with his men and looked around. There weren't any signs of a disturbance. Everything seemed in place—so where was Chopper? Bugsy understood that men in their position only go missing twice, either they were locked up or they had been murdered. And he had checked, Chopper wasn't incarcerated.

"What you want us to do, boss? We searched all the locations, and he ain't nowhere to be found. We can continue to look for him," said Avery.

"He'll turn up sooner or later," Bugsy said. "Let's just go."

As they began to exit the residence, Bugsy saw something that caught his attention. He walked farther into the kitchen and noticed that one of the cabinets was ajar. Bugsy bent down and pulled out a heavy black duffel bag and placed it on the kitchen's island, already knowing what was inside. Bugsy unzipped the bag and exhaled. He was staring at fifteen kilos of cocaine that didn't belong to Chopper.

"Fuck," Bugsy cursed. Meyer was right. Chopper had been the snitch all along. Bugsy couldn't bring his mind to understand why his righthand man would flip on him for the Juarez cartel. Even with the evidence staring him in the face, he still wanted to speak to Chopper for an explanation. This could be a setup. "Yo, none of y'all say a word to my brother about this shit. We need to find Chopper, and I'll handle him."

Avery nodded. "You want us to take the yayo?"

"Nah, leave it. Because if I find out that Chopper had anything to do with the Juarez cartel and my son's murder, I'ma bury him with it."

Bugsy exited the home and climbed back into the vehicle. He had a bad feeling.

The four Navigators pulled away from the curb. So many things were swirling inside of his head. Could his best friend set him up to endure so much pain? With Maxine's betrayal, he now felt that anything was possible. Bugsy felt relieved that no one in his organization knew where Alicia lived. He had to continuously switch vehicles to throw rivals off, and he would regularly change routes on his way to Alicia's place. Sometimes what was an hour and a half drive would be two hours, sometimes longer to make sure he wasn't being followed by anyone. The last thing Bugsy wanted was to bring the heat to Alicia's front door. Not again. Bugsy had lost his son, his family, Maxine, and much more, but he would not lose Alicia. Not twice.

The kids ran up and down the urban block in Germantown, Philadelphia. It was a sunny, spring day and the block was active with residents moving about. It was a one-way street in a blue-collar neighborhood. The corner bodega had plenty of foot traffic that afternoon, and the locals sat on their front porch or steps talking and gossiping, while the kids played. Teenagers rode their bikes up and down the block, popping wheelies and talking shit to each other. As the day progressed, a couple youngsters stared at an old, rusty, dark-colored 1967 Chevy Nova parked at the corner for several days now. No one claimed the car, and it hadn't been moved. The neighbors grew suspicious of the vehicle, wondering who did it belonged to? Or was it simply abandoned?

Two boys went up to the car, and they noticed a pungent smell coming from it—like something was putrefying from it.

Then one boy looked down and saw a crimson stain under the trunk, and he uttered to his friend, "Is that blood?"

Curiosity overtook them, and they scrutinized the vehicle. They opened the unlocked doors and looked at the interior and saw it was clean. There wasn't anything valuable in the front or backseat and nothing in the glove compartment. Now it was the trunk they wanted to check, hoping there was some prize to steal.

"Yo, pop the trunk," one said.

The younger boy fumbled underneath the dashboard, looking for the release switch. The only problem was, there was no release switch for the trunk of the vintage car. It was an old vehicle, so the boys had to do things the hard way. They left and came back an hour later. It took tools, a crowbar, and a screwdriver, but finally, they forced open the trunk and immediately got the shock of their lives. Their eyes grew wide with sheer shock as they were aghast by the gruesome sight, a headless body was in the trunk. The younger vandal screamed and ran down the block, hollering at the top of his lungs while the other remained. This brought the neighbors to the car, where several folks puked at the mere sight of a decapitated body.

Philadelphia police officers and nearly a half dozen homicide detectives flooded the street, and they, too, were stunned. The body in the trunk had no identification, along with no head; his fingertips on his left hand had been amputated, but why leave the right? There were visible signs of torture, but not only that, someone had sprinkled cocaine all over the body and made sure his murder was drug-related. The scene was becoming the talk of the town, and detectives wanted to quickly identify the body.

The cellphone rang late in the evening, interrupting Bugsy's time with Alicia. The two were nestled together on the couch watching Power on Starz's when, unfortunately, business came calling. He looked annoyed, and Alicia looked more annoyed. This was supposed to be their time together, but when a 9-1-1 text came through, Bugsy knew it was necessary to respond.

"I need to make a call. I'll be a minute, baby…promise," he said.

She could only sigh her feelings. Bugsy stepped into the next room and called back. "What's up?"

Avery said, "Yo, they found Chopper…."

"Where?"

"They found his body in the trunk of an old car in Philadelphia, but they didn't find his head."

Bugsy's heart sank. "They sure it's him?"

"Police ran his fingerprints. It's him."

Bugsy sulked, hearing the tragic news. He was devastated, someone had gotten to his righthand man.

The news of Chopper suddenly put him in a gloomy mood. He went back into the living room with Alicia, and she immediately knew something was wrong with him.

"Is everything okay?" she asked him.

"Yeah, everything's cool," he lied.

He took a seat next to his woman, pulled her back into his arms, and continued watching Power. Although his eyes were on the TV and he had Alicia in his arms, Bugsy's thoughts were on Chopper. Chopper was his best friend and most loyal confidant. Bugsy was broken up inside but had to swallow any emotions bubbling up inside. The cartel sent him a message—*we're close, and we're coming for you and everyone you love.*

Chapter 47

A week later, there was more bad news for Bugsy. The Juarez cartel had attacked another one of their stash houses and came off with the biggest heist yet. Sixteen of their men had been gunned down, and they took a quarter of a million dollars and ninety kilos. A week after that, another spot had gotten hit, five men dead and eight kilos gone. It seemed like the Juarez cartel was everywhere. They were striking fast and striking hard. The siblings were losing money hand over fist. Within the month, all the money Bugsy and Lucky had stolen from their parents was now in the hands of the Juarez cartel. Now it was feeling like he was drowning in problems and warfare. When Bugsy would hit them, they would hit back twice as hard and take from him twice as much. Angel had an unlimited supply of shooters and resources. Bugsy was losing money, product, time, and men. An emergency meeting had to be called with the siblings.

"We need to reach out," Meyer had suggested.

"Reach out to who?" Bugsy wanted to know.

But Bugsy and Lucky already knew who Meyer was talking about, and immediately they were against it. Everything was falling apart, and they couldn't get ahead of it. The siblings thought they could stand in Scott and Layla's shoes, take the reins, and surpass their parents' accomplishments. However, warring with the cartel had exposed them and magnified who built the West empire. This war with the Juarez cartel was showing them that their parents were the entrees, and they were the appetizers.

Alicia didn't have to ask Bugsy twice to get Lulu so the baby could spend the weekend with them. He, too, needed an escape.

"We want my niece for the weekend," he asked his sister.

"So come and get her."

"Why can't you bring her to us?"

Lucky wasn't having it. "All the way to Connecticut? You done bumped your fucking head. I have two nannies, Bugsy. I don't need you."

"Nannies ain't family, Lucky. Besides, what are you doing anyway that you can't make the drive."

"I said no!" she snapped. "If you want Lulu, then come here. In fact, you can watch her at your Manhattan apartment. I don't want my daughter that far away from me."

Lulu was Lucky's child, so she called the shots. Bugsy could only agree to her demands.

It was a balmy Thursday evening when Bugsy steered his Bentley into the Upper West Side of Manhattan, with Alicia riding shotgun. She couldn't wait to see Lulu again.

Following behind the Bentley was Avery and another soldier, Skinny Paul, in Bugsy's Escalade, and a second SUV with two of

Bugsy's most skilled triggermen. The couple arrived at Bugsy's plush apartment high-rise building and parked out front. Parked on the other side of the street was Lucky seated in her G-wagon with Lulu, Maria, and Yusef. She was on her cellphone engaged in a conversation with Opie about her side hustle, with the current state of the wholesale business, this call was imperative. She instructed Maria to get out of the car with Lulu and take her baby to Bugsy and Alicia. She didn't want to interrupt her conversation.

Alicia climbed out of the Bentley to greet the nanny and take Lulu from her hands, Bugsy sat behind the wheel and watched everything. His head swiveled as Avery sat parked right behind him, and Nate sat parked behind Avery. Bugsy felt exposed, but he was sure everything was secured—not getting the memo that things were never secured.

"I'm gonna go and check on Lucky," Avery said. "Stay alert, nigga." Skinny Paul nodded and watched as Avery did a slow jog across the street. He peered in Lucky's G-wagon and said, "I think your brother wants you."

Lucky rolled her eyes at being interrupted. She pointed toward her cellphone and pivoted, giving Avery her back. Yusef said, "I'll go see what he wants."

Avery nodded and then casually walked into the corner store to buy smokes.

In the shadows watching everything were Angel's killers. They sat in three cars, nearly a dozen shooters, waiting for the right moment to strike. They had pictures of Bugsy, Lucky, and Meyer. They observed Bugsy behind the wheel of the Bentley, and they watched the nanny walk with the baby in a car seat approaching Alicia, and they saw another figure seated inside an SUV talking on a cellphone. The mistake was, they became confused. The woman in the G-wagon had different hair, short and curly hair, so they assumed she was another nanny. They focused their attention toward Alicia, who looked a little lighter than the picture and whose hair was styled differently. They quickly convinced themselves that Alicia was Lucky—and that the nanny was returning the child back to its mother.

A Mac-11 was cocked back along with several other fearsome weapons. The men were ready to strike. They exited the vehicles, and heatedly approached their targets. They came in like a violent wave, ready to wipe everything out in its path. Immediately Bugsy saw them coming from the rearview mirror. But before he could react, the first shots went off, exploding toward Alicia, Maria, and Lulu—his worst nightmare became a reality.

Rat-ta-Tat! Tat! Tat! Tat! Tat! Tat! Tat! Tat!

The intense gunfire exploded upon them, and instantaneously all three girls—Alicia and Maria carrying Lulu went down. Bugsy furiously leaped from his Bentley with his gun in his hand, only to be quickly cut down by a bullet in the face. His body jerked before he instantly collapsed. Bugsy's men in the vehicles behind his were immediately taken out too, Mexican men tore into the cars with their Mac-11's. They didn't stand a chance.

Lucky watched everything from her Benz, the nightmare unfolded around her like it was in slow motion. Her gun-toting thug, Yusef, he too was violently mowed down by machine gunfire. There was chaos all around her. Lucky gripped her pistol to save her child, but suddenly, she couldn't move. She sat there, frozen like ice. Her eyes were on several Mexican thugs raising hell in broad daylight on a very populated street. They just didn't give a fuck! She was sure that once she emerged from the vehicle, she would die too. They all were dead; all bodies were sprawled on the black pavement, but she couldn't see her child. As she was wrestling with her guilt, she heard more gunshots, more chaos ensuing. And then she saw what looked like the cavalry, which was the ironic appearance of the FBI. They came from out of nowhere, in blue flight jackets, and battled with the cartel. They had continued their surveillance of the family. When the smoke cleared, four of Angel's men were dead, and nine eluded capture.

Angel was pleasantly surprised when his peoples brought him the baby unharmed. It wasn't his orders, but strangely he was pleased that they had the wherewithal to think so clearly in an intense situation. They were only there to kill Bugsy. Killing Lucky and bringing him his baby was a bonus. Capturing and torturing Chopper had paid off. He didn't give up much, but he did give up Bugsy's West Side residence. It didn't take Angel long to realize that Chopper gave up that residence because Bugsy wasn't ever there. Angel had his men sit on that residence day and night, but to no avail; there wasn't any movement. But patience is a virtue, and he knew that eventually, they would get lucky.

He had called off his other men from Lucky's location, believing she was dead. Angel had his men waiting at the gym she used before she'd gotten pregnant. It was a long shot. His men sat outside that location day and night, but there weren't any signs of her until fate would have it, they both converged at the right place at the right time.

With Lulu in his arms, he looked at the adorable little girl and knew it was his baby, and he wondered by his hands, could he murder what was a part of him? Lulu had been wailing, and she was scared. She had been through a horrible ordeal, but the moment Angel took her into his arms and rocked her soothingly, her crying had stopped. Lucchese looked up at her father with the sweetest and innocent eyes. She clung to him tightly as if she knew what was unspoken.

Lucky didn't know that the killers thought Alicia was her. With the FBI all over her ass and the city block swamped with media cameras and reporters, Lucky couldn't think straight. There was death all around. They had to rush Bugsy to the hospital. He was in bad shape. She immediately called Meyer several times, but there was no answer from him. She tried not to panic, but with Lulu's body not amongst the dead, she knew her daughter had been kidnapped, and her heart couldn't beat right. She was awash with worries and pain. And when she got to escape the spotlight of the reporters, the police, and the FBI, she got on her cellphone and dialed Angel. Surprised that he answered her call, she immediately pled for her daughter's life.

"Please, don't kill her...bring my baby back to me!"

Angel was shocked that she wasn't dead. His men swore to him that they took her head off with the Mac-11, watched her brains explode onto the street. But they were mistaken.

"I thought your child was already dead. What was his name...Lou, right? That's right, Lou, short for Lucchese West," he toyed with her.

"I'm so sorry! Please, I'm sorry! I'm sorry I lied to you...please!" she apologized profusely.

"You lied, and I told you that there would be consequences for lying to me."

"I'll do anything to get her back," she declared humbly.

"I'll trade her life for yours," he said.

Lucky quickly objected. "Our child needs her mother, Angel. What you're suggesting is cruel."

"On the contrary," Angel countered, "My choice is generous considering the other option is death for you both. I told you what my cartel would do should they discover that an heir is not of only Mexican blood. You have my word that the baby will live."

She was in a tight bind. Lucky cried real tears, the ultimatum sinking into her bones like cancer. She wanted to regurgitate the last year of her life and abort it. Lucky was too young to have these issues and worries—just nonstop drama, and she wasn't here for it. She asked, "Who will raise Lucchese once I'm gone? You've murdered the only people I would have considered worthy, and that's Bugsy and Alicia."

"Then your parents can raise her!"

"No!" Lucky shouted. "Angel, absolutely not! Do not let my parents get near our baby. Promise me that, please."

Angel shrugged, already vexed with the direction of the conversation. "Her life for yours, and there are no negotiations."

"This is low, even for you," she said.

"You can only run for so long, Lucky. Eventually, I will find you. So do us all a favor, speed up the process, and save your child's life."

There was a deep sigh over the phone, and then she relented, saying, "I'll do it."

"Good. I'll call you back with the location."

Chapter 48

Chris Brown's *"Back to Sleep"* blared throughout the strip club, and Meyer was having the time of his life. Lollipop ground her thick hips against him and pushed her tits into his face, arousing Meyer, his dick hard underneath her. In the private room, he paid for what he had gotten for free. He licked her nipples, cupped, and smacked her ass cheeks—treating her like the whore he thought she was.

When Meyer got bored with Lollipop, he turned his attention to the other strippers in the club. Meyer gripped a wad of cash and made it rain. The club was packed, and the sexual debauchery was thick with promiscuous females from wall-to-wall. The stage had two girls in stilettos, pasties, and G-strings poll dancing, putting on a perverted show for the customers. Meyer was lit, throwing money around like it was confetti, drinking from a bottle of Grey Goose. He pulled a big booty stripper in his grasp, and she quickly twerked while Meyer stuffed hundred-dollar bills in her G-string. Lollipop stood aside and watched him trick on the next bitch, growing angry that he could easily dismiss her. But there wasn't anything she could do about it. She knew that she and Meyer weren't exclusive, but it still stung to watch him disrespect her in front of her coworkers.

The big booty stripper backed her ass up against Meyer, and he grabbed a handful of her wobbly butt cheek, squeezing with delight. He took another swig from the bottle. Meyer danced wildly against her and threw more money around. Lollipop couldn't watch anymore of it, so she spun around and marched toward the dressing room. Meyer didn't even notice her absence.

"You wanna fuck me?" the stripper asked him.

Meyer chuckled. They all wanted him—his money. They knew his status, and they wanted a piece of the young don, even if it was a small fraction of his time. She put it on Meyer; she reached behind her and squeezed his crotch, fondling him. There were no limits with her, she was a freak like that. His cellphone vibrated against his hip, but Meyer paid it no attention. It rang again, and still, he didn't care. He allowed the caller to go to his voicemail. The young, half-naked dancer had his undivided attention. Anyone else would have answered their phone immediately, knowing they were at war with the cartel. But Meyer needed this escape, to enjoy himself. Business took a backburner.

A few hours later, and still in the club, Meyer finally checked his phone. He saw he had dozens of missed calls and numerous unheard voice and text messages. Something had happened. He knew it. And when he finally got in contact with Lucky, she informed him of the nightmare that had transpired earlier; Alicia was dead, Bugsy was shot in the face, and Lulu had been kidnapped by Angel. Meyer was left in a state of disbelief.

Immediately he left the club and jumped into his car, and he sped toward the hospital. Guilt, anger, madness—lots of emotions competed for dominance. He clenched his fist around the steering wheel tightly and gritted his teeth. He did like a 100 mph toward the hospital, his hands were shaking badly. His niece, kidnapped by Angel Morales, meant that she would not be alive for much longer. And Bugsy was shot in the face, how could anyone survive that? They needed help. He didn't care what his siblings said, they needed their parents back in the picture. So, while he raced to the hospital to be with his brother and sister, he got on his cellphone to call Layla, but there was no answer. His calls kept going straight to her voicemail, and he couldn't leave a message because her voicemail was full. Next, he called Scott, but received the same results, no answer and unable to leave a voicemail.

"Fuck!" he screamed out.

He sobered up quickly and finally arrived at the hospital after driving like he had a police siren on his hood. He charged into the lobby and threw names at the staff. Lucky was there to meet him, and she told him the sad news. Bugsy was already out of surgery, one bullet had gone in and out of his right cheek, taking out a few molars with it. He suffered severe injuries to his right leg. There was one bullet lodged near a major artery making it difficult for the surgeons to remove it, so it had to stay. Bugsy had shattered bones and lost a lot of blood. He was in critical condition and sedated—touch and go for a moment, being monitored around the clock.

"I'm gonna kill these muthafuckas!" Meyer angrily screamed out; his rage echoed through the hospital. "Did you speak with Angel? Has he harmed Lulu?"

Lucky refused to tell Meyer about Angel's proposal. She said, "No word yet, but I'll let you know. Right now we have to be strong for Bugsy."

The location was in New Jersey, some backwoods outside of Trenton. The hour of the meeting was at 6 p.m. Angel explained to Lucky what would happen should she try to be slick, and she assured him that she had no more magic in her bag of tricks. She promised that she would come, and she would be there alone.

Chapter 49

A ngel didn't know what to expect from Lucky. Would she show up in exchange for the life of her child? The child she so sneakily and defiantly gave birth to. He wondered. He had his men prepared for war. And soon, Angel got his answer—and the supposed exchange had turned into a bloodbath. Eight of Lucky's men never made it out of the building alive. Angel clarified that the Juarez cartel was not to be fucked with. It angered him that Lucky could be so stupid, to think it would be that easy. What was she thinking?

Still, he contemplated Lulu's fate, strategizing. In the safety of his estate in Mexico, he had Lulu with him, with his family. She was a happy baby and loved being held. She would wrap her small arms around Angel's neck; they were making a connection, a connection that Angel tried his hardest to fight. She was his blood, but he didn't speak it.

Bugsy finally opened his eyes to see he was in the hospital. His body ached, and he felt paralyzed. He couldn't move without pain. He couldn't even speak. He saw Lucky, Meyer, Avery, and two of his men inside the room with him, but he didn't see Alicia. Immediately, he knew she was dead. He had seen her get hit, struck down by a machine gun in broad daylight. It was a brazen hit. He watched her body drop, and his heart sank. She was gone. She was gone because of him. Right away, guilt overcame him, and his emotions were strangling him. He looked at Lucky and Meyer, and he tried to speak, but he couldn't. The moment he opened his jaw or tried to, it felt like his mouth was pulling to the right. His jaw had been wired shut on his right cheek. It was the side the bullet entered and exited.

Meyer moved closer to his brother. He planned on being there for Bugsy as Bugsy had been there for him in his time of need. Quietly he explained to him that the FBI was lingering around the hospital, and they wanted to speak to him. They had to be extra careful.

"She's gone, Bee...they got to her, but I'ma handle it. You just get better and try not to speak. They got your shit wired shut, so just chill."

Alicia's death was hard enough on Bugsy, but when Meyer broke the news to him about Lulu being kidnapped, Bugsy could only speak with his eyes. His tears flowed uncontrollably, blinding the educated thug until everyone in the room appeared blurry. His body contracted from the sheer pain of another loss, another innocent soul taken over dollars and drugs. Instantly, he was ready to go back to war. Bugsy wanted to die on the battlefield, the guilt of life was now a heavy burden.

Lucky stood there, silent. She and Bugsy locked eyes. He knew his niece was dead and that they couldn't protect her. Bugsy reached out to his sister, and she grabbed his hand. He knew what she was going through.

Lucky sat in Bugsy's hospital room with Meyer and Avery. She and Bugsy were fortunate to be alive, but how long would she keep getting lucky? Soon her luck was bound to run out. Lucky sat there quiet, her mind racing with worries and concerns. She sent her soldiers to help her resolve the problem. Lucky made the phone call to several reliable triggermen, including Opie, and gave them the meeting address. Lucky had her men there at noon, setting up around the perimeter, lying in wait, with explicit instructions to bring her child back home. There was no way she would meet Angel alone and turn herself over to him. She knew what the cartel would do once they got their hands on her, and it wasn't humane.

The meeting time came and went. Still, there was no word from any of her men. Slyly she had been calling them, but everyone had gone radio silent. *God, what have I done?* She asked herself. *I should have just traded myself in.* Everything was happening at once, and it was an overwhelming feeling.

Detectives had recently left the room frustrated because Bugsy refused to cooperate with them. It had been a massacre on the city block, and the mayor was highly upset with the shooting. It was a high-profile case, leaving several people dead, and the ugly event was a stain on the city's renewed reputation. They couldn't have full-blown shootouts on the Upper West Side of Manhattan. It was bad for tourism and local businesses.

Lucky sat there detached with uncertainties. She hardly spoke all afternoon. She kept busy with her phone. Her brothers didn't pay her too much attention. They figured she was heartbroken over Lulu and thought that she needed space. Once again, Lucky tried to contact her men, but to no avail. However, minutes later, her cellphone rang with Opie's number showing, she almost felt relieved. She quickly excused herself from the room and stepped out into the hallway. She answered the phone with, "Opie, please tell me something good."

Right away, she heard a sinister chuckle, and Angel said, "This isn't Opie bitch. Opie and everyone else are dead."

Lucky's heart felt like it was in her throat. She was speechless. She felt it was confirmed, Lulu was dead. Angel continued with, "You are a piece of work, Lucky. You are a stubborn little bitch, and you will learn not to fuck with me. So, I left you a gift at the nurses' station…a box. Go to it now."

Lucky felt faint. Angel knew she was at the hospital with Bugsy, he had eyes shadowing her. She scanned her surroundings but saw no threat, no men coming for her. Angel wanted to play mind games. She had no choice but to do what he said. Lucky powerwalked down the hallway toward the nurses' station. She saw a small white box with a red bow tied around it, it was placed at the edge of the counter. No one paid any attention to it. The staff went about their business, unaware of the package.

Angel was still on the phone as Lucky picked up the small white box and hesitated to open it. She took a deep breath and removed the cover and instantly was appalled. It was a tiny finger, an infant's finger. It was Lulu's finger.

"Do I have your attention now? You fucked with the wrong narco."

Lucky immediately broke into tears and wept. "What the fuck do you want from me?" she screamed into the cellphone.

Lucky became so loud that she startled the nurses.

"I already told you, your life for your daughters…so, do we have a deal? And don't lie to me again, or I'll take apart precious Lucchese limb by limb and send you the parts express mail."

Lucky felt like she was about to have a panic attack. They already took her daughter's finger; she couldn't imagine the pain and torture her baby girl was going through. She scowled and chose. There had to be a sacrifice. Lucky heatedly replied to Angel's shock, "Do what you must! But it will be on your fuckin' conscience. And when I find you, I will send you personally to hell!"

Angel hung up on her. She refused to die in her daughter's place. Lulu was as good as dead, and Lucky signed the death certificate. It was apparent Lucky didn't care for the girl, she was a heartless bitch, and her outburst threw him off guard. He looked at his lieutenant and gave the order.

Lucky broke down in tears. She wanted her revenge and couldn't do it from the grave. She created unwanted attention on herself with her grief, and the nurses tried to console her.

"Get off of me!" she snapped at the nurses and pushed them away. She turned around to march back to her brother's hospital room, but before she could take one step, she felt the knife jab into her lower abdomen abruptly, and she jerked in shock from the blow. Her eyes widened in shock. Her attacker pulled it out briskly and repeated the action, stabbing Lucky several times in her stomach while everyone watched on in wide-ranging horror. It was a brazen attack from a cartel soldier. He scowled at Lucky as he continued to put the sharp blade inside of her, violently penetrating her flesh, desperately trying to drain the life from her.

The attack and the staff's screaming alerted everyone around, including several undercover agents. Lucky bowed over in pain, clutching her stomach, her blood was overrunning everywhere. She fell to her knees, knowing she was about to die.

"Freeze! Drop the fuckin' knife…drop it now!" one federal agent shouted at the man that brazenly tried to kill Lucky in public.

The assassin calmly dropped the knife and put his hands up in the air, willingly surrendering to the authorities. They wrestled him to the ground and handcuffed him. He showed no resistance.

Angel knew that the hospital would be crawling with law enforcement, and this soldier pledged his life to the Juarez cartel. He was only doing his job.

Meyer and Avery came rushing out of Bugsy's room after hearing the commotion and the "Code Blue" over the intercom system, and there was Lucky collapsed on the floor in a pool of blood; beside her, there was a baby's finger and a gift box.

"What the fuck!" Meyer screamed madly.

Epilogue

everything had hit faster than lightning could strike. Bugsy was shot, Lucky was stabbed, Lulu was murdered and dismembered, and Meyer was about to lose his fucking mind. His sanity was slipping. The FBI was trying to influence him to give them a statement. They wanted to take him down to their headquarters and question him, but Meyer resisted. When the federal agents tried to strongarm him, he called his mother's counsel. Fitzgerald Spencer handled his interests and backed the FBI off his client.

Things turned into a media circus at the hospital. Lucky's attempted murder made headlines, and the press was having a field day reporting the family's misery. The West family was New York City's gangsta Kardashians; the people couldn't get enough of hearing about their hardships and legal drama.

Meyer wanted no dealings with anyone. He became standoffish and hostile toward everyone. Meyer lingered around Bugsy's room and soon noticed something strange. He covertly watched Avery dial a number repeatedly but detected that he was

300

not conversing with anyone. Meyer realized Avery was desperately trying to reach someone—but who? Bugsy and Lucky were down, and Meyer was in the same room with him, so who on earth could Avery be trying to reach? The unusual look on Avery's face made Meyer suspicious of him. He was always looking around, especially Meyer's way, but Meyer played it cool. He didn't show Avery too much attention. He didn't want to spook him. So Meyer diverted his eyes and focused on his brother.

Avery's cellphone finally chirped, and he didn't hesitate to answer. He excused himself from the room and went into the hallway. Shortly after that, Meyer eased out the hospital room and observed Avery traveling down the hall to a quiet area, he bent the corner and then he disappeared from Meyer's sight. Meyer carefully followed and subtly looked around the corner of the corridor to see Avery talking on his cellphone. Meyer hid himself a few feet away from the conversation and intently listened. Avery was giving someone on the other end of the phone updates.

"The plan ain't going down the way you wanted it to. It's all fucked up…yeah, no doubt. Instead of Angel killing Bugsy, they got his bitch…Alicia. I think that's the bitch's name. Yeah, man, she's gone."

There was silence on Avery's end for a moment. Meyer wanted to make out who was on the other end of the phone, but he couldn't. Avery continued with, "Bugsy came close, though. There was a shootout with the Juarez cartel at the old place, and Bugsy caught a few slugs, one in the face, but he ain't dead. He's a tough sonofabitch! Yeah, he's the real Lucky, that should have been his fuckin' name, muthafucka got nine lives." Avery chuckled at his own comment.

Avery listened more and then said, "Lucky got the worse end of it, though. One cartel member caught her slipping and stabbed her like over a dozen times in the hallway."

The more Meyer heard him speak, the more his blood boiled—straight venom shot through his veins. Fuckin' Avery was the rat! He soon heard more.

"Nah, she ain't dead yet, either. She's in surgery right now. She's really fucked up, though, and I doubt if she makes it through the night."

More laughter escaped from Avery's mouth. He then said, "What Layla said? Tell Layla she's crazy as shit...yeah, Angel is gonna finish what he started so y'all ain't gotta worry. He's a coldblooded muthafucka. He murdered Lucchese and sent Lucky her daughter's finger right before his man put that knife through her."

Meyer clenched his fists and seethed like he never seethed before. But he continued to listen. And heard Avery say, "Yo, y'all in the right place. Stay in Australia for some time cause it's hot out here right now. The FBI is crawling everywhere, and they on this case, like stink on shit. I'll hit y'all up when Bugsy and Lucky are finally dead...oh, no doubt. I'm keeping an eye on Meyer, too. He good for now, ain't nobody fuckin' wit' him, they gotta go through me first."

Finally, Avery hung up the call, but before he could turn around and march back to the room, Meyer was already behind him, and his belt angrily wrapped around Avery's neck tightly. Meyer quickly dragged him into the stairwell. Avery struggled and fought desperately to breathe and stay alive. He got a glimpse of the sleeve tattoos on the wrists and knew it was Meyer attacking him. His breathing was quickly becoming restricted as Meyer tightened the belt around his neck and pulled with all his strength. The whites of Avery's eyes were showing. He couldn't break free from the leather noose; it felt like an anaconda was wrapped around his neck. It took several minutes for Meyer to squeeze the life out of Avery, and he did it right under the nose of the FBI. Avery's body went limp, he was lifeless. Meyer was breathing hard like he just ran a marathon. He undid the belt from around

Avery's neck, and the body dropped right by his feet. He scowled and exclaimed, "Fuckin' snitch!"

Meyer coolly exited the stairwell and walked back to his brother's room, leaving Avery's body to be found by some poor unfortunate passersby. What he'd just overheard was almost impossible to process. His parents had set in motion the events to eventually lead to the murder of their firstborn son, and firstborn daughter. And had caused the deaths of both of their grandchildren.

Meyer knew that he had to stop them by any means necessary.

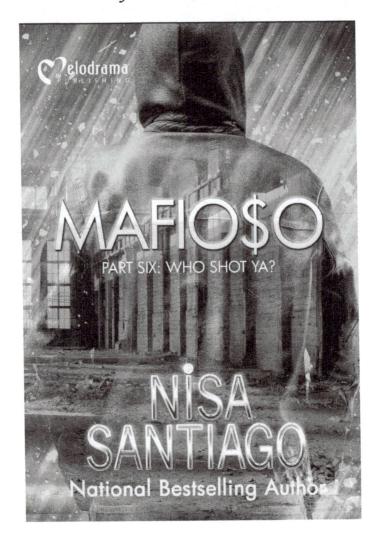

Made in the USA
Coppell, TX
02 August 2020

32314021R00167